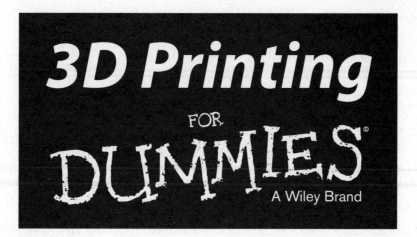

3D Printing

FOR

DUMMIES®

A Wiley Brand

**by Kalani Kirk Hausman
and
Richard Horne**

3D Printing For Dummies®

Published by: **John Wiley & Sons, Inc.,** 111 River Street, Hoboken, NJ 07030-5774, www.wiley.com

Copyright © 2014 by John Wiley & Sons, Inc., Hoboken, New Jersey

Published simultaneously in Canada

For general information on our other products and services, please contact our Customer Care Department within the U.S. at 877-762-2974, outside the U.S. at 317-572-3993, or fax 317-572-4002. For technical support, please visit www.wiley.com/techsupport.

Wiley publishes in a variety of print and electronic formats and by print-on-demand. Some material included with standard print versions of this book may not be included in e-books or in print-on-demand. If this book refers to media such as a CD or DVD that is not included in the version you purchased, you may download this material at http://booksupport.wiley.com. For more information about Wiley products, visit www.wiley.com.

Library of Congress Control Number: 2013952422

ISBN 978-1-118-66075-1 (pbk); ISBN 978-1-118-66077-5 (ebk); ISBN 978-1-118-66068-3 (ebk)

Manufactured in the United States of America

10 9 8 7 6 5 4 3

Contents at a Glance

Table of Contents

Part II: Outlining 3D Printing Resources 61

Introduction

● ●

*U*nlike traditional manufacturing which involves injecting material into a pre-formed mold or removing material from base material objects, additive manufacturing (3D printing) starts with a virtual 3D model that is transformed into solid form one layer at a time. Each layer is built on top of the layer before, creating a solid form representing the virtual 3D model in all of its complexity and detail without requiring additional forms of machining and treatment necessary in traditional forms of manufacturing.

Although 3D printers have been available for years, only recently have they become available at a price most home users can afford. Because they are becoming more widespread, and because innovations in this technology now permit the creation of products in a much wider array of materials — and even combinations of materials — 3D printing is poised to make an impact on average consumers in a big way. *3D Printing For Dummies* was written with the average reader in mind. It's a survey of the existing capabilities of additive manufacturing, for both private and commercial purposes, and a consideration of the possibilities of its future.

About This Book

In this book, we review many different technologies currently available for additive manufacturing. These are early-generation technologies with numerous limitations and caveats to their use and the selection of materials available for use in 3D printers in both commercial-scale and consumer-grade options. We also explore the process by which you can build your own 3D printer using the open-source self-REPlicating RAPid-prototyping (RepRap) family of designs. This will not make you an expert in all aspects of 3D printing, but will provide you with an opportunity to explore the many types of additive manufacturing systems. Hopefully, you will be excited by the amazing potential of 3D printers – excited enough to build your own printer and start sharing your own creativity with friends and family!

Foolish Assumptions

You might find it difficult to believe that we have assumed anything about you — after all, we haven't even met you yet! Although most assumptions are indeed foolish, I made these assumptions to provide a starting point for the book.

It is important to understand that the current level of sophistication in 3D printers is close to the first automated looms that found their way into factory settings in the early 1700's. Commercial 3D printers have less variance, but for consumer-grade equipment a certain amount of "tinkering" will be needed from time to time to keep things running. Working with 3D printers is very rewarding, but you should learn how to adjust and tune your home or office printer so that when things go awry you will be able to fix them yourself. It is not necessary to be a do-it-yourself handyman, but a certain familiarity with basic tools will help you when you build, assemble, or use your own 3D printer.

The book assumes you will have the ability to download or access programs in a web browser if you want to try out some of the applications we review, such as TinkerCAD. However, it is not necessary to have a computer of your own to enjoy this book — all you need is an open mind and enthusiasm about the future and what additive manufacturing can produce!

Icons Used in This Book

As you read this book, you'll see icons in the margins that indicate material of interest (or not, as the case may be).This section briefly describes each icon in this book.

Tips are nice because they help you save time or perform some task without a lot of extra work. The tips in this book give you timesaving techniques or pointers to resources that you should check out to get the maximum benefit from 3D printing.

I don't want to sound like an angry parent or some kind of maniac, but you should avoid doing anything marked with a Warning icon.

Whenever you see this icon, think *advanced* tip or technique. You might find these tidbits of useful information just too boring for words, or they could contain the solution you need. Skip these bits of information whenever you like.

If you don't get anything else out of a particular chapter or section, remember the material marked by this icon. This text usually contains an essential process or a bit of information that you must know.

How This Book Is Organized

We divide this book into several parts based on topic. The following sections describe what you can expect to find in each part.

Part I: Getting Started with 3D Printing

Part I explores fundamental 3D printing technologies and options for additive manufacturing within the current state of the art. It is intended to provide you with a general overview of what additive manufacturing provides today.

Part II: Outlining 3D Printing Resources

Part II expands your exploration of additive manufacturing to include different materials that can be used in current and near-future 3D printing technologies, and examines options available to create new virtual 3D object models to be printed.

Part III: Exploring the Business Side of 3D Printing

Part III examines the potential for disruption in existing businesses and new business opportunities that becomes possible through new additive manufacturing capabilities. We also explore current lines of research, building new options to the current state of the art.

Part IV: Employing Personal 3D Printing Devices

Part IV explores consumer-level 3D printer options including both commercial and open-source alternatives available for home and small business uses in fabricating creative and artistic designs exploring this magnificent new capability. We discuss considerations you should take into account when building your own RepRap-style 3D printer.

Part V: Creating a RepRap 3D Printer

Part V walks you through the creation, assembly, and calibration of a RepRap style printer.

Part VI: Part of Tens

Part VI offers lists of ten interesting, disruptive, or impossible (in traditional manufacturing) applications of additive manufacturing.

Beyond the Book

A lot of extra content that you won't find in this book is available at www. dummies.com. Go online to find the following:

✔ **Online articles covering additional topics at**

    www.dummies.com/extras/3dprinting

Here you'll find examples of how to use available software to design and prepare 3D models for printing and to set up your own personal digital storefront using free services already in place.

✔ **The Cheat Sheet for this book is at**

    www.dummies.com/cheatsheet/3dprinting

Here you'll find a roadmap to additive manufacturing and the construction of your own RepRap-style 3D printer.

✔ **Updates to this book, if we have any, are also available at**

    www.dummies.com/extras/3dprinting

Where to Go from Here

The goal of this book is to get you thinking about 3D printing and the potential it offers in your own life, home, or work. We stand at the start of a new Industrial Age, where traditional mass manufacturing will give way to personalized, individualized, ecologically-friendly and on-demand manufacturing close to home. You do not have to read this book cover-to-cover, although I think you will find interesting and amazing items on each page. In any event, we hope you walk away with dozens of ideas for improvements, uses and new capabilities made possible by the emerging capabilities of 3D printers.

Part I

Getting Started with 3D Printing

getting started with

3D Printing

In this part...

- ✔ Explore the world of 3D printing, including many of the different types of additive manufacturing and their applications.

- ✔ Discover current uses for the ever-growing spectrum of 3D-printing alternatives available today.

- ✔ Examine alternatives currently in existence for 3D printing.

- ✔ Discover ways that you may be able to use additive manufacturing in personal and professional settings.

Chapter 1

Seeing How 3D Printers Fit into Modern Manufacturing

*A*n amazing transformation is currently under way in manufacturing, across nearly all types of products — a transformation that promises to remake the future into a sustainable and personally customized environment. In this fast-approaching future, everything we need — from products to food, and even our bodies themselves — can be replaced or reconstructed rapidly and with very minimal waste. This is not the slow change of progress from one generation of iPhone to the next, but instead a true revolution, mirroring the changes that introduced the world to the Industrial Age and then bought light and electricity to our homes and businesses.

This will not be a "bloodless coup" by any means; any truly fundamental change that spans all aspects of the global economy will, by its nature, be disruptive. But traditional inefficient ways of producing the next year's model will surely give way to entirely new opportunities impossible to imagine before. The technology behind this transformation is referred to as *additive manufacturing, 3D printing,* or *direct digital manufacturing.*

By whatever name, in the coming decade this technology will be used to construct everything from houses to jet engines, airplanes, food, and even replacement tissues and organs made from your own cells! Every day new applications of 3D printing are being discovered and developed all over the world. And even in space: NASA is testing designs that will function in zero gravity, on the airless moon, and even to support human exploration of other planets like Mars. (See Figure 1-1 for a glimpse.) Hold on tight, because in the chapters ahead we cover a lot of incredibly new and fantastic technologies — and before the end, we show you how you can get involved in this amazing transformation yourself by building and using a 3D printer at home.

Figure 1-1: A line drawing of NASA's planned 3D-printed lunar construction.

Embracing Additive Manufacturing

So, what is "additive manufacturing," you might ask? Additive manufacturing is a little like the "replicators" in the *Star Trek* universe, which allow the captain to order "Tea, Earl Grey, hot" and have a cup filled with liquid appear fully formed and ready for consumption. We are not quite to that level, but today's 3D printers perform additive manufacturing by taking a 3D model of a object stored in a computer, translating it into a series of very thin layers, and then building the object one layer at a time, stacking up material until the object is ready for use.

3D printers are much like the familiar desktop printer you already use at work or in your home to create copies of documents transmitted electronically or created on your computer, except that a 3D printer creates a solid three-dimensional object out of a variety of materials, not just a simple paper document.

Since the time of Johannes Gutenberg, creating multiple printed documents has brought literacy to the world. Today, when you click the Print button in a word processor application, you merge the functions of writers, stenographers, editors (spellcheck), layout, illumination (coloring and adding in images), and press reproduction all into a single task, and with the click of a few more buttons, you can post the document you create onto the Internet and allow it to be shared, downloaded, and printed out by others all over the world.

3D printing does the exact same thing for objects: Designs and virtual 3D models for physical objects can be shared, downloaded, and then printed out into physical form. It's hard to imagine what Johannes Gutenberg would have made of that.

Defining additive manufacturing

Why is additive manufacturing called "additive?" Additive manufacturing works by bringing the design of an object — its shape — into a computer model, then dividing that model into separate layers that can stack atop another to form the final object. It reimagines a three-dimensional object as a series of stackable layers that, when added together, forms the finished object. (See Figure 1-2.) Whether this object is a tea cup or a house, the process starts with the base layer and then builds up each additional layer until the full object has been completed.

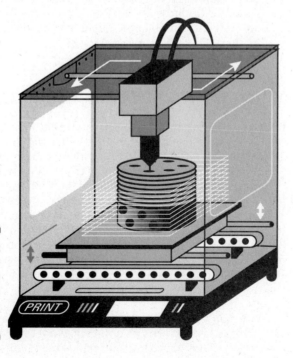

Figure 1-2:
A line
drawing
of how 3D
printing
works.

My children did this before they ever saw my first 3D printer. They discovered they could use crackers and cheese spray for more than just a snack — they could build towers and grand designs simply by layering crackers and cheese on top of each other. These edible structures show the potential in additive manufacturing. Each cracker was given a personalized application of cheese to spell out names, draw designs, and even to build shapes and support tiny pyramids. The resulting snacks were both unique and also customized to exactly the design each child wanted.

3D printers build up layers of material in a few different ways: Either they fuse liquid polymers with a laser, bind small granular particles using a laser or a liquid binding material, or they extrude melted materials out like a tube of toothpaste squeezed onto a toothbrush. However, 3D printers perform their additive manufacturing using many more materials than just toothpaste or cheese spray. They can fabricate items using photo-curable plastic polymers, melted plastic filament, metal powders, concrete, and many other types of material — including biological cells that can form amazingly complex structures to replace, repair, and even augment our own bodies.

Just as the rings of a tree show the additive layers of growth to the tree each year, additive manufacturing builds up objects one layer at a time. In this way we can create a small plastic toy, a whole car, and very soon an entire house (with all of its furnishings), or even complete airplanes with interlocking parts. Research today on conductive materials suggests that wires will soon become just another part of the additive manufacturing process, by allowing them to be printed directly into an object itself instead of having to be installed later.

Contrasting traditional manufacturing

How does this additive manufacturing compare to the traditional methods of production that have worked just fine since the First Industrial Revolution in the 1700's transformed manufacturing from hand production to automated production, using water and steam to drive machine tools? Why do we need to take up another disruptive technological shift after the Second Industrial Revolution in the 1800's transformed the world through the increased use of steam-powered vehicles and the factories that made mass manufacturing possible? Today, we stand at the opening moment of the next transformation, a Third Industrial Revolution, where mass manufacturing and global transfer of bulk goods will be set aside in favor of locally-produced and highly personalized individual production fitting society's transition to a truly global phase of continuous self-upgrade and incremental local innovation.

The First Industrial Revolution's disruption of society was so fundamental that governments had to pass laws to protect domestic wool textile production in England against new power-woven cotton textiles being imported from the East Indies. The spinning jenny and automated flyer-and-bobbin looms allowed a small number of people to weave hundreds of yards of fabric every week, whereas hand weavers took months to card plant fibers or shorn hair, spin the material into thread, and then weave many spools of thread into a few yards' worth of fabric. Suddenly, these new industrial technologies like the automated loom shown in Figure 1-3 were putting weavers out of work, sparking the formation of the Luddite movement that tried to resist this transformation. Fortunately, the capability for the new technologies to provide clothes to families eventually won that argument and the world was transformed.

Figure 1-3:
An example from past industrial revolutions.

A few years later, the Second Industrial Revolution's disruption of society was even more pronounced, because automation provided alternatives not limited by the power of a man or horse, and steam power freed even massive industrial applications from their existence alongside rivers and water wheels, and allowed them to become mobile. The difficulties traditional workers faced with these new technologies are embodied in the tale of folk hero John Henry, chronicled in the powerful folk song "The Ballad of John Henry," who proved his worth by outdigging a steam-driven hammer by a few inches' depth before dying from the effort. This song and many like it were heralded as proof of mankind's value in the face of automation, and yet the simple fact that the steam hammer could go on day after day without need for food or rest, long after John Henry was dead and gone, tells the tale of why that disruption has been adopted as the standard in the years since.

Here at the edge of the transformation that may one day be known as the Third Industrial Revolution, the disruptive potential of additive manufacturing is obvious. Traditional ways of mass manufacturing, which makes products by milling, machining, or molding raw materials; shipping these materials all over the world; refining the materials into components; assembling the components into the final products in tremendous numbers to bring per-unit costs down; shipping those products from faraway locations with lower production costs (and more lenient workers' rights laws); storing vast numbers of products in huge warehouses; and finally shipping the products to big-box stores and other distributers so they can reach actual consumers, is comparatively inefficient in the extreme. (See Figure 1-4.)

Figure 1-4: Cargo transportation required for traditional mass-manufactured goods.

Because of the costs involved, traditional manufacturing favors products that appeal to as many people as possible, preferring one-size-fits-most over customization and personalization. This limits flexibility, because it is impossible to predict what the actual consumption of products will look like by the time next year's model is available in stores. This process is also incredibly time-consuming and wasteful of key resources like oil, and the pollution resulting from the transportation of mass manufactured goods is costly to the planet.

Machining/subtractive fabrication

Because additive manufacturing can produce completed products — even items with interlocking moving parts such as bearings within wheels or linked chains — 3D-printed items require much less finishing and processing than traditionally manufactured items. The traditional approach uses *subtractive* fabrication procedures, such as milling, machining, drilling, folding, and polishing to prepare even the initial components of a product. The traditional approach must account for every step of the manufacturing process, even a step as minor as drilling a hole, folding a piece of sheet metal, or polishing a milled edge, because such steps require human intervention and management of the assembly-line process — which therefore adds cost to the end product.

Yes, this means that fewer machining techs will be needed after the Third Industrial Revolution occurs, but it also means that products can be produced very quickly, using far fewer materials. It's much cheaper to put down materials only where they're needed, rather than to start with blocks of raw materials and mill away unnecessary material until you achieve the final form. Ideally the additive process will allow you to reimagine 3D-printed products from the ground up, perhaps even allowing you to use complex open interior spaces that reduce materials and weight while retaining strength. And additive manufactured products are formed with all necessary holes, cavities, flat planes, and outer shells already in place, removing the need for many of the steps in traditional fabrication.

Molding/injection molding

Traditional durable goods, such as the components for automobiles, aircraft, and skyscrapers, are fabricated by pouring molten metal into molds or through tooled dies at a foundry. This same technology was adapted to create plastic goods: Melted plastic is forced into injection molds to produce the desired end product. Molding materials such as glass made it possible for every house to have windows, and for magnificent towers of glass and steel to surmount every major city in the world.

However, traditional mold-making involves the complex creation of master molds, which are used to fashion products as precisely alike as possible. To create a second type of product, a new mold is needed, which can in turn be used to create only that individual design over and over. This can be a time-consuming process. 3D printers, however, allow new molds to be created rapidly so that a manufacturer can quickly adapt to meet new design requirements, to keep up with changing fashions, or to achieve any other necessary change. Or, alternatively, a manufacturer could simply use the 3D printer to create its products directly, and modify the design to include unique features on the fly. This direct digital manufacturing process is currently being used by GE to create 24,000 jet-engine fuel assemblies each year, an approach that can be easily changed mid-process if a design flaw is later discovered, simply by modifying the design in a computer and printing out replacement parts — something that would require complete retooling in a traditional mass-fabrication process.

Understanding the advantages of additive manufacturing

Because computer models and designs can be transported electronically or shared for download across the Internet, additive manufacturing allows manufacturers to let customers design their own personalized versions of products. In today's interconnected world, the ability to quickly modify products to appeal to a variety of cultures and climates is not insignificant.

In general, the advantages additive manufacturing offers can be grouped into the following categories:

- Personalization
- Complexity
- Sustainability
- Recycling and planned obsolescence
- Economies of scale

The next few sections talk about these in greater detail.

Personalization

Personalization at the time of fabrication allows additive-manufactured goods to fit each individual consumer's preferences more closely — in terms of form, materials, design, or even coloring, as we discuss in later chapters.

Nokia, for example, recently released a 3D-printable case design for its Lumina 820 phone, making it available for free download and modification using the Creative Commons licensing model. (See Figure 1-5.) In no time, people within the 3D-printing community created many different variations of this case and posted them to services like the Thingiverse 3D object repository. These improvements were rapidly shared among members of the community, who used them to create highly customized versions of the case, and Nokia gained value in the eyes of its consumer base through this capability.

Creative Commons Licensing refers to several copyright licenses developed by the nonprofit Creative Commons organization to allow designers to share their designs with others, reserving specific rights and waiving others to allow other creators to share and expand on their designs without complex formal copyright licensing for traditional intellectual property controls.

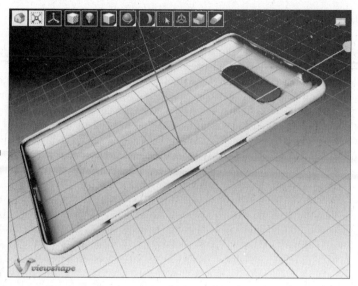

Figure 1-5:
The free down-loadable, 3D-printable phone case from Nokia.

Complexity

Because every layer of an object is created sequentially, 3D printing makes it possible to create complex internal structures that would be impossible to achieve with traditional molded or cast parts. Structures that are not load-bearing can have walls that are thin or even absent altogether, with additional support material added elsewhere during printing. If strength or rigidity are desired qualities but weight is a consideration (as in the frame elements of race cars), additive manufacturing can create partially filled internal voids with honeycomb structures, resulting in rigid, lightweight alternatives. Structures modeled from nature, mimicking (say) the bones of a bird, can be created using additive manufacturing techniques to create wholly new product capabilities not possible in traditional manufacturing.

When you consider that this technology will soon be capable of printing entire houses as well as the materials therein, you can see how easily it can affect more prosaic industries. Consider moving companies — in the future, moving from one house to another may be a simple matter involving transferring nothing more than a few boxes of personalized items (kid's drawings and finger-painting, Grandma's old tea set, and baby's first shoes) from one house to another. There may come a time when we don't need a moving company; we'll just contact a company that will fabricate the same house and furnishings (or a familiar one with a few new features) at the new location. That same company could reclaim materials used in the previous building and furnishings as a form of full recycling.

Sustainability

By allowing strength and flexibility to vary within an object, 3D-printed components can reduce the weight of products and save fuel — for one aircraft manufacturer, for example, just the redesign of its seatbelt buckles is estimated to save tens of thousands of liters of aviation fuel across the lifetime of an aircraft. And by putting down materials only where they will need to be, additive manufacturing can allow a reduction in the amount of materials lost in post-production machining, which will conserve both money and resources.

Additive manufacturing also allows for the use of a variety of materials for many components, even for the melted plastic used in printers like the RepRap device we show you how to build later in this book. Acrylonitrile butadiene styrene (ABS), with properties that are well known from its use in the manufacture of toys like the LEGO brick, is commonly used for home 3D printing, but it is a petrochemical-based plastic. Environmentally-conscious users could choose instead to use plant-based alternatives such as polylactic acid (PLA) to achieve similar results. Alternatives such as PLA are commonly created from corn or beets; however, the current research into producing industrial quantities of this material from algae may one day help reduce our dependence on petrochemical-based plastics.

Additionally, other materials — even raw materials — can be used. Some 3D printers are designed to print out objects using concrete or even sand as raw materials! Using nothing more than the power of the sun concentrated through a lens, Markus Kayser, the inventor of the Solar Sinter, fashions sand into objects and even structures. Kayser uses a computer-controlled system to direct concentrated sunlight precisely where needed to melt granules of sand into a crude form of glass, which he uses, layer by layer, to build up bowls and other objects. (See Figure 1-6.)

Recycling and planned obsolescence

The Third Industrial Revolution offers a way to eliminate the traditional concept of planned obsolescence that is behind the current economic cycle. In fact, this revolution goes a long way toward making the entire concept of "obsolescence" obsolete. Comedian Jay Leno, for instance, who collects old cars, uses 3D printers to restore his outdated steam automobiles to service — even though parts have been unavailable for the better part of a century. With such technology, manufacturers would not even need to store copies of old parts; they would simply download the appropriate component design and print out a replacement when needed.

3D printers take advantage of sustainable construction methods, but beyond that, they can allow manufacturers to re-use existing materials and components, with personalized and customizable attributes added to retain consumer interest. This could easily impact the cycle of reinvestment for

Image courtesy Markus Kayser

Figure 1-6:
A natural-glass bowl formed using sunlight through the Solar Sinter to fuse sand.

major-purchase goods. By removing the endless cycle of planned obsolescence with new seasonal models, we would reduce fundamental goods production in some trades and also reduce endless consumer debt accumulation to keep up with the cyclic purchasing of durable goods.

Instead of industries — automobiles, houses, furniture, or clothing — endlessly pushing the next year's or next season's product lines, the future could well be focused on industries that retain investment in fundamental components, adding updates and reclaiming materials for future modifications. In this future, then, when a minor component on a capital good like a washing machine fails, a wholly new machine won't need to be fabricated and shipped; the replacement will be created locally and the original returned to functional condition for a fraction of the cost and with minimal environmental impact.

Economies of scale

Additive manufacturing allows for individual items to be created at the same per-item cost as multiple items of the same or similar designs. This is unlike traditional mass manufacturing, where fabrication of huge numbers of identical objects drops the per-item cost passed along to the consumer. Traditional manufacturers also choose areas of the world where labor laws and safety mandates are less restrictive in order to bring costs down further through reductions in labor expenses — and this, of course, is not an issue with additive manufacturing.

Additive manufacturing, as it matures, may engender a fundamental transformation in the production of material goods. Supporters present the possibility of ad-hoc personalized manufacturing close to consumers; critics argue at the damage this transition would make to economies that currently exist because of

- ✔ mass manufacturing in lower-cost areas
- ✔ bulk transportation of goods around the world
- ✔ storage and distribution networks

Traditional manufacturing depends on these factors to bring products to consumers.

By placing production in close proximity to consumers, shipping and storing mass-produced goods will no longer be necessary. Cargo container ships, along with those costs associated with mass-manufacturing economies, may become a thing of the past.

It would be possible to repurpose these immense cargo ships to serve as floating additive manufacturing centers that could park offshore near their consumer base as we migrate away from traditional mass manufacturing fabrication centers. One example of the potential in this shift would be that manufacturers of winter- or summer-specific goods could simply float north or south for year-round production to meet consumer demand without the issues and costs associated with mass manufacturing's transportation and storage cycles. Following a natural disaster, such a ship could also simply pull up offshore and start recycling bulk debris to repair and replace what was lost to the elements.

Exploring the Applications of 3D Printing

There is no doubt that additive manufacturing technologies will transform many industries and may even return currently outsourced manufacturing tasks to the United States. This in turn may well impact industries involved in the transportation and storage of mass quantities of products, but the fundamental technologies behind additive manufacturing may also transform the materials (and quantities thereof) used in the production of goods.

When we look ahead at the possible impact of the Third Industrial Revolution — 3D printing, crowdfunding, robotics, ad-hoc media content, and a host of other technologies — we see a means to not only alter the course of production but also to fundamentally shatter traditional manufacturing practices. In the chapters ahead, we show you the current state of the art of

3D printing — what the technology can and can't do now — and what it might one day do to transform the world we know into an agile, personalized, customized, and sustainable environment.

We discuss with you the different types of materials that can be used to conduct additive manufacturing, and provide some ideas of the materials that may soon become available. I show you how to create or obtain 3D models that are already available, and how to use them for your own purposes and projects. Many 3D objects can be designed using free or inexpensive software and photos of real objects — objects from photos of historical locations, antiquities in a museum, or just pictures of your child's clay creation from art class. There are a number of considerations to take into account before creating your own 3D-printed object, whether you have a 3D-printing service create them or decide to print them at home for yourself, and we look forward to sharing these with you.

We have given you a taste of the disruptive potential present in additive manufacturing, but many more opportunities will emerge as well. However, the transition from one paradigm to another will be difficult wherever it interacts with a legal system based in the earlier industrial age. When anything can be created by anyone, anywhere, many legal issues arise related to intellectual property and legal responsibility.

Working with RepRap

The first 3D printer was patented in the late 1980s, but the rate of change was fairly minimal for 30 years. Labs and research departments used early 3D printers in *rapid prototyping* systems that produced solid mock-ups quickly. But things really took off after British researcher Adrian Bowyer created the first *self-replicating rapid prototyping (RepRap)* system using salvaged stepper motors and common materials from the local hardware store. That "self-replicating" part means that one RepRap system can be used to print many of the components for a second system.

Later in this book Richard and I show you how to assemble your own RepRap, configure it, and use it alongside free open-source software to build many items including another RepRap 3D printer if you choose.

Chapter 2

Exploring the Types of 3D Printing

In This Chapter
▶ Exploring basic forms of additive manufacturing
▶ Recognizing specialized forms of additive manufacturing
▶ Seeing where current technologies are lacking

*W*henever you discuss additive manufacturing, direct digital fabrication, rapid prototyping, or 3D printing, you are actually talking about the same process — translating a 3D design stored in a computer into a series of thin layers, and then manufacturing a real, physical object by creating those layers, one at a time, in a 3D printer. This same process takes place whether you are printing small plastic kittens to give away at my daughter's birthday party (see Figure 2-1) or a full-scale airplane wing of lightweight metals.

The applications for this technology are rapidly increasing. Carrying additive manufacturing machines onboard naval vessels allows seamen to print replacement components while at sea. The U. S. Army is fielding its own rapid prototyping *fablabs* (fabrication laboratories) on the front lines to create quick adjustments to existing technologies, such as a small plastic clip that covers the on/off buttons on flashlights. The clip is useful in preventing soldiers from accidentally turning on their flashlights during stealth missions and accidentally giving away their positions. In the future, this technology may be used in the vacuum of space: NASA is looking at techniques to build objects up layer by layer from designs rather than depending on spare parts for everything astronauts will take with them into space, to the moon, or even to other planets such as Mars.

This chapter discusses the current applications for this technology — and some of its existing limitations.

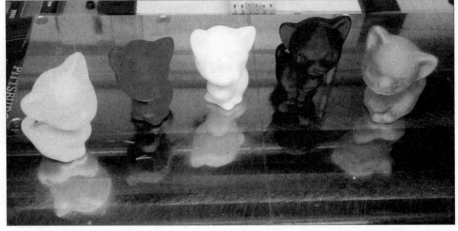

Figure 2-1:
Plastic
kittens
3D-printed
for a child's
birthday
party
giveaways.

Exploring Basic Forms of Additive Manufacturing

In order to translate a 3D virtual model's design into the series of layers that will make up an object, all 3D printers require the unique coordinates for every part of the object to be fabricated.

Some 3D printers work across a level surface called the *build plate*, while others create objects atop successive layers of granulated material. The RepRap printers I show you how to build at the end of this book will be of two types: *Cartesian* (which uses motors to move in the X, Y, and Z directions, see Figure 2-2) and *Delta* (which relies on mechanical linkages to three motors to move an extruder around within the entire build volume). Even Delta-and Polar-type 3D printers still require X, Y, and Z coordinates into which they will extrude the build material for the final object.

These printers are designed to accommodate the properties of the materials they use to create objects. The most common types are

- Photopolymer
- Granular
- Lamination
- Fused deposition modeling

I talk about each of these in the next few sections.

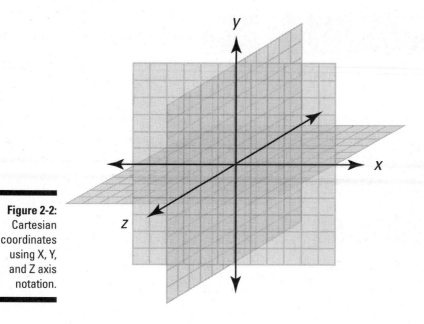

Figure 2-2:
Cartesian
coordinates
using X, Y,
and Z axis
notation.

Photopolymer

Photopolymers are materials that can transform from a liquid to a solid almost instantaneously when the right kind of light shines on them. These materials are great for additive manufacturing.

The first type of additive manufacturing was termed *stereolithography* by its inventor Charles Hall, who founded and leads 3D Systems today. From the word *stereolithography* comes the standard 3D-printed object file type, STL, invented by Mr. Hall in the late 1980s. Today's 3D printers and software still use the STL file type for most common printing operations; a few more modern file types are emerging as new variations on full-color and blended-material 3D printing become possible. SLA fabrication is often used for high-resolution object fabrication, providing highly detailed surfaces, as in the case of jewelry master designs for molding and casting.

Stereolithography uses focused UV light to transform liquid photopolymer plastic into solid form. (See Figure 2-3.) The process takes place upon a movable platform above a reservoir of the photopolymer plastic. The platform submerges into the reservoir just enough to create a thin layer of liquid. An ultraviolet laser passes back and forth over the liquid to create the first layer of the object. By lowering the platform to allow more liquid to cover the first layer, the second layer can be constructed atop the first. Each layer must connect to the one below or to a support structure that can later be removed in order to keep the object from floating out of position as the new layers are added and more fluid polymer is poured atop it.

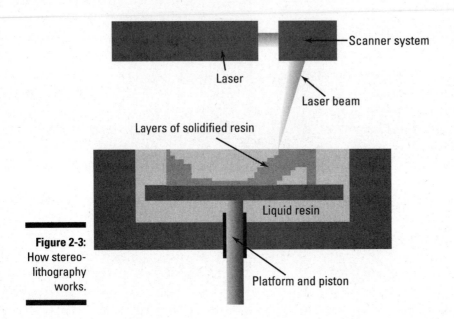

Scanner system

Laser

Laser beam

Layers of solidified resin

Liquid resin

Figure 2-3:
How stereo-
lithography
works.

Platform and piston

Stereolithographic formation of objects provides excellent detail (see Figure 2-4), but the materials are currently limited to polymers that can be cured to solid states using focused light. More recent developments include DLP light projection of an entire layer at once across the bottom of the build volume, curing each layer as the object is raised out of the polymer liquid from atop a full-screen light source.

High-resolution variations of stereolithography use lasers focused so tightly that individual elements of the final object are microscopic in size. Such multi-photon lithographic designs have created entire buildings so small they could be lost entirely in a single drop of water. The rendering of the Brandenburg Gate shown in Figure 2-5, for instance, is only a fraction of a millimeter in size.

Objet's PolyJet system also uses photopolymerization, but in this case it uses ink-jetted materials to build up the layers. This system does not rely on a bath of liquid, but instead keeps the materials in separate cartridges within the printer during operation — and can even mix materials as it sprays them, hardening the applied spray using ultraviolet light after each pass. (See Figure 2-6.) With this approach, you can create seemingly impossible print-outs — such as a ship in a transparent bottle or a fetus gestating within a transparent mother's belly.

Figure 2-4:
An example of stereolithography printed using the FormOne printer.

Brandenburg Gate
Berlin, Germany

Figure 2-5:
An example of multi-photon lithography using the NanoScribe 3D printer.

Image courtesy of NanoScribe

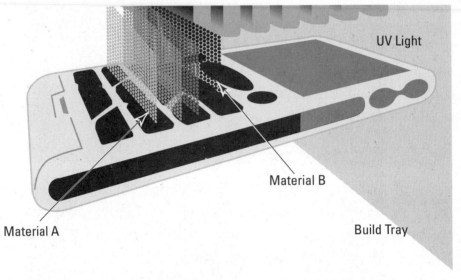

UV Light

Material B

Figure 2-6:
Objet's
photopoly-
mer PolyJet
printer can
mix multiple
types of
materials.

Material A

Build Tray

The PolyJet's capability to mix materials also allows for the creation of different functionalities within the same printed material (refer to Figure 2-6). This means that complex objects, such as a prosthetic — a flexible joint sandwiched between rigid, hard-plastic body components — can be printed all in the same process. Using this approach, you can create combinations of materials — part rubbery and part solid, for instance — all at once, if desired. Good examples of this type of prototyping include a cellphone with a hard plastic shell and a rubberized grip, or the wheels on a toy car, a rigid wheel and a rubber tire all as a single print.

The level of detail and personalization in these multi-material printers can be seen in major movies. Objet's printer, for instance, was used to create the armor that fit Robert Downey Jr. like a glove in the *Iron Man* movies. Also, the Objet printer allowed the effects team for the blockbuster *Prometheus* to quickly produce and custom-fit the film's bubble-like spacesuit helmets for a variety of actors, including Noomi Rapace and Michael Fassbender.

Granular

Another technique, popular for plastics, metals, and even ceramics, relies on the use of a granular powder. This technology has been used to create large objects from James Bond's car in *Skyfall* to flexible artwork like the 3D-printed full dress worn by model Dita von Teese. The granules can be solidified in a variety of ways, including:

 ✔ By binding the granules with bonding materials like glues.

 ✔ By *sintering* (combining powders by heating them below their melting point) as shown in Figure 2-7.

 ✔ By melting (combining powders by heating them above their melting point to create a full melt pool of material) using a laser or electron beam to provide the energy necessary to fuse the powder only where the final object needs to be.

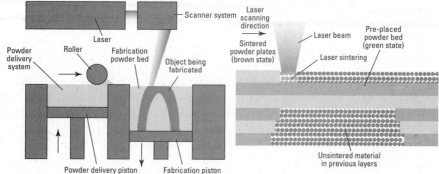

Figure 2-7:
Laser
powder
sintering.

Binding powder

Powder-binding printers use ink-jet sprays to apply a rapidly-solidified binder into the powder bed, creating the new solid object from this sprayed glue and the base powder material. Once the entire model has been completed, unused powder is removed and recovered for re-use (as seen in Figure 2-8), and if the final object exceeds the build volume of the printer, then final assembly can take place. Using the 3D-printing process to create many of the interlocking features already assembled — instead of making them individually and then assembling them — saves effort in comparison to traditional manufacturing processes.

Plastic-powder objects remain granular and so can be easily crushed unless dipped into resin to fill the spaces between the granules. For metal and glass casting, the resulting "solid" shapes are stabilized by heating them to fuse the binder and powder, or when using simple metal powder by infusing the powder-binder mixture with additional liquid metals (such as bronze) to create a stronger alloy or more pleasing appearance. This is popular for jewelry making, where precious metals like gold and silver are too expensive to keep in granular form to fill the powder bed. The use of powder granules from a more common source also further decreases the cost of materials that go into the creation of truly personalized and unique items.

Image courtesy of the Francis Bitonti Studio

Because the powder bed supports the solidified bound material, this type of production allows for the creation of large, complex designs without concern that thinner elements will break apart during fabrication. One vendor, VoxelJet, uses the powder bed's support to allow for continuous creation of objects — their system uses a binding jet that operates across a tilted granular bed and a conveyer belt that moves the entire volume of powder slowly through the printer. In this way, the printer builds models by just adding more powder, layer by layer, along the incline (see Figure 2-9) and selectively binding the powder according to the 3D design. This capability can even be used to fabricate solid objects that are longer than the entire printer's depth

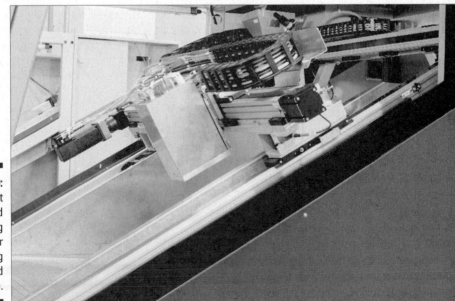

Figure 2-9:
A VoxelJet
powder-bed
binding
3D printer
prints along
an inclined
plane.

Image courtesy VoxelJet

by continually printing the front end of the model as the rear extends beyond the conveyer behind the printer.

Blown powder

Another technique used in metal fabrication involves blowing metal powder into a laser or electron beam, adding the blowing powder into the melt pool formed by the heat source. This is particularly useful when the materials require exceptionally high levels of heat to melt — examples include tantalum or titanium in aircraft manufacturing or as the edge cladding of turbine blades (whether for repair and enhanced operation). Like the other forms of additive manufacturing, blown powder can be applied very exactly to create complex final parts with no more effort than creating a simple design using the same amount of material, as seen in Figure 2-10.

Figure 2-10: A titanium cooler block created using EOS's Direct Metal Laser-Sintering (DMLS) 3D Printer for WithinLab.

Image courtesy WithinLab

Lamination

Another type of additive manufacturing, *lamination,* uses a rather different approach. Instead of laying down layers of powders or melting pools of material, lamination cuts out individual layers of material and then combines them, one atop another, with a form of glue. Metal foils, plastic sheets, and even common paper can be used to create laminated objects, as illustrated in Figure 2-11.

Wire freeform electron beam "welding"

In space, the lack of strong gravity precludes the use of powder-bed printing, and blowing powder would create a small, unwanted second rocket exhaust. To get around these issues, NASA has been investigating a close relative of blown-powder 3D printing: a system that carefully injects wire into the electron beam. By using a metal wire (as do terrestrial electron-beam welding systems), researchers have been able to perform the same type of additive manufacturing without gravity or atmosphere — without the hazard created by metal powder being dispersed into the cabin's air supply.

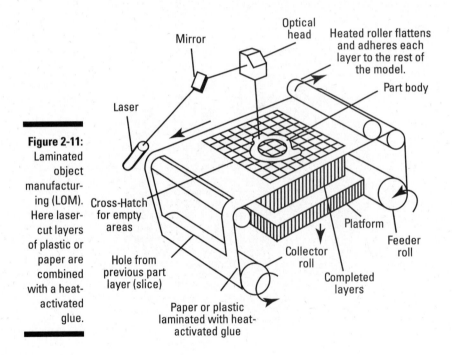

Figure 2-11: Laminated object manufacturing (LOM). Here laser-cut layers of plastic or paper are combined with a heat-activated glue.

Mirror

Optical head

Heated roller flattens and adheres each layer to the rest of the model.

Laser

Part body

Cross-Hatch for empty areas

Platform

Feeder roll

Hole from previous part layer (slice)

Collector roll

Completed layers

Paper or plastic laminated with heat-activated glue

The final product will only be as strong as the material it's made of — paper, foil, or plastic, together with the glue — and laminated object-manufacturing systems lack resolution in the Z axis (as the object gets taller) because each layer can be no taller than the thickness of the sheet of material plus the layer of glue. Still, these systems can be very attractive to clients who need models for rapid prototyping of products and would prefer an inexpensive and rapid assembly to a higher-resolution alternative.

Fused deposition modeling

Perhaps the best known form of additive manufacturing is *fused deposition modeling* (FDM), which was invented by Stratasys in the late 1980s. Using the same STL files created by 3D Systems for their stereolithography system, the fused deposition modeling 3D printer squeezes melted thermoplastics through a small nozzle to create an object. The process is much like the way you squeeze out toothpaste to cover your toothbrush. By building up layers of melted plastic, the object can be created and rapidly cooled to room temperature in a matter of minutes. (See Figure 2-12.)

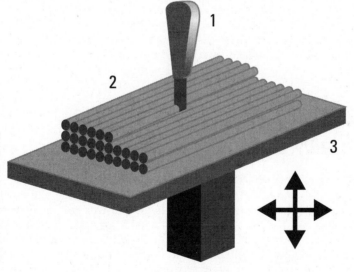

Figure 2-12:
A line-art illustration of fused deposition modeling (FDM).

Because the term *fused deposition modeling (FDM)* is trademarked, the same process is also called *fused filament fabrication (FFF)* by hobbyists and researchers.

The RepRap 3D printer uses fused thermoplastic to build objects at home, including many of the parts necessary to build another RepRap printer. We show you how to build your own RepRap 3D printer in the last chapters of this book!

The thermoplastic used in this type of 3D printer is typically sold in spools of thin filament, varying in widths between 1.75 and 3.00 mm. This filament can be made up of acrylonitrile butadiene styrene (ABS) polymer, polylactic acid (PLA) bioplastic, water-soluble polyvinyl alcohol (PVA) for support, nylon, and composite materials. One such experimental wood/plastic composite filament can be sanded and painted like wood, and even given a grain-like pattern by varying the temperature at which it is squeezed out.

Many 3D printers — like the Cube that will soon be available at Staples office supply stores — require the use of proprietary cartridges already loaded with high-quality filament. The proprietary approach ensures that the filament is the proper thickness and that it melts at the precise temperatures, which makes printing easy, but the cartridges can be expensive. Many open-source advocates in the RepRap community prefer buying less expensive generic filament, which allows the use of materials not yet available in cartridge form — such as glow-in-the-dark plastics. Some more complex versions of RepRaps and their commercial offspring (such as the MakerBot Replicator) can print using multiple types of filament at the same time; the flexibility of generic filaments can be valuable — especially if you're willing to take the time to sort out the variations in quality among vendors of generic filament. We discuss these issues more thoroughly later in the book, when we show you how to build your own 3D printer.

Recognizing Specialized Forms of Additive Manufacturing

In addition to thermoplastic, printers can also extrude other materials in melted, gel, or semi-liquid states to fabricate a wide range of amazing objects from highly-detailed wax jewelry models for lost-wax casting (where dissolvable master objects are embedded in clay and hot metal is poured in, forcing out the wax or plastic and leaving the final object to cool and harden), to foods and candy. Even body parts and complex organs are being tested for the possible bioprinting of living tissues.

Manufacturing with a variety of materials

If printing new parts for our bodies wasn't amazing enough, NASA is looking at ways to use additive manufacturing beyond our planet to create bases on the moon and Mars, using little more than the local rocks melted and fused together using microwaves from collected solar energy. (See Figure 2-13.) If a material can be stacked, melted, sintered, squeezed out, bound in powder

Image courtesy Contour Crafting

Figure 2-13:
Additive manufacturing may take us to the moon and beyond.

form, or deposited by a robot, then some form of additive manufacturing can use it to create entirely new types of products — even trash, such as the thermoplastic used in milk jugs and plastic bottles, can be used to create amazing new objects.

Even raw materials here on earth are being explored as sources of new types of additive manufacturing, from natural glass (made by using concentrated solar energy to melt sand) to fabrication based on the natural production of silk. Researchers at MIT's Mediated Matter Group are studying the way that nature builds up its own creations by observing how silkworms build cocoons and how spiders spin webs — and then applying what they learn to create entirely new types of additive manufacturing solutions. An example is the extraordinary suspended SpiderBot 3D printer shown in Figure 2-14.

Printing in color

If "a picture paints a thousand words" then color transforms those words from a monotone recitation of the lunch menu into a driving, emotionally compelling ballad. Color creates variation both significant and sublime in paintings, photographs, and now in 3D-printed objects as well. Many types of additive manufacturing produce objects in bland colors — like white or the natural color of the material used, such as metal and concrete — but others can make use of different colored materials such as the filament used in fused thermoplastic fabrication systems. Melting one or two types of filament alongside each other can produce objects that fade from one color to the other. Churning different types of filament together within the melting element can produce 3D-printed items that are as attractive as they are fascinating in their creation.

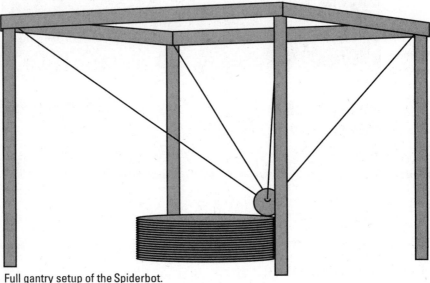

Full gantry setup of the Spiderbot.

Measured lengths of filament can be affixed to one another to give a printed object a layer of one color and another layer of an entirely separate color. Other materials such as nylon can be dyed different colors, making each object completely unique and allowing for even more personalized variation among printed objects. More deliberate variations can include a serial number printed into each object's design at the time of manufacture.

Additive manufacturing techniques that employ inkjets to apply sprayed powder binders — or use cut paper layers for lamination — can take this process one step further: They can use inkjet printing in the most familiar way — printing in color. The binder doesn't have to be a clear adhesive between white granulated powder, when the addition of color can illustrate additional data or create eye-catching prototypes for review and consumer response before the final product goes to market.

The same is also true of multi-material fabrication techniques, which can provide a prototype with several different surface treatments, allowing potential users to touch and feel a model that reflects the final design in far greater detail than two-dimensional renderings can. These prototypes can also be rapidly adjusted in response to feedback and testing, with a new object printed in a few hours' time to verify that requested changes accomplished the desired goal.

Fabrication using direct digital manufacturing can then take the design directly from the test site and begin rolling out the first production models or creating the molds for mass manufacturing, including new changes discovered during the process of review and testing. This flexibility would be impossible for traditional manufacturing. For the traditional manufacturer, changes identified mid-process would require retooling; the direct digital manufacturer could simply adjust the model in use and continue producing objects with the new feature already in place. For that matter, a second digital production line could turn out the modified replacement for existing products. Imagine the time you'd save when a recall for a part on your car results in nothing more than a trip to the dealership to have the proper replacement printed out for your specific make and model. No need to keep all possible variations in stock, or to keep your car for days while the proper replacement is shipped from the manufacturer.

Seeing the Limitations of Current Technologies

The potential for additive manufacturing is little short of miraculous, but there are still a number of factors that will affect how rapidly the transformation from traditional manufacturing to additive manufacturing occurs.

Considering fabrication rates

The cultural expectations of instant fabrication were set by Hollywood, where the simple utterance of "tea — Earl Gray — hot" by an actor on *Star Trek* was quickly rewarded by a cup of hot tea. These expectations are still too high. Today's technologies take minutes, even hours, to create a plastic cup — never mind the water and tea to fill it. (See Figure 2-15.) The object might be hot, though, depending on the technique used to fabricate it, so perhaps it's only a matter of time before we can order up a cup of hot tea *Enterprise*-style. But it may be a while.

Newcomers to 3D printing are often taken aback by how long it takes to print even a small plastic item. Some of the items shown in magazines and in TV specials about 3D printing can be amazing, but they may also be made up of hundreds of individual little pieces, each of which takes time to design and then print out — assuming everything works perfectly the first time. The benefit of additive manufacturing is that any complex features that would have taken a long time to produce through traditional means (holes through the object, stamped serial numbers, and so on) can simply be printed and may take no longer than printing the same model without those details.

Exploring size constraints

Most 3D printers only have a specific volume within which they can create their output — for some printers, our *Star Trek* teacup might be too large; others (like the VoxelJet) can produce a full-scale lamppost in a single print. Realistically, most additive manufacturing systems currently have a *constrained build volume* (the biggest thing they can make must fit within the printer) although this concept might soon be eliminated if open-form systems like the SpiderBot can be perfected.

Adding robots to the additive manufacturing process seems almost redundant — after all, additive manufacturing systems are specialized types of robots to start with. As with improvements in traditional manufacturing lines however, additive manufacturing will benefit from industrial robotics to handle the extracting and finishing objects, enhance analytical software and design systems to design our future homes and the items that fill them, and (in the form of expert systems) help clients select just what they want from their new purchase before the purchase is made.

Identifying object design constraints

In addition to having to fit within the printer, your Ultimate Tea Cup will have to be printable in the first place. This is where experience in design and materials science can help — not every hollow object with a handle will work as a cup. Depending on what it's made of, the item might prove to be a better garden trowel.

All forms of manufacture have their unique concerns. Anyone familiar with injection molding, for instance, knows that there must be channels for air to escape the mold when filler material is forced in. Additive manufacturing is no different. Several unique factors have already become commonplace.

For some 3D-printing types, an effective support structure that can later be removed is necessary, as is a specific amount of overhang so that each layer can be aligned atop the one before it without gaps or drooping edges. The software used to design printable objects also takes some experience to master, although it need not be expensive. A number of alternatives for home use do not require the thousands of dollars per copy that many professional packages command — and you can expect that whole range of software to improve rapidly. New software is starting to handle full-color object designs, complex internal voids and structures, interlocking components in the same build volume, and the specified qualities of an object based on its unique materials mix at each point in the build. We discuss the software requirements and some of the options for 3D printing later in the book.

Understanding material restrictions

The variety of new materials that can be used in 3D printers is expanding too fast to enumerate here. In the year prior to the publication of this book, Objet PolyJet system alone exceeded 100 different types of materials. Other manufacturers are not slowing their efforts at ever-expanding suites of options for materials and fabrication techniques.

Where the bioprinters of a year ago were hard-pressed to produce a functional artificial cartilage, today the first 3D-printed organs are being tested. By next year, you might be able to print a steak for your home barbecue as easily as I might 3D-print a replacement for my aging knee. (See Figure 2-16.) A few years down the road, 3D-printed heart replacements or new muscular enhancements printed directly into our bodies may be as common as 3D-printed silverware . (See Figure 2-17.)

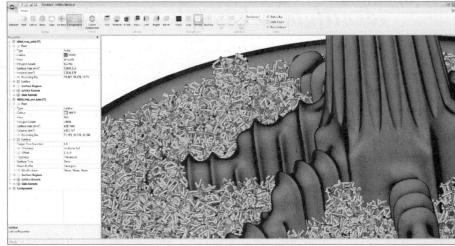

Image courtesy WithinLab

Figure 2-16:
A complex bio-compatible replacement bone socket being designed in the Within Medical software.

Image courtesy the Francis Bitonti Studio

Figure 2-17:
3D printed silver forks.

Today's fabrication techniques are being refined, but they aren't perfect. Compared to injection-molded items, the fused thermoplastic objects created by today's printers have minor weaknesses along each layer's boundary. Both bound and sintered granular materials have a more complex — and potentially fragile — inner structure than their solid forged alternatives, but they also weigh far less and may prove to have surprising new capabilities that their predecessors' makers could never have dreamed of. The use of new sustainable materials like polylactic acid (a biodegradable plastic derived from plant sugars) can even assist in recycling and may aid in the adoption of additive manufactured products. All revolutionary change brings about both new requirements and new capabilities.

Chapter 3

Exploring Applications of 3D Printing

*T*he promise of additive manufacturing is that one day, any product can be created in a fully personalized manner locally on demand. Enthusiasts of additive manufacturing see that day as just around the corner. Supporters of 3D printing see in this promise the possibility for 3D printing to repatriate manufacturing functions — and manufacturing jobs — back to their local communities; reductions in waste materials; the elimination of a need for "spare parts"; and the potential to use biodegradable, sustainable alternative materials in place of the durable petroleum-based plastics that currently pour into landfills.

Despite the advantages of this new paradigm, critics of additive manufacturing exist. Some are already implementing agitprop campaigns to discredit or cast doubt on 3D-printed objects by asking questions like "when a car crashes because of a 3D-printed part — who is legally liable?" Beyond the fundamental assumption that a car would only fail because of a 3D-printed part, what these same critics are trying to prevent from rising to the public's attention is that a number of parts and components that are already being designed, tested, prototyped, and in some cases even being manufactured using additive manufacturing — and this has been the case for decades in some fields.

No matter how you look at it, additive manufacturing will have an impact on the way people manufacture goods. Already it has been used to augment existing mass-manufacturing factories and processes. One day, perhaps, this technology will be the only means of manufacturing goods, and every product will be subject to local fabrication and full personalization, but we're not there yet. Even barring the emergence of a modern-day Luddite movement, traditional manufacturing practices have a deep hold on the economy and will continue to exist for some time essentially unchanged. But even in these traditional settings, additive manufacturing has already caught hold and is busily helping to create products used daily.

In this chapter, I discuss applications of additive manufacturing technologies as they exist today.

Creating Objects Directly Using 3D Printing Today

As we discuss in Chapter 2, a number of different types of additive manufacturing are already available for use in directly manufacturing objects using plastic, resin, metal, and many other types of material. This lends itself to several obvious current-use applications, including prototyping, direct digital fabrication, and more.

Rapid prototyping

The earliest use of 3D printing was in the production of digitally-designed objects as prototypes of new designs before production begins. (See Figure 3-1.) The advantages of rapid prototyping with additive manufacturing are apparent in processes such as these:

1. Evaluation of a design while it is still in the computer.

2. After evaluation, creating a solid prototype based on the design that can be handled and operated.

3. Comparing the printed prototype to components of existing systems to ensure correct fit and function.

Creating a solid object for consumers to evaluate speeds up the rate at which new designs can be compared side by side. 3D-printed versions of alternate designs or iterations can be reproduced and compared much faster than individual examples of each design can be turned out — saving weeks in the production schedule.

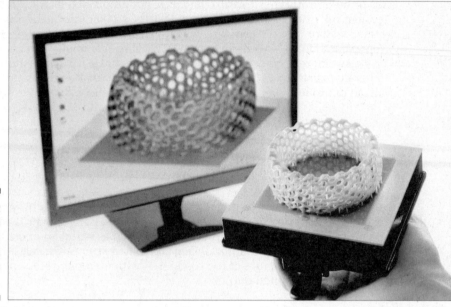

Figure 3-1:
Rapid
prototyping
a new digital
design for a
bracelet.

Image courtesy of FormLabs

Often a prototype does not need the material strength of the final object design, so a plastic or resin design can be used to test an object before investing in the cost and materials required for metal reproduction. Jewelers and other designers can test their designs in wax or biodegradable plastic for a few cents — and then create only their final model in gold, silver, or other valuable materials, after the client has already approved the fit and function. (See Figure 3-2.)

Figure 3-2:
Custom
personalized
silverware
created and
tested using
3D printing
before final
production
for the
client.

Image courtesy of the Francis Bitonti Studio (Designer: Michael Schmidt, Architect: Francis Bitonti)

3D-printed prototypes can also illustrate additional details for product evaluation, using color and other indicators, so that information such as stress load or thermal measure within a structured object can be clearly represented for non-technical review. This same capability can be used to show different model design options, to illustrate the visual impact of different artistic or coloring options, and to build marketing materials ahead of production to allow review by test audiences.

Direct digital fabrication

The use of additive manufacturing to create prototypes allows for rapid transition through the stages of the design process, but in some cases it does not stop there. With metal fabrication systems, additive manufacturing can be used to create end-use — final — products and designs, rather than just plastic prototypes. With this approach, details such as serial numbers, branded marketing designs, even interlocking and joined structures, can be included in the physical structure of the product — with no tooling steps needed beyond the 3D-printed output.

Production of a single unique design, called a *one-off*, or other limited-production runs for specialty products used in racing, medical, and space technologies, can be very costly in traditional manufacturing. (See Figure 3-3.) Because the same mold or tooling is only used a few times (possibly only one time), there are no opportunities for efficiencies of scale that bring down per-item costs in mass manufacturing of goods.

Figure 3-3: A lightweight intake cooling system for racecars, created with a complex interior set of voids to reduce weight.

Image courtesy of WithinLab

Direct digital manufacturing also allows updates to be made in the middle of a production cycle, without re-tooling the production line. Once the digital model has been modified and uploaded to the 3D printer, all future produced items can include the change automatically. GE has started using this capability in the design of its future aircraft jet engines, where rapid updates can be performed and the line kept in operation to save time overall in the production of high-precision engine components because multiple components can be combined and printed at a single time without requiring the traditional methods of brazing and welding to combine individual assemblies.

Restoration and repair

Additive manufacturing has its place in current direct digital fabrication, but that same function can be used to re-create objects that were once available but have long since been lost from available inventory stocks to make room for the next year's model.

Whether the component is a compressor cover on Jay Leno's steam-powered car from last century or a replacement flipper for a pinball machine, both are long gone for the corner store, even if they were ever available locally to the public. (See Figure 3-4.) However, by scanning in the broken bits of an existing design or by creating a new replacement part from measurements and CAD design, additive manufacturing can bring new life to these outdated designs as NASA recently did to create new examples of the massive hand-welded Saturn V engines that once allowed us to reach the moon.

Figure 3-4: A replacement flipper for an old pinball machine, shared as THING #1789 on Thingiverse (a large open-source 3D model repository).

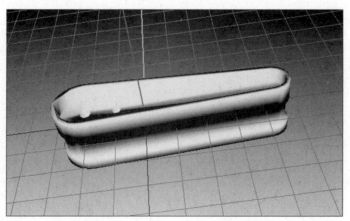

By creating designs that can take the place of original equipment, it is even possible to improve on the original to make the repaired item quite literally better than it was when it was new — new materials can be used, reinforcements can be added, and any number of modifications can be made entirely within the computer before a part is ever created. By creating the part in lightweight and inexpensive plastic, its fit can be tested and further adjustments made before a final object is created in material desired.

The amazing potential of this new type of parts management is that manufacturers would no longer need to store copies of all possible parts in warehouses and other locations. Instead, they would simply download the appropriate component design and print out its replacement when needed. Instead of days or weeks until the proper replacement can be shipped to your local dealership, you could call up the mechanic to schedule a recall item replacement, and they would print out the part to have ready when you arrived on your way home.

A complete warehouse full of individual parts could be replaced by a small shop stocking only raw materials and a bank of 3D printers. No more concerns for items being out of stock, and available options could include different materials for special needs or even personalized designs created by individuals based on standard fittings or connectors. (See Figure 3-5.)

Figure 3-5:
Three funnels I created to allow re-use of proprietary liquid soap dispensers with generic soap, shared as THING #32186 on ThingiVerse.

Making proprietary become generic

Another capability made possible by 3D printing is the creation of connectors and fittings that can make proprietary containers reusable by allowing them to be refilled using inexpensive generic materials, or repurposed by refilling them using alternative materials altogether using items like the funnels shown in Figure 3-5. This creates issues for manufacturers who price their goods based on selling cartridge refills, and will certainly bring up claims that any failures in operation may be the result of substandard materials used to refill the original containers. But these are well-worn paths of complaint for both traditional refills and 3D-printed connectors to assist in refilling proprietary consumables, seen anytime non-factory parts are used to upgrade a car's engine, or when generic refills are used in the office ink-jet printer.

Beyond simply taking advantage of repairing outdated designs and printing replacement parts, 3D printers could also provide manufacturing techniques that could re-use existing materials and components, with "this week's model" body style or other personalized and customizable attributes added to an existing durable product to retain its interest to consumers. By printing a new case, cover, or structure, we can displace the endless cycle of "keeping up with the Joneses" with new models. This will reduce fundamental goods production in some trades but also reduce endless consumer debt accumulation to keep up with purchasing, with designers and boutique opportunities providing the potential for individual artists to create entirely new industries to cater to user personalization.

The future could well be focused on industries that retain investment in fundamental components, adding updates and reclaiming materials for future modifications and re-use in the place of outlets endlessly pushing the next year's or next season's product lines — whether automobiles, houses, furniture, or clothing.

Fabricating Tomorrow Using 3D Printing

Building better and cheaper goods for existing produce cycles provides many advantages, while the true power of additive manufacturing lies just ahead in the new opportunities, products, and services that will be made possible as this suite of technologies becomes more prevalent and capable. The following subsections describe opportunities for near-future 3D-printed innovations.

Household goods

Today, I might 3D-print a hammer to use to hang a photograph on my wall. The photograph could be 3D-printed in full color, using an image from my own collection, as a single object that includes a frame — and even a cover pane of transparent plastic to give it the same look and feel as a more common framed picture. As more materials and complex assemblies can be created through additive manufacturing, everything from the furnishings to items filling those shelves can be fabricated with full color, shape, and function present in the original materials from which their designs were derived. (See Figure 3-6.)

Figure 3-6: A metal table illustrating both function and fluid complex form.

Image courtesy the Francis Bitonti Studio (Designer: Michael Schmidt, Architect: Francis Bitonti)

As additive manufacturing technology improves in sophistication — to the point of printing complex, multi-material objects such as integrated electronics and composite interlocking structures — the range of "printable" objects expands. Eventually it will become possible to 3D-print many items that we commonly use around the house — and the house.

Buildings

Soon, much larger 3D printers extruding concrete may fabricate complete structures intact — not only the furnishings but also entire buildings. The technique would not require human contractors working to assemble individual components and then affix those assemblies to a foundation. The final building structure would emerge from the printer.

Figure 3-7 illustrates this concept, showing an elevated gantry to support the concrete extruder operating above the structure as it is created. Current estimates based on the test equipment suggest that a new house could be constructed in as little as 20 hours' time, making this technology very desirable as the ever-growing population needs new homes.

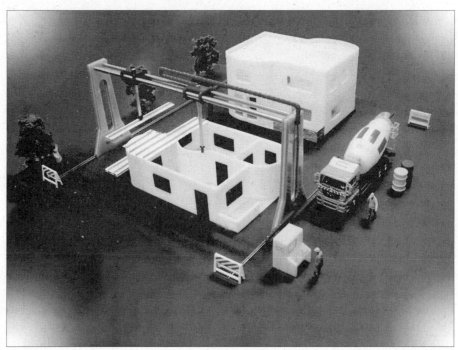

Figure 3-7:
A 3D printer
for houses.

Image courtesy of Contour Crafting

Emergency shelter following natural disasters such as hurricanes, earthquakes, and tidal waves could be replaced by solid shelters formed from natural materials present in the local environment like the open structural framework in Figure 3-8. This illustration is a small-scale creation formed by focusing concentrated sunlight onto natural sand like that found on beaches and in deserts around the world. The 3D printer merely moves the focal point across the sand to sinter together individual granules into solid structures.

Figure 3-8:
A structure created by using sunlight to fuse sand.

Image courtesy of Markus Kayser

Additive manufacturing techniques also allows for the formation of complex interior structures and spaces to accommodate wiring, plumbing, and improved insulation. It's quicker and more efficient than creating such spaces in traditional concrete slabs poured in wood frames. Figure 3-9 illustrates the creation of a corrugated concrete wall that could be left with empty air pockets or filled with other materials (from foam to loose dirt) to provide greater thermal protection. This means that the same structural support capacity can be created using far less material and without the scraps, cut-offs, and remainder material left by the traditional construction process. There will come a time when plumbing and wiring can be fabricated directly into the structure itself.

Image courtesy of Contour Crafting

Figure 3-9:
Corrugated
walls of 3D
extruded
concrete.

Even now we are on the verge of printing out homes — or entire high-rise buildings — using 3D printers that will climb up the buildings they are creating, lifting themselves to build one floor at a time (as illustrated in Figure 3-10). This model is constructed much as the Egyptians once constructed the great Pyramids, but such printed buildings could have complex curved walls that currently frustrate traditional stick-frame construction.

Extreme recycling

In addition to using sustainable materials and producing far less waste, additive manufacturing will soon make it possible to create everything that exists in a home so that we might no longer need to "move" in the same sense of the word as we migrate around the world. You might be able to collect a small number of irreplaceable items (like your kids' drawings on the refrigerator or Grandmother's wedding dress), and then contract with a recycling service to recover the materials and components from your old home and its furnishings.

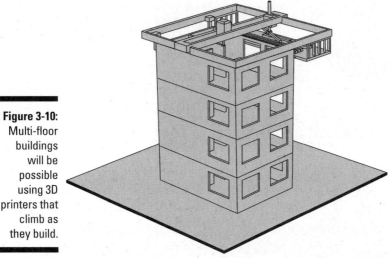

Image courtesy of Contour Crafting

Figure 3-10:
Multi-floor buildings will be possible using 3D printers that climb as they build.

Meanwhile, as each item is scanned and catalogued, its clone can be fabricated at the new site — perhaps with a few changes, such as that new family room addition. Moving in at the new site need not require getting used to a new layout, but instead will be more like coming home to the same house filled with the same things, only now located in a completely new setting. Hope the neighbors are friendly!

Examining Molding and Casting through 3D Printing

The capability for extreme recycling — where nearly everything we own can simply be re-created as desired — is still a ways ahead, but today additive manufacturing is already being used to create customized durable goods and many tools in use at traditional manufacturing facilities.

Because of the amazing level of detail possible using inexpensive plastic resins, 3D printing can be used to capture intricate designs that show precise details. Beyond just being used for prototyping, these models can also be used to create precise master molds for injection-molding bulk goods.

The benefits of digitally fabricated items include:

✔ **Flexibility:** Individual molds can be re-created as multi-cavity molds by simply creating multiple copies of the base design several times in the computer model and then printing a new model, with updates that improve corner-radius issues or add channels to increase flow efficiency.

✔ **Repeatability:** As older molds slowly degrade (for example, with the softening of the sharp edges), new molds can be created — even years later — with perfect repeatability of the original mold.

✔ **Scalability:** Digital designs can be printed at any desired scale, allowing the creation of precise duplicates at half scale or double scale — or duplicates that include specific distortions to facilitate specialized brand identification (or other artistic manipulation of the original image).

Lost-material casting

3D-printed materials such as thermoplastics and extruded wax designs can be used for lost-material casting for creating jewelry designs for gold, silver, or other valuable materials. After the final design is created in a computer, it can be printed out complete with additional material to form basins, sprues, gates, and runners all included as a single object. This object is embedded in casting clay and once the clay has set, the cast mold can be heated to allow the plastic or wax to evacuate the casting mold cavity. Again, repeatability is exceptionally helpful in mass manufacture, with no need to assemble subcomponents to create complex core and cavity arrangements in permanent molds.

Sintered metal infusion

For artistic metal designs, inexpensive granular material such as steel can be sintered into a solid form. Because sintering does not involve a full melting of the material, the resulting sintered object is essentially a porous mesh of steel particles bound into the desired shape — which may be quite fragile, depending on the technique used to sinter the granular material. Embedding these objects into casting clay makes possible the introduction of a more artistically desirable material such as bronze into the mold, filling the void defined by the steel granules. After polishing, the resulting metal amalgam can produce an alloy with desirable artistic or material traits. Such processes can bind together materials with very dissimilar properties in ways that would not be possible through traditional alloy injection molding.

Applying Artistic Touches and Personalization

The ability to create customized one-off designs or low-volume production runs with minor variations helps to create designs customized to individual characteristics and preferences. This can include manufacturing details such as logos and serial numbers directly fashioned into the object itself, or can include custom complex material forms not possible through traditional molding, casting, or forging manufacture.

Medical implants

Perhaps the most variable, personalized, and specialized application of manufacturing is the creation of medical implants, which must fulfill a function while performing in harmony with the organic structures of the body. (See Figure 3-11.)

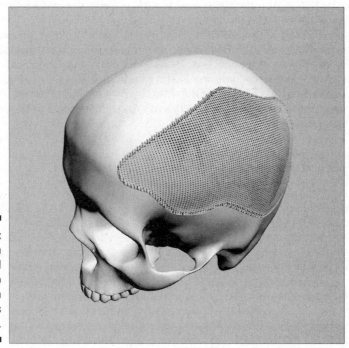

Figure 3-11:
A custom
3D-printed
cranial flap
implant with
a porous
structure.

Image courtesy of WithinLab

3D printing is only limited by the overall size of an object. Thus the object's interior geometry can be solid like that of a traditional cast object — or can be hollow or more complex. The result is a quicker way to create an object with optimum balance between strength and weight — or to minimize materials cost and waste. In medical implants, metals are often used because they are not reactive to the body's natural processes. Metals such as titanium are popular, but have such a high melting temperature that most designs are traditionally cast as solid models. This approach is not only costly for the subject, it also raises the possibility of post-operative damage from vibration and movement of the implant against biological materials like bone.

Figure 3-12 shows an example in which WITHIN Labs used *selective laser sintering (SLS)* to create a titanium artificial hip implant in a 3D printer. This implant has a highly complex metal geometry that allows bone to grow into the implant itself, forming an improved bond with much greater mechanical strength than is possible with traditional screws and adhesives.

Figure 3-12:
A acetabu-
lar cup
pelvic
implant,
showing
complex
metal
lattices.

Image courtesy of WithinLab

Item personalization

Personalization is not restricted to iPhone cases and other material objects. Another, far more specialized application is biological prosthetics for reconstructive purposes or for replacement of missing limbs.

After massive injury to a body, 3D printing allows the re-creation of a subject's features from old photographs or through modeling based on remaining body elements. This technique can return the ability to eat and drink normally to individuals who have suffered injuries or diseases affecting the facial tissue, or provide a completely new ear for people born with *microtia* (a functional inner ear but no external ear, which causes hearing impairment or loss). Researchers using 3D bioprinters are testing bioengineered ears using collagen and living cells to form a new cartilage structure that can be implanted to restore proper functioning.

External prosthetics for limb replacement have traditionally been little more than solid forms with as much articulation as their designers could provide. A company called Bespoke has started creating custom coverings, called *fairings*, designed by creating a 3D model from a scan of the remaining limb. By mirroring the existing limb, Bespoke's design integrates artistic designs with a balanced appearance created by an artist working with the recipient. Fairings can be created in plastic, or even chromed metal, using 3D printing to create a look that fits the recipient's unique personalized preference. (See Figure 3-13.)

Figure 3-13: An example of a personalized prosthetic fairing, covering a replacement leg with a very artistic design mirrored from the remaining limb.

Clothing and textiles

Going beyond appliances to whole-body coverings, artists are developing new materials such as 3D-printed artificial leather and flexible lattices that can be worn in personalized clothing or footwear fitted to the recipient's exact form.

Designer Michael Schmidt and architect Francis Bitonti teamed up to create a stunning 3D-printable gown custom-fitted to the specific proportions of fashion model Dita von Teese, shown in Figure 3-14. This dress was created using a curved latticework design based on the Fibonacci sequence, a mathematical relation that defines many of nature's most beautiful shapes. Applying the lattice to a scan of the model's body allowed the creation of a 3D-printed mesh complete with interlocking flexible joints that wraps her perfectly.

Figure 3-14:
A completely 3D-printed gown worn by fashion model Dita von Teese.

Image courtesy the Francis Bitonti Studio (Designer: Michael Schmidt. Architect: Francis Bitonti)

At the current state of the art, the artist added Swarovski crystals to enhance its appeal on the catwalk, but advances in multi-material printers may make that treatment unnecessary in the near future. If this technology becomes more common, we will soon simply step into a scanner and then select the desired material to create a custom-fabricated 3D-printed pair of pants that won't bunch at the waist or fall down on the hips, regardless of the wearer's body dimensions.

Deploying Technology to Strategic Locations

Customization goes beyond personalized objects, implants, and clothing to include almost any design for an object or device. Many times, issues are only discovered after a design is already in use, which can prove very troubling when the manufacturing facility is unavailable and far away.

Military fabrication

Ships in the U.S. Navy operate for extended periods of time far away from land, and sometimes need parts or modifications that aren't readily available. Some ships have started employing on-board additive manufacturing systems to assist in the prototyping of modifications and to do direct digital fabrication of components to be deployed operationally.

Eventually, improvements to additive manufacturing will allow in-place repairs to equipment that is currently inaccessible without major work at a service yard. Metal cladding, for example, can use this process to add material to an existing metal object, allowing the repair of damaged or corroded mechanical equipment. Submarines may yet be equipped with specialized 3D printers that crawl along the spaces between the inner and outer hulls, providing mid-operational repairs that are currently impossible.

Similar needs have been found for smaller equipment as well, leading the U.S. Army to create the Mobile Expeditionary Lab, a 20-foot shipping container packed with rapid-fabrication systems that can be used by soldiers in the field without access to parts shops and metalworks in conflicted areas. Early successes of this capability include creating new brackets to adapt equipment to fit on local vehicles, or a small cover that prevents a soldier's flashlight from being accidentally turned on while moving around during maneuvers. Bringing this capability to the location can best identify needs and test designs that fit the locale (a desert, say, as opposed to a jungle). Presently the Army can get a new product, component, or update into use within days. Designs at the lab are uploaded to the Rapid Equipping Force's home location where they can be reviewed, updated, or sent for full scale fabrication with a tremendously shortened chain between the troops and their gear.

In space

Few environments provide a greater challenge than in space travel, as we look outward beyond our own planet to the moon, Mars, and beyond. If the only wrench that fits the radio mast gets lost during repairs, it's exceptionally difficult to have a replacement delivered. No wonder additive manufacturing is under deep investigation by NASA and other spaceflight services. Being able to make what astronauts need in flight and en route, using basic materials and a 3D printer that can work without gravity or in a vacuum, is potentially a vital feature of future spacecraft.

The cost of lifting anything from the surface of Earth is still (pardon the expression) astronomical. When planning a mission to another planetary body, the use of native materials like lunar soil (called *regolith*) and energy from the sun is very appealing. If we can adapt the same systems used with sand and dirt here on earth so that they can be used on the moon, then we can send robotic systems ahead to print out roads and structures to house our astronauts without further cost for lifting materials to orbit and to the escape velocity beyond that. (See Figures 3-15 and 3-16.)

Figure 3-15: Lunar construction of roads and buildings using additive manufacturing.

Image courtesy of Contour Crafting

Image courtesy of Contour Crafting

Figure 3-16:
A small-
scale model
of a lunar
habitation
printed out
of concrete.

Part II
Outlining 3D Printing Resources

In this part...

- Survey the various 3D printing materials, including thermoplastics and nylon, liquid photopolymers, and dry granular materials for metal and ceramic objects.

- Explore several different methods to create or capture 3D models, including scanning, designing in CAD software, and photogrammetric shape extraction using multiple photographs.

- Check out the possibilities in bioprinting, which may allow us one day to print food, animal products, and even living tissues and organs.

- Review the places you can find 3D-printable objects, such as Internet sources and online repositories.

- Begin to find or make objects for 3D printing yourself!

Chapter 4

Identifying Available Materials for 3D Printing

Although 3D printing is still in its infancy, the number of different materials available are rapidly expanding — with new options being made available almost every week. In the final chapters of this book, we describe how you can build your own 3D printer that uses melted plastic filament to fabricate solid objects.

The specific type of thermoplastic used for 3D printing determines the temperature that must be used to melt it. Melting temperature, in turn, has an impact on the strength of the final object and the type of surface needed to let the first layer hold properly through the printing process. In a 3D printer, only the final stage of the extruder heats up, with the filament remaining at room temperature until it reaches the FFF/FDM extruder's hot-end.

Ambient air temperature can affect the final product's quality, with some professional printers heating up an enclosed build volume (the maximum space a 3D printer can fabricate solid objects within) to help each new layer bind more completely to the previous layer. The build plate can be heated in some printers to help the first layer adhere to the plate and limit warping, but the build plate can also be covered by a material to assist the plastic's grip. Some types of filament can use common painter's tape to assist first-layer adhesion to keep the object in place during the print process, while other types of filament may need a more exotic material like the heat-resistant polyimide Kapton tape DuPont developed for NASA's spacesuits.

Other materials are commonly used to help the first layer bind properly, including ABS Cement, hairspray, and even scrap filament dissolved in a compatible solvent and painted on the build plate to create a thin film. The materials simply need to be compatible with the thermoplastic being used.

For other types of 3D printers, layer binders may be present in the process itself (SLA, for example, binds the liquid to the build platform as it is solidified) or they may be unnecessary, as in granular binding where the unbound powder stabilizes the object during print. The variety of techniques for securing a print at its very start mirror the variety of types of materials that can be used in the object's fabrication as well, with different material types available for different techniques of fabrication.

Enumerating Extruded Materials

As we discuss in Chapter 2, fused deposition modeling (FDM) systems like RepRap 3D printers (which we create in Chapter 12) use extruded materials — such as melted thermoplastic — to create objects,. Although thermoplastics are presently the most common types of filament, new types of filament are made available every day.

Filament like that shown in Figure 4-1 can generally be obtained as spools of plastic with a 1.75mm or 3mm diameter, but select your material with care. Many failed 3D prints can be directly attributed to flaws in the filament:

- ✔ Lower-quality filament manufacturing processes can result in filament spooled while still slightly moldable — which may stretch it into an oval shape around the spool's axis.
- ✔ Filament extruded in varying thickness can distort the object being printed.
- ✔ Dirty filament can drag soil into the extruder.

Professional-grade (and many proprietary consumer-grade) 3D printers work only with filament in pre-spooled cartridges. Although such filament is more carefully quality-controlled and protected by the cartridge casing, these cartridges carry a higher price and provide fewer options than can be found in generic filaments.

Thermoplastics

Thermoplastics make up most of the types of filament used in fused deposition modeling. Filament made from these thermoplastic materials can be created in many different colors, even transparent or glow-in-the-dark.

Figure 4-1:
Spools of
thermoplas-
tic filament
of various
material
types,
including
PLA, ABS,
and nylon.

Variations in the material qualities of different filament types create potential difficulties if you decide to change from one filament type to another (PLA to ABS, for
example) during a single print. Even so, halting a printout in the middle to change
the color of filament is a common way to enhance the attractiveness of the final
product. Figure 4-2 illustrates a 3D-printed puzzle bolt that makes another use of
paused printing — adding the nut to the bolt as it is being fabricated.

Polylactic acid (PLA)

One of the most commonly used thermoplastics in 3D printing is PLA, an
environmentally friendly and biodegradable polymer created from plant
sugars from crops such as tapioca, corn, and sugarcane. This material can be
printed using a print bed covered with painter's tape and does not require a
heated build plate. PLA melts at a very low temperature, around 160 degrees
Celsius, although it bonds better around 180 degrees Celsius, and most PLA
printers direct a small fan at the extruder to cool the material as it is added,
preventing the hot end of the extruder from re-melting the previous layers.

PLA can be more brittle than some other thermoplastics, although specialty
versions are being developed for increased flexibility and a reduced carbon
footprint during the material's creation. PLA is popular in cash-poor areas of
the world because of its ease of creation from whatever natural plant sugars

are available locally. PLA is used to create rain-collectors and pipe fittings in many less-developed parts of the world, along with simple sanitation products like toilet seats. It is somewhat more brittle than ABS, less flexible than nylon, and so remains one of many options in use today in developed areas.

Figure 4-2:
A 3D-printed puzzle for children that includes a printed nut added to a dual-ended bolt paused during fabrication and then completed.

Model: Thing #13923 at the ThingiVerse repository, shared under the Creative Commons license by its designer Aeva

Acrylonitrile butadiene styrene (ABS)

ABS plastic is used in a variety of industrial applications for extrusion and injection molding, including in children's toys like the popular Lego bricks, so its properties are well known and the quality of filament can be more easily controlled during manufacture. ABS

- melts at a higher temperature than PLA (150 degrees Celsius but bonds better at 220–225 degrees Celsius)
- extrudes more easily, with less friction as it passes through the extruder
- can be printed onto Kapton tape or a thin layer of ABS cement

ABS plastic shrinks as it cools. Thus a heated build plate produces better results by limiting the contraction of earlier layers to prevent warping of large objects.

If used in a confined area. ABS has a mild odor during extrusion that can affect chemically sensitive birds and people. ABS is also said to produce more airborne microscopic particles than PLA without adequate air filtration.

Polycarbonate (PC)

Polycarbonate materials such as Lexan are a recent addition to the available thermoplastics used in 3D printer filament. Polycarbonate applications include CD and DVD media and automotive and aerospace components, due to its high resistance to scratches and impact. Higher strength and durability, however, require extruder temperatures of 260 degrees Celsius or higher, which some printers cannot sustain. Although polycarbonate plastics are used in the creation of "bulletproof glass" when poured into forms, the layering in 3D printers creates microscopic voids between layers so the final result will not be as strong as molded industrial equivalents. Polycarbonate objects can also undergo a change in state when exposed to ultraviolet light, becoming more opaque and brittle over time.

Polyamides (nylon)

Nylon filament is another recent addition to 3D-printing options, especially useful for objects that require flexibility and strong self-bonding between layers. Nylon thermoplastic filament requires extrusion between 240 and 270 degrees Celsius, and has excellent layer adhesion. Nylon is also resistant to acetone, which dissolves materials like ABS and PLA. In addition, polyamide materials can be opaque, transparent, or even dyed to different colors using common clothing dyes meant for nylon fabrics. In addition to its resistance to acetone as a solvent, nylon can produce good flexible vessels such as vases and cups because its excellent layer-bonding aids in the creation of watertight objects.

Richard's "tie-dyed" nylon filament (Figure 4-3) allows for the creation of unique objects with color combinations along the length of a filament without requiring splicing or halting print jobs in the middle. This is a very popular option for the hobbyist doing 3D printing at home; clothing dyes are easily available.

Polyvinyl alcohol (PVA)

A popular option for water-soluble support is polyvinyl alcohol, a biodegradable industrial adhesive material extruded between 180 and 200 degrees Celsius. Some varieties of PVA are conductive and can be used to 3D-print electrical circuits directly into fabricated objects. However, PVA-printed material dissolves easily in water and so must be isolated from atmospheric humidity. PVA is most commonly used as a support material for other types of thermoplastic, so that it can later be simply dissolved away in water to reveal the completed plastic object.

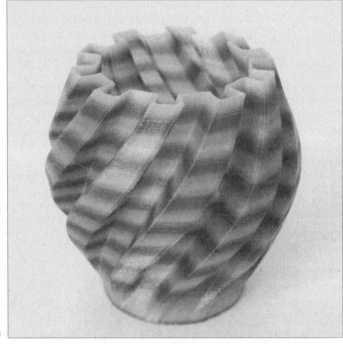

Figure 4-3: A dyed nylon 3D-printed object from Richard's experimentation using off-the-shelf clothing dyes.

High-impact polystyrene (HIPS)

Another soluble support material that has recently become available is HIPS, a variation of styrene, the same material used in packing material and food containers. High-impact polystyrene (HIPS) has similar properties to ABS but dissolves in limonene, a biologically derived solvent made from citrus plants, rather than using acetone like ABS. HIPS filament is relatively new and its use is still experimental. Like PVA, HIPS is used primarily as a soluble support material in combination with other types of thermoplastic.

High-density polyethylene (HDPE)

HDPE is the thermoplastic material used to create bottles and other recyclable items marked as "Number 2." Because HDPE is easily found in recycle bins and in landfills, the use of HDPE scavenged from recyclables like milk jugs is generating interest. HDPE binds easily to itself, but it has difficulties binding to other materials, so it often requires the use of an HDPE sheet as the build plate. Because it is more difficult to work with, HDPE is not popular for 3D printers but its sheer availability as a byproduct of many industrial applications is encouraging efforts to apply this material for additive manufacturing — especially once home filament extruders become more available.

Students at the University of Washington have used extruded HDPE to create boats for a local milk-jug regatta competition and recently won a contest to use recycled HDPE in 3D printers to fabricate toilet seats and water-collection components for Third World areas. The sheer variety of containers fabricated using HDPE makes this material readily available for recycling in many parts of the world, allowing one nation's trash to be recycled as useful products once techniques for adapting recycled HDPE to 3D printing are more mature.

Experimental materials

Recent attention to 3D printing is providing an almost constant influx of new options for materials, including variations of PLA and ABS with new qualities and capabilities. PLA varieties include flexible variations, even some that produce specific smells in the final printed objects. ABS alternatives include glow-in-the-dark and color-diode materials that shift colors in response to temperature variation like 1970s mood rings, and carbon-fiber composites that make conductive 3D-printable material that's suitable for embedded electronics.

Composite materials can also provide results that appear to be natural. An example is the use of wood fibers in the experimental Laywood-D3 filament, which produces an extruded solid form that can be sanded and painted like real wood. Varying the temperature of the hot end during printing also allows layers to blend darker and lighter regions to create grain-like patterns in the final objects. A German researcher, Kai Parthy, has also created new materials that result in a sandstone-like appearance for architectural modeling, as well as extruded objects that are ductile and transparent — suitable for use as home-printed light pipes embedded in 3D-printed objects.

3D-printed light pipes using transparent 3D-printed plastics are used by The Walt Disney Company in their remarkable Printed Optics (shown in Figure 4-4) to bring low-voltage, cool LED illumination directly to their displays in ways that traditional Edison-bulb designs simply cannot match. The Printed Optics program is developing this technology to make toys more responsive to children's interactions, adding responsive elements to traditional components of their theme park settings, and to provide illumination using low-power LED bulbs more individually fit to specific purposes within its array of exhibits.

Extruded alternatives

In addition to thermoplastic materials, other options for 3D printing include pastes, gels and even clays and clay alternatives such as Play-Doh. The Hyrel3D printer can extrude objects made of air-dry clays and plasticine, using a proprietary screw-drive emulsifier; Cornell's open-source Fab-Home design can create customized foods and other products using almost any material that can be pureed and squeezed out of a syringe — from cake batter and bread dough to printable scallop and celery pastes.

Figure 4-4:
3D-printed light pipes in Disney's Printed Optics program developing alternatives to Edison-style bulb illumination.

The RepRap printers we discuss later can also make use of Richard's open-source Universal Paste Extruder to create 3D-printed muffins, corn chips, and even chocolates like the bunny shown in Figure 4-5.

Other alternatives use fused filament fabrication (FFF, which is another term for the proprietary FDM technique), with wax and granular materials in paste form such as sugar, salt, and some ceramic powders that are also usable in sintering and granular binding fabrication.

Identifying Granular Materials

Granular materials are used in sintering, melting, and additive applications of binding glues. With them, you can create objects in a wide variety of materials, including glass particles, plastic powders, various metals and alloys — almost any type of material that can be rendered into a fine powder or granular state.

Figure 4-5: 3D-printed white-and-dark chocolate bunny, created using a RepRap 3D printer and Richard's Universal Paste Extruder.

Plastic powders

Commercial printers like the multi-color ZPrinter bind together plastic powders by using an ink-jet of liquid glue. To further solidify the resulting objects, post-processing typically includes a dip in cyanoacrylate resin to fill in the gaps between particles. Without the resin filler, these objects typically lack the structural strength of other forms of additive manufactured products. The use of ink-jet binders allows for color mixing not possible through other forms of fused or sintered production. Other printers, like the VoxelJet system shown in Figure 4-6, can use materials like granulated plastic and fine sand to create their results.

Sugar and salt

Artistic uses for food-printed items include more than simple extruded chocolate. Granular binding of sugar and salt provides the fine control of details needed to create complex structures like the sugar sculpture shown in Figure 4-7. Although sintering and melting of sugar granules is also a way to fabricate objects, the application of heat caramelizes most sugars and creates a color transformation during the process.

Figure 4-6:
The
VoxelJet
VX4000,
which binds
granular
powder
using an
overhead
binder-
application
system.

Image courtesy of VoxelJet.

Figure 4-7:
3D printing
using bound
sugar
granules.

Image courtesy of The Sugar Lab.

Metal powders

Creations for the aerospace, automotive, and medical fields require the use of material much stronger than plastic — typically these are biocompatible metals such as titanium, or materials that can withstand very high temperatures or provide great strength-to-weight ratios for racing cars or aircraft components. Many materials like titanium and tungsten are difficult to use in traditional manufacturing, where their high melting points and other factors prevent easy integration using traditional manufacturing techniques. Using sintering and melting techniques by laser or electron beam, very high-resolution details can be achieved even when the materials don't alloy well or melt at matching temperatures. Figure 4-8 illustrates a granular binding of titanium particles, done by sintering to create a custom medical implant.

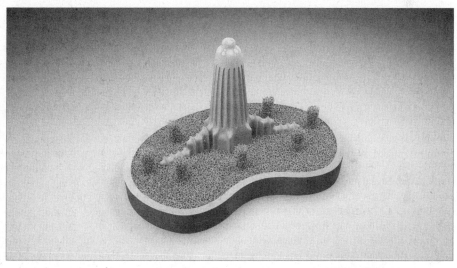

Figure 4-8:
Fine detail in a titanium joint implant using metal powders and an EOS metal-sintering system.

Image courtesy of Within Technologies

Sand and natural granular materials

Silica and other minerals can be used to create items through additive manufacturing techniques that include granular binding, sintering, and melting of the individual granules into an aggregate natural form of glass. Researchers like MIT's Markus Kayser are currently exploring the use of naturally occurring sand, fused using only light from the sun, to create sustainable objects and structures in some of the poorest parts of the world where structural materials are costly and difficult to obtain. Figure 4-9 illustrates his Solar Sinter in operation, creating a rough, solid, natural-glass object from sand taken directly from the Egyptian desert without any further processing.

Image courtesy of Markus Kayser

Figure 4-9:
Laser sintering of granular sand creates a rough form of natural glass.

Exploring Photo-Cured Resins

Photopolymer liquid resins used in stereolithographic (SLA) systems are so closely coupled to their particular applications that they're typically sold directly by the manufacturer to ensure compatibility. The resin's opacity affects how much light is necessary to cure a layer of the object being printed — and how deeply each layer penetrates into the fluid pool. The frequency of light provided by the laser or DLP projector will affect absorption by the resin. In high-precision, multi-photon lithographic systems like the NanoScribe (used to create the microscopic lattice shown in Figure 4-10), interaction among multiple illumination sources cures individual points within the build volume.

Understanding Bioprinting

Of all the types of additive manufacturing, perhaps the one with the greatest level of current interest is the emerging capability to print using living cells. The growing field of bioprinting may one day create picture-perfect steaks without the need for methane-producing feed lots, form leather clothing without the need to kill the original wearer of the skin, or fabricate replacement structures — even whole organs — from an individual's own cells rather than relying on organ donors. No generic bioprinting materials exist, nor standards for their use — because this technology offers the potential to use an organism's own cells as the building blocks for more complex tissues and organs.

Figure 4-10:
Photonic crystalline lattice created using two-photon lithography photographed through a microscope.

Image courtesy of NanoScribe

PolyJet materials

In addition to liquid pools of photopolymer resins cured from the top or bottom of the pool by using external light sources, Objet Corporation has created a whole different technique: Ink-jet applicators apply the resins, and then a UV light immediately cures the sprayed layer into a solid state.

This PolyJet application can mix different materials in much the same way that traditional 2D printers mix ink colors — only now, rather than mixing (say) blue and yellow to create green, the PolyJet printer can mix a flexible material and a rigid one to create objects with variable strength and flexibility: Complex areas with greater strength can be integrated with more flexible regions, all printed as a single object. Objects produced this way need no post-fabrication treatment using glues or other traditional techniques for assembly.

PolyJet printers currently allow use of the widest range of potential materials in a single print — presently over 104 different options. By mixing different materials, Objet can create a complete model ship in a transparent bottle or a medical model of a transparent body with only the significant details rendered as opaque visible objects.

Bioprinting food and animal products

Food underlies the fundamental ability to sustain a population and the production of foodstuffs. In particular, proteins from meat require significant resources to produce — feed grains, fresh water, and land, in addition to the management of byproducts like methane and animal waste from the farming of livestock. As the world looks to an ever-increasing number of hungry mouths and a dwindling supply for fresh water and open land, the ability to create living tissues like meat without the need for animals appeals both to economics and to the religious beliefs of much of the world's population.

Current attempts to grow muscle tissue using 3D-printed gelatin structures and living cells are not yet sufficiently mature to produce a recognizable steak (or even a good hamburger), but we are only just taking the first steps. Modern Meadow is a company attempting to create no-kill bioprinting alternatives to meat and leather production, using additive manufacturing techniques.

Leather is another area under investigation, as there are many ongoing efforts worldwide to curtail the use of animals to provide fur, leather, and other bodily materials to use for clothing and other human purposes. Organizations such as PETA reflect a growing interest in alternatives, but many parts of the world remain poverty-stricken and cannot afford more costly alternatives to traditional manufacturing of shoes, cords, and animal-hide shelters. When bioprinted leather becomes possible, the properties of this material could be extended to a wide range of applications without a single animal being harmed, while also eliminating much of the cost and waste associated with farming.

Replacement tissues and organs

Biological tissues can be used for more than simple food and clothing — in particular, to repair or even enhance our own bodies. Unlike donor tissues, bioprinted alternatives will be fashioned from our own cells so anti-rejection medications and waiting lists for biocompatible matches will be relics of a bygone era. Early successes in bioprinted tissues and organs have included blood vessels, trachea, and even bladder equivalents due to the simplicity of their cellular structure.

Organovo has recently announced progress toward a 3D-printed liver by merging several types of tissues in a complex structure that may soon lead to a 3D-printed replacement for the body's principal filter. Other efforts at 3D-printed heart tissues and lung tissues may also give us techniques to address common frailties brought on by age. 3D-printed biocompatible implants are already being tested for cosmetic and reconstructive purposes.

Researchers are considering new surgical techniques that would involve keyhole-type orthoscopic procedures that could replace or repair organs in our bodies without requiring dangerous open-body exploratory surgery.

There are, of course, potentially negative uses of the same techniques. An athlete might be given additional muscle tissue or enhanced connective tissues merely to enhance performance. The ability to visit a bioprinting cosmetic surgery office to have a "face-lift" that results in applying the current top supermodel's facial structure under your own could result in copyright-infringement lawsuits that presently seem bizarre.

Of course, our culture and legal systems will need time to adapt to the potential of these technologies, as techniques expand to enhance and extend human lifespans, to modify our appearance and our height, or to craft entirely new capabilities within our own bodies. The initial steps toward all of these are already being researched today.

Identifying Alternative Materials

Because the field of additive manufacturing offers application in almost every area of manufacturing and production, alternatives to traditional materials will rapidly follow transitions away from traditional techniques for creating objects.

Recycled materials

As 3D-printed buildings become available in the form of extruded concrete structures, a more efficient approach to construction becomes possible. Elements such as power conduits and plumbing can be created directly within the structure itself during printing. Rapid assembly systems might create components on one side of a new building and assemble them on the other while the 3D fabricator builds up one layer of concrete after another with the proper voids already in place for the other components. (See Figure 4-11.) New ways to use recycled materials would be a natural fit for this process.

In addition to stimulating the development of new materials, additive manufacturing can make more efficient use of existing materials by

- ✔ reducing need for new materials by reducing waste
- ✔ re-using, recycling, and repurposing materials already in use

Image courtesy of Contour Crafting

Figure 4-11:
A 3D printing corrugated concrete wall section including spaces for electrical lines or plumbing.

Artist Dirk Vander Kooij, for example, has taken the plastic from old refrigerators to create extruded furniture in his Endless line. Other inventors have been working on devices that home users can use to create new 3D-printing filament from inexpensive bulk pellets or even their old failed prints and waste thermoplastic materials.

Thus, additive manufacturing offers the chance to "green" the making of new materials and products in several ways:

✔ Reducing the need for materials in the initial manufacturing process by eliminating post-fabrication machining and waste-material cut-offs

✔ Allowing the efficient creation of complex structures with interior voids not possible in traditional casting or injection-molding

✔ Recovering and recycling materials for use in 3D printing

Such advantages can help realize longer-term sustainability in the face of reduced resources in the post-peak-oil economy projected to begin around 2020.

Research is currently proving early successes in using recycled paper, glass, and pulverized concrete to create new material for additive manufacturing. In addition, more environmentally favorable materials are emerging, such as the fully biodegradable plant-sugar based PLA thermoplastic. As bioprinting continues to expand its capabilities, new types of foods and other animal-based goods may become possible without resorting to killing live animals or maintaining massive quantities of livestock with fresh water and edible grain that could be put to use feeding the ever-growing number of humans.

Storing food

NASA is currently funding research into a 3D printer that can produce foods such as pizza from powdered basic materials that can be emulsified into pastes using only water. The pastes would be extruded layer by layer, even cooked by the heated build plate of a special-purpose 3D printer designed for operation in the long-term exploration of the moon and other planets in the solar system. The shelf life of such powdered foods is targeted for 30 years or more, allowing the creation of food stockpiles that can be distributed as needed ahead of major storms.

Caring for people

In the wake of a major catastrophe, a mobile additive manufacturing facility could provide food and shelter even as damaged structures and debris are collected and recycled into the material that will form replacements for all that was lost to the flood, earthquake, or tsunami. Injuries may be repaired using 3D bioprinters to create compatible tissue based on living cells collected from the injured — avoiding issues of tissue matching or potential rejection.

In daily use, 3D printers may take on the role of custom formularies, creating whole courses of medications precisely matched to individual patients' needs. Instead of taking two pills of medication X each day for ten days and then one pill of medication X and one pill of medication Y in a particular course of treatment, a patient could simplify the regimen: Specialized 3D printers will soon be able to create each day's medications in the minimum possible number of pills, delivering exactly the combination, dosage, and proportions of medications needed for each day's treatment so that individual patient needs can be uniquely treated by the personalized course of medications filled into each pill.

Chapter 5

Identifying Sources for 3D-Printable Objects

*T*oday, 3D printers are becoming more commonplace in businesses, schools, libraries, and homes. Online services like Shapeways, Ponoko, and iMaterialise can transform 3D models into solid form even if you lack a printer of your own. However, those 3D models do not spring into the world fully formed — they must be created. Once created, they can be shared with others around the world as easily as a song in MP3 format or a photograph on a photo-sharing site.

In this chapter, I review several ways to create 3D models suitable for printing or sharing with others. But keep in mind that not all object designs are intended to be captured, shared, or otherwise produced without the original designer's permission. Before you create an object or sell a design of your own, make sure that it truly is yours to use. In Chapter 11, we discuss the more common licensing models used in the 3D-printing community, but we must stress that you should always remember to use the creative work of others only as they have requested. That being said, it's easy to find designs with few such restrictions — such as those whose creators have stipulated only that their designs be attributed them as the creators — so you have a wealth of models to get you started in 3D printing!

Exploring Object Repositories

A virtual 3D object model is encapsulated using standard file formats, such as the common STL and OBJ file types. Individual 3D model files can be transmitted via e-mail, stored in a repository, or shared using any other service that handles ASCII data, although the software-specific file types require access to the proper software to open and manipulate the virtual model. Other file formats for individual software include SKP for SketchUp, SLDPRT for SolidWorks, STP for 3DStudioMax, BLEND for Blender, and DXF for AutoDesk products, which can also be used to save and share 3D models online.

Collections of these files are referred to as *repositories,* which can be provided by individual vendors to supplement their own products (the Maker's Tool Works MendelMax RepRap design from Chapters 11-15 is shared as: `https://github.com/Makers-Tool-Works/MendelMax-2.0/`), open-source sharing sites like Makerbot's ThingiVerse, or via individual personal file-sharing services like GitHub. (Richard's own 3RD delta printer RepRap design, for example, is shared at his personal GitHub site at `https://github.com/RichRap/3DR-Delta-Printer/`.)

Vendor repositories

Perhaps the first treasure-trove of 3D-printable designs most people discover are the online repositories of designs provided by vendors of 3D printers. When 3D Systems, for instance, sells a new Cubify 3D printer, the company wants to make sure that the buyer can download sample models to test the new printer!

In these repositories you can find free file downloads for a variety of 3D-printable objects — cases for your iPhone, buttons you can sew onto your favorite shirt, or jack-o-lantern decorations for Halloween fun. The vendor provides free designs that you can download, modify with a variety of software applications — which I cover later in this chapter — and print out in solid form.

Cubify.com also allows designers to upload 3D models that customers can download by paying for a copy of the designer's original file, which forms a new type of marketable commodity, one that's composed entirely of virtual object designs and that does not require inventory, storage space, or shipping for delivery to the customer.

Other types of vendors sometimes use 3D-printing repositories to provide parts for their products to the consumer, reducing costs and allowing personalization of the final design by the consumer. The Cartesian MendelMax

RepRap kit we discuss later in the book is a good example of this approach: MendelMax provided the models for the brackets used to mount electronic end-stop switches (see Figure 5-1), posting the models as files at an electronic repository. Users can download the files and create the actual objects later.

Figure 5-1:
Four brackets for electronics that are printed to complete the MendelMax 2.0 RepRap 3D-printer kit.

In this way, vendors can also provide designs to enhance or personalize their products, as Nokia did with the 3D-printable phone case we discuss in Chapter 1. Here the vendor increases the desirability of a product line by allowing consumers to design their own cases or purchase designs provided by someone else to print at home or through an online service.

This type of repository also allows mid-process modifications to be provided for consumer adoption without requiring the reassembly of a packaged kit. Instead, consumers can simply be provided with a notice of the upgrade and the location from which it can be downloaded. A few years from now, a part recall at your local auto dealership will be handled by a quick visit where the dealership can download the proper modified part for your particular vehicle from the manufacturer's repository, print it out, and install the new part without ever having to stock and store the multitude of different parts needed to fit all makes and models affected by the recall.

Some vendors even provide designs to customers to help repair their objects. In this way vendors can sometimes work around an expensive product recall, as might happen if a stroller manufacturer made a repair available by providing customers with a printable model for a small replacement part on their own part design repository. Using a metal-fabrication system, customers could print the repair in a matter of hours from their local 3D printing center, instead of having to wait for weeks for a tiny replacement part to be shipped to their homes. Other parts might be designed for fabrication using plastic on consumer-grade home 3D printers, as in the case of the cellphone case.

Community repositories

Another source for 3D-printable objects can be found at the many community repositories on the Internet. Users of these repositories upload models for a variety of reasons — for educational purposes, say, or artistic expression, or even to distribute functional parts like the components used to build a new 3D printer. Closely coupled with the so-called "Maker Movement," many of these repositories support open-source designs and shared licensing models where derivatives of object designs can trace their pedigree back to the original designer with pride.

Many of the models I use as examples when I speak about 3D printing come from community repositories like the ThingiVerse open-source design repository created by the co-founders of the MakerBot 3D printer business, Bre Pettis and Zack Smith. Figure 5-2 illustrates a handful of object designs from ThingiVerse, which houses hundreds of thousands of downloadable models, both original and derivative. These object models are grouped into categories such as Art, Fashion, and 3D Printers but you can easily waste an afternoon browsing through the lists of possible designs to create and show your friends.

Many upgrades for off-the-shelf 3D printers are shared via repositories such as ThingiVerse, and even designs for entire 3D printers, if their creators have decided to share them as open-source designs. The 3D-printer kits we describe later in the RepRap-building part of the book can also be constructed using downloaded 3D-printable object models and off-the-shelf components from local electronics and hardware stores. The kits just eliminate the need to search for compatible components or materials you might have to cut to length yourself. Commercial repositories are great for getting first-time 3D printers up and printing quickly, but for self-built systems, kits save the time needed to track down unusual parts such as toothed belts and stepper motors.

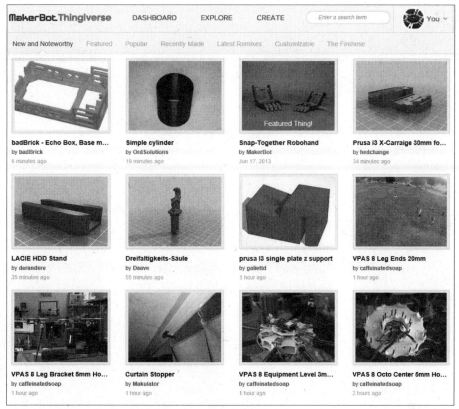

Figure 5-2:
An example
of Makerbot's
ThingiVerse
community
repository.

Designing in the Computer

Until a few years ago, designing 3D models involved *computer-aided drafting (CAD)* software (such as Autodesk Revit, shown in Figure 5-3) that required powerful computers and expensive specialized software. For years, CAD was well beyond the capabilities of most people outside of a dedicated group of specialists.

Additive manufacturing allows the creation of complex internal structures rather than simple, solid-block components — an improvement over traditional CAD tools which cannot always create models to rival the true capabilities of 3D printers. New tools are becoming available in specific arenas, as in the case of medical implants that must be highly customized to fit an individual's bone structure while also allowing complex lattices and other forms of fabricated non-solid models. (Figure 5-4 illustrates a complex structural lattice applied to what was originally just a hollow sphere with sliced-off sides.)

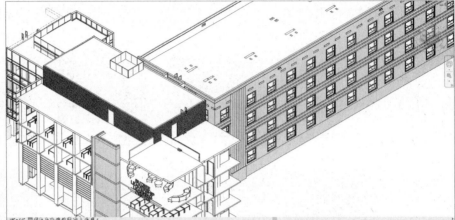

Figure 5-3: A CAD design in Autodesk Revit.

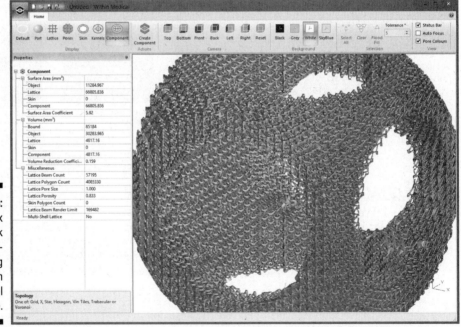

Figure 5-4: A complex latticework object created using the Within Medical software.

Beyond high-end and special-purpose CAD software that require extensive training and practice to use properly, much more user-friendly and available alternatives have been recently developed for home users. Options include the SketchUp package originally developed by Google, Blender, and a host of other applications that can be obtained for little or no cost. Public school teachers in the SOLID Learning program often use the browser-based TinkerCAD program (see Figure 5-5) because it is free, does not require a client installation on their computers, and has a simple, easy-to-understand user interface.

Figure 5-5:
TinkerCAD being used to prepare a 3D-printable mold from scanned dinosaur tracks at the Glen Rose excavation.

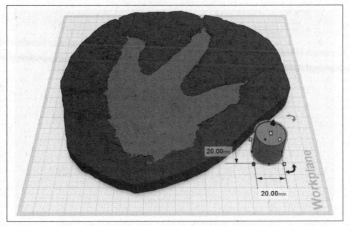

Dinosaur track scan provided by Dr. Louis Jacobs.

In addition to computer-based design applications, Autodesk has also released a series of free-to-use options for popular tablet devices. These rely on cloud-based processing instead of calculations done by the tablet device itself — so you can get an excellent result in very little time. Figure 5-6 shows the CAD-like interface of the 123D Design program.

Not all 3D-modeling programs require strict dimensioning and hard edges, because additive manufacturing allows a much more flexible build environment than traditional manufacturing could accommodate for home designers. Another free application in Autodesk's tablet suite is 123D Creature, which Kirk's kids love because they can use it to create 3D-printable monsters using a simple drag-and-drop interface. (See Figure 5-7.)

Many programs for 3D design and modeling can export files into common 3D printable formats like the STL encoding used with our RepRap examples, allowing designers to make use of their favorite tools when building complex and beautiful work to print, share, or sell. 3D printing is already allowing individual designers to sell their artwork and other designs directly to the public without the limitations of design and production present in traditional manufacturing alternatives.

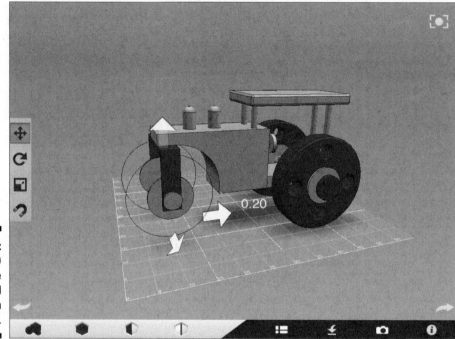

Figure 5-6:
Editing a 3D
model in the
tablet-based
123D Design
application.

Scanning Objects

It is also possible to capture existing objects into the computer so they can
be modified or simply re-created using a 3D printer. This is particularly useful
in the case of artwork or other unique formations that could not otherwise
be designed easily in a computer model. The Glen Rose dinosaur track in
Figure 5-5, for example, came from a laser scan of the original fossilized
impression, which was used to create an electronic copy (see Figure 5-8) of
the track that can be shared without risk to the original.

Optical scanning captures only the outer shape of an object, but it is possible
to use ultrasound imaging or CT scan data to create models of internal structures as well. Researchers have recently created a model of the first exposed
full skeleton of a living animal, for example, by 3D-printing the bone structure
taken from a CT scan of the subject. Similar data is being used to reconstruct
the facial features of mummified remains in Egypt and of the newly discovered remains of King Richard III. Using CT scans and a stereolithographic
system, researchers at the University of Dundee were able to print King
Richard III's skull into solid form, re-creating what this long-dead former
monarch looked like in life.

Figure 5-7: A
3D monster
model in
the tablet-
based 123D
Creature
application.

Early 3D capturing systems relied on a probe that contacted the printed object at many different locations, defining a "point cloud" around the object's shape to define its basic geometry, which is then filled in with greater detail as the scanner measures finer points between the original markers. These systems are still used in machinery analysis and other durable environments. More recent scanners use illumination from lasers or *structured light* — projections that measure the distance from the camera to different parts of an object, so there is no risk of harm to the object under investigation from the contact points of the scanner. Figure 5-9 is an example of a handheld self-contained scanner provided by Creaform being used to scan a human face. Coupled with software on a computer, this structured-light scanner can build a 3D model from repeated measurements of an object's surface structure as the scanner is simply waved above an object of interest.

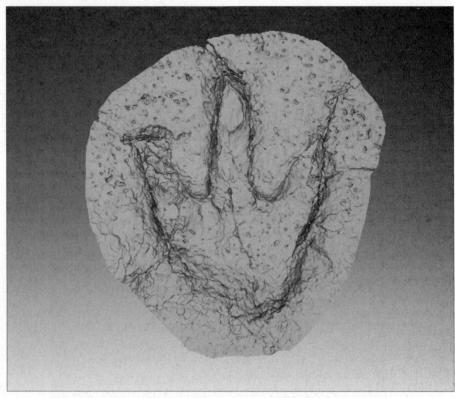

Figure 5-8:
A scanned
virtual
copy of the
Glen Rose
dinosaur
track.

Optical scanners can have difficulty scanning highly reflective surfaces or scanning objects lacking in detailed features. While a mirrored surface would appear as just a longer path to whatever is reflected, a large sphere would appear identical to the scanner from one point to another; the software would have trouble stitching the various different angles together to create a whole model (See Figure 5-10). When scanning large objects with limited features, it is possible to help the scanner by attaching small reflective dots to the object in various locations; the scanner can use the dots to calculate the orientation of various parts of the scan as we did for our reclining model shown in Figure 5-10.

Commercial 3D scanners provide very high-resolution models of scanned objects; such devices can be as small as a handheld scanner or can involve larger, more complex systems that map multiple angles at the same time. Scanners can image the inside surface of pipes, map out mineshafts and subterranean caverns, or even scan entire build sites for large structures, using laser tools similar to RADAR called LiDAR. Such systems are used to map mining operations to calculate ore removal, or in surveying to create digital terrain maps.

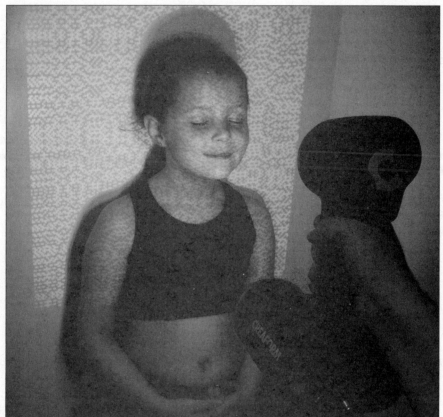

Figure 5-9:
A hand-held
Creaform
Go!Scan
structured-
light
scanner
capturing a
human face.

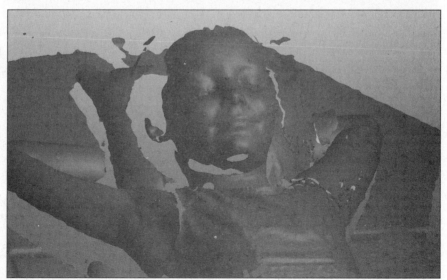

Figure 5-10:
Software
stitching
together
multiple
scans of
the reclin-
ing subject.
Hair does
not scan
well and
will require
edits before
printing.

Commercial systems such as Creaform, FARO, Artec, XYZ/RGB, and a host of other alternatives provide very high-resolution object models suitable for industrial applications and manufacturing. However, a home user can use inexpensive lower-resolution scanners — like the one built into the Kinect video game controller — to model objects for 3D printing. Together with software such as SCENECT, ReconstructMe, or Microsoft Fusion, the Kinect game controller's movement-mapping system can be used to generate scanned 3D models at home. An example is the image of Kirk's desk shown in Figure 5-11.

Figure 5-11:
A model of the monitors and speaker on Kirk's desk, scanned using a Microsoft XBox Kinect video game controller.

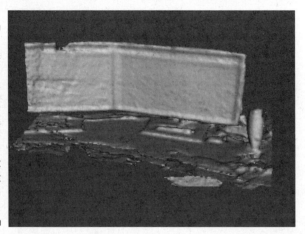

Capturing Structure from Photographs

Very high-resolution modeling for computer graphics can be performed using 3D scanners, but to capture objects in motion — such as a runner leaving the starting blocks — requires another technique — *photogrammetry*. Photogrammetry uses multiple 2D photographs to calculate the shape of objects within the field of view. By taking multiple photographs at the same moment, objects in motion can be captured as easily as the still objects required for 3D scanners.

Photogrammetric results are often not as exact as scanned equivalents because all points are calculated based on differences between two photos taken at slightly different locations. Professional photogrammetric studios like the one shown in Figure 5-12 can make use of carefully measured locations for each camera — and highly calibrated depth-of-field measurements on the lenses and lighting — to provide the best possible capture of living subjects. Models using systems like this can capture details down to individual hairs on a subject's arm, depending on the type of lenses and number of cameras used.

Advances in computing power, particularly in video card GPGPU processors, have made photogrammetry available to home users without high-end supercomputers.

Figure 5-12:
Photogram-
metric
studio
using 110
Canon DSLR
cameras
synchro-
nized by 6
laptop com-
puters.

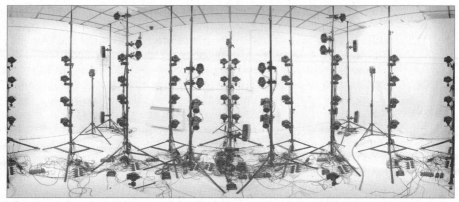

Image courtesy of Lee Smith/Infinite Realities

Early Structure from Motion techniques have been collected into commercial software packages such as AgiSoft's PhotoScan, shown in Figure 5-13, which is the same package used to capture 3D models for movie CGI, and for video game designers and artists who want full-body, full-motion captures of their subjects.

Figure 5-13:
Photogram-
metry on
Kirk's local
computer,
using
AgiSoft's
PhotoScan
to calculate
an object
from a
series of
photos
taken from
around the
object.

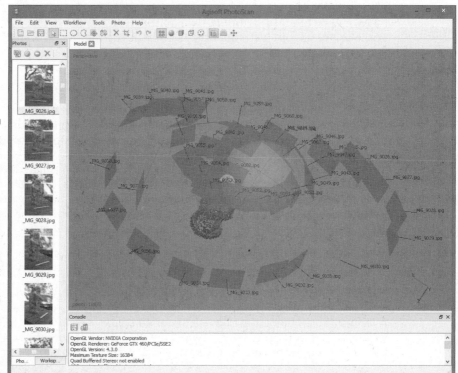

As computing power continues to increase, photogrammetric applications have developed greater capability to locate similar features between several different photos and calculate the relative position of the camera for each photograph without requiring the fine calibration needed for a professional studio. A hobbyist recently used his Google Glass camera to snap repeated photos of a museum statue, which he then reconstructed into a 3D model using Autodesk's free, cloud-based 123D Catch application.

No one was aware of this capture of the museum artifact because he was using a script that captured a photograph of what was directly in front of him every time he blinked. This capability strikes fear into the designers of next year's car-body models — not to mention fashion designers — because their unique creations may already be captured fully by the time a model walks off the runway during the first public display of a new design. As additive manufacturing continues to mature, a fabricator downtown or around the world could already be printing out copies of the designs in wearable materials before the model even reaches her dressing area.

As part of its cloud-based 3D modelling services, Autodesk's popular 123D Catch application allows tablet and PC users to perform photogrammetry even when their local computer lacks the resources necessary to process all of the detail matches in a reasonable amount of time. Using an example photographic set, for example, Kirk extracted the model of a warrior's statue (shown in Figure 5-14) at home — in a little over five days. The same translation was possible in just under three hours using the free "Create 3D Model" feature built into the browser-based Autodesk 360 interface.

Photogrammetric surface calculations can be used to capture 3D models of statues, moving people, and animals, even when a high-resolution 3D scan would not be quick enough to capture all the details of the subject. However, the same systems can stitch together photographs to build models of buildings — and even areas of land for agricultural review. Using a quadrotor or other type of UAV equipped with a camera, architects can capture a 3D model of a business park by simply flying the vehicle overhead and then later building the model in a photogrammetry solution. Using ROV submersibles, researchers in the local marine archaeology department are starting to use this capacity to map out wreckage and debris on the ocean floor to plan their recovery dives before the first person even enters the water.

Preparing Models for Printing

A 3D-printable object must have a manifold shape — it must be completely without holes and (in essence) "watertight" to print successfully. A hole though the object is fine, so a 3D-printed doughnut is possible, but a hole in

Figure 5-14:
A 3D model created using photogrammetry and a series of photographs.

the surface of an object must be filled or patched to create a continuous outer surface before it can be printed. When a scanner calculates a 3D object's shape, it does so using only the scanned surface (the outside) and so minor holes and other imperfections may require additional cleanup before the design is complete.

Some models need preparation before they're ready to be 3D-printed — whether they were created using CAD, scanned into the computer, or calculated from photographs through photogrammetry. Holes in the surface may need to be repaired; misaligned faces may need to be resolved (since a model has only an outside without an inside, the results can be mixed up if two models intersect); extraneous details may need to be trimmed away, leaving only the part you want to print. Figure 5-15 shows the added details captured in the same photos that Kirk took of the warrior's statue from Figure 5-14, which he had to clear away and then fill the hole left where the warrior's base meets the earth.

Figure 5-15:
The full
3D model of
the warrior
statue
before being
cleaned up
and made
ready for 3D
printing.

The model of King Richard III's skull was prepared using the excellent commercial Geomagic FreeForm application, but a number of free software tools are also available to assist educators, home users, and hobbyists just getting into 3D printing. The next sections offer an overview.

3D model viewers

One of the easiest additions to your suite of tools will be some type of 3D object viewer, so that you can inspect your object before the 3D printing begins. The 3D printer's control interface will use a system like this to lay out items on the build plate before printing begins, but other options can make quick choices between models easier. 3D models can be viewed in 3D printer control software like MakerBot's MakerWare, the open source Repetier interface, or in standalone products like the free STL Viewer application.

Mesh modelers

Mesh is the term used to describe the surface of a 3D model, which is defined using numerous small triangles. Many tools can export 3D designs into formats such as PLY, STL, OBJ, COLLADA and other file-storage types, and a tool like the free, open-source MeshLab can help convert these into the file type your 3D printer needs. Other mesh modelers — such as the free MeshMixer from Autodesk — can help cut away the parts of a scan or photogrammetric mesh you don't want, or close the holes in an incomplete mesh.

Mesh repairers

In addition to MeshMixer and MeshLab, there are tools that excel at helping to create a manifold object surface by extending a surface to fill in gaps — or to fill in overlapping areas where two manifold surfaces meet. One of the more common tools is the commercial NetFabb Studio, which has a basic free version for noncommercial personal use. Such tools easily automate the preparation and repair of 3D objects, a very handy capability for users new to 3D modeling.

NetFabb also includes toolpath management for RepRap printers, although we will show you alternatives recommended for each type of printer in our build chapters later in the book.

Part III
Exploring the Business Side of 3D Printing

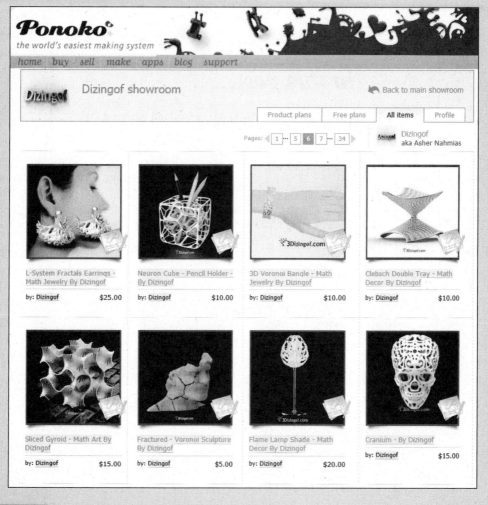

Explore the ways additive manufacturing affects product designers now and in the future at www.dummies.com/extras/3dprinting.

In this part...

- Find out how 3D printing is changing the world of business and manufacturing.
- See how to create a unique 3D-printed design and sell it on a personal online storefront.
- Consider the possibilities of using a design based on an expired patent.
- See the ethical side of additive manufacturing.
- Explore the future of 3D-printed designs.

Chapter 6

Commoditizing 3D Printing

*B*eyond the ability to print out small plastic animals for your children's parties, 3D printing offers a number of moneymaking opportunities not possible even a few years ago. The earliest commodity application of additive manufacturing was in the arena of prototyping, where its ease of one-off fabrication for testing earned it early fame as "rapid prototyping." Many products are tested by creating a physical model through additive manufacturing, allowing consumers to try out the fit and arrangement of controls and mechanical features using an actual model of the intended product. Today, 3D printing still facilitates the creation of rapid prototypes of different designs, but its capabilities have been expanded to include metal and ceramic materials suitable to the fabrication of durable production goods. This chapter examines many of the emerging uses for today's additive manufacturing systems, which are already opening up entirely new industries for exploration and commoditization.

Democratizing Manufacturing

Massive corporations such as Microsoft use additive manufacturing to prototype designs for their latest video-game controllers; small businesses can try out new products that would not have been possible with traditional manufacturing chains — skipping the multiple rounds of designers, sculptors, casting fabricators, and a host of other specialists and technologies well beyond the budget for small startups trying to break into a new market. 3D printing truly is democratizing the production process (bringing it "to the people") by providing a mechanism by which any individual can design an idea on free and open software and then render that idea into a solid form for testing, as a model for traditional manufacture — or fabricate that design directly into a marketable product.

The following sections discuss a few modern commercial applications of additive manufacturing.

Derived designs

3D printers capable of fabricating solid objects from metals and ceramics allow modern jewel crafters to design and create intricate pieces of jewelry. Small-volume production runs allow jewelers to make one-off custom pieces designed to fit the personal makeup of an individual client. Even people without skills in alloying or casting metals or other manufacturing processes can create new works. The flexibility of 3D printers means that a completely original design can be created in the computer or fabricated by mixing elements of other designs to create a new design for fabrication.

May individualized designs can be created by merging 3D-printed models, such as putting rabbit ears on a frog or your own head atop DaVinci's statue of David (or a 3D scan of your little brother). This type of item personalization is being applied to 3D-printed chocolates and many other gift items offered for sale by enterprising entrepreneurs using nothing more than a Kinect scanner, free design software, and a consumer-level 3D printer.

Curated artifacts

Some entrepreneurs are using 3D printers to create solid versions of digital models for sale or to exhibit in galleries as showpieces. The Smithsonian Institute's own digital curation team is currently scanning items from its vast collection, creating 3D models of objects (see Figure 6-1) that can then be reproduced for display elsewhere without risk to the originals — many of which are simply too fragile or too rare to risk being transported around the world. Fourteen million items have so far been identified for eventual capture by the Smithsonian's two-person digitization team, which is using laser scanners to capture high-resolution models from items both in the storage areas of the Smithsonian and artifacts from other museums and locations around the world.

Although the Smithsonian's digitization project is not a profit-generating effort, other museums and display venues are starting to take advantage of similar capabilities to create collections of the world's rarest artifacts without any risk of damage or loss but which can be licensed for use in other

Figure 6-1:
Digitization of a bronze statue of Thomas Jefferson and its full-scale reproduction.

Image courtesy of the Smithsonian Institute

museum displays. Many designs are being captured and shared for free, as in Figure 6-2, which shows a portion of the artifacts museums have uploaded to the ThingiVerse 3D-model repository for public sharing and download. Using such models, it would be possible to have examples of the world's greatest historical artistic and cultural achievements arranged around the living room or displayed in a classroom to enrich students' learning experiences. As long as the licensing for a 3D model allows its commercial re-use, it is possible to sell objects created directly from a 3D printer to schools, museums, or private collectors.

Creating models

A rapidly-developing opportunity for profitable work in 3D printing is exhibited by the digitization team known as the "Laser Cowboys" at the Smithsonian Institution, who capture 3D models of the Institute's vast body of artifacts. Many different jobs are being created around the capture of 3D models for artifact curation, stylistic modeling of new designs for durable goods, creation of cityscapes for urban planners, and capture of living organisms for the medical industry.

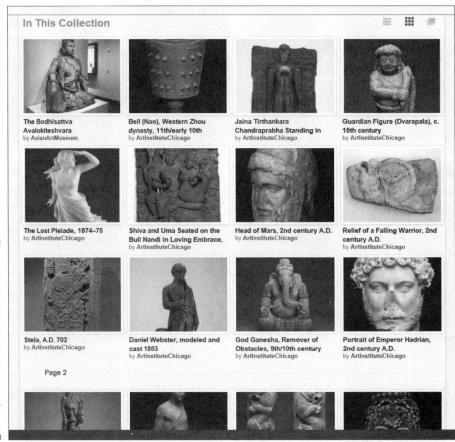

In This Collection

The Bodhisattva
Avalokiteshvara
by AsianArtMuseum

Bell (Nao), Western Zhou
dynasty, 11th/early 10th
by ArtInstituteChicago

Jaina Tirthankara
Chandraprabha Standing in
by ArtInstituteChicago

Guardian Figure (Dvarapala), c.
15th century
by ArtInstituteChicago

The Lost Pleiade, 1874–75
by ArtInstituteChicago

Shiva and Uma Seated on the
Bull Nandi in Loving Embrace,
by ArtInstituteChicago

Head of Mars, 2nd century A.D.
by ArtInstituteChicago

Relief of a Falling Warrior, 2nd
century A.D.
by ArtInstituteChicago

Stela, A.D. 702
by ArtInstituteChicago

Daniel Webster, modeled and
cast 1853
by ArtInstituteChicago

God Ganesha, Remover of
Obstacles, 9th/10th century
by ArtInstituteChicago

Portrait of Emperor Hadrian,
2nd century A.D.
by ArtInstituteChicago

Page 2

Figure 6-2:
Museums
share
3D models
of their
artifacts for
download
via the
Thing-I-
Verse
repository
site.

Not all of these types of jobs involve simply laser mapping to create the digital model, as Figure 6-3 demonstrates. UAVs are being flown over entire cities to create printable 3D models of buildings through photogrammetry, CT Scans are being used to create 3D models of ancient skeletal remains, and ultrasound imaging of fetal development allows a mother to see what her unborn child looks like well before the baby's delivery. These are just some of the many different opportunities for new industries growing around the use of additive manufacturing, creating the need for new skill sets and new job opportunities.

The studio shown in Figure 6-4 provides an example of new industry coming out of the 3D model space, where the capture of living subjects sitting still or in motion is providing entirely new techniques for animation and movie-making. Hollywood is seeing many uses of 3D printing in recent films, such

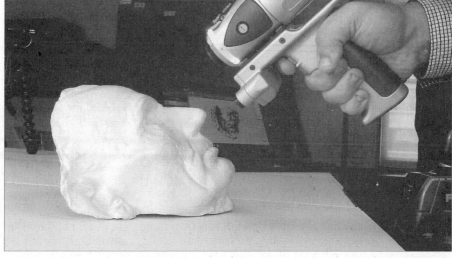

Figure 6-3:
A FARO
laser arm
being used
to create a
3D model
of this life
mask.

Image courtesy of the Smithsonian Institute

as the custom-fit gloves created for the *Iron Man 2* suit of armor or the clear, personally fit helmets used in the movie *Prometheus*. Animators for the movie *ParaNorman* were able to use full-color 3D-printed models for the faces of the stop-motion animated cast, with different expressions simply printed as additional copies of the character's head and then substituted in the proper frames captured to create an animated scene. Even the magnificent car seen in the James Bond movie *Skyfall* was created using high-resolution scans and a very large-format printer to create a prop in place of an actual 1960 Aston Martin DB 5, which would have been too costly to destroy in an explosion for the movie.

Figure 6-4:
3D high-
resolution
capture
studio for
facial
models.

Image courtesy of Infinite Realities/Lee Perry Smith

3D printing has also become fare for story lines in television shows. 3D-printed firearms show up in "CSI," 3D-printed counterfeiting plates in "Hawaii Five-O," and 3D-printed action figures of characters Howard and Raj in "The Big Bang Theory." Re-creating specific prop models from television and movies is also generating new opportunities for commoditization, but simultaneously raising issues of intellectual property rights and control over trademarked or copyrighted designs. An example is engineer Todd Blatt, whose self-created model of the alien cube from the movie *Super 8* resulted in legal takedown notices from Paramount. The studio had already licensed rights to reproduce collectables, including the cube, to another business — creating potential legal conflict resulting from Mr. Blatt's personally-designed model that could otherwise be simply downloaded and printed at home by fans of the movie. (We discuss the intellectual property implications of 3D printing in greater detail in Chapter 7.)

Selling 3D models instead of physical objects is another option for commodification of 3D printing, providing a valuable "product" (the design) that can be used to print objects using local 3D printers or printing services. As additive manufacturing expands into more types of materials and areas of use, individual boutique design shops can provide 3D-printed overlays and cases for our technologies — a rich spectrum of opportunities for new industry — and generate profit by selling access to 3D models that can be used to create physical objects.

Research is currently being conducted into techniques to restrict the number of copies that can be made from a 3D model and the types of materials that can be used in its fabrication, but the availability of personal or small-industry 3D printers creates easy ways to violate imposed restrictions on the current state of the art, where (say) a cartridge of aluminum powder could simply be swapped for titanium powder by a technician.

Microsoft is currently working on techniques that involve the creation of specific inner patterns of voids within 3D-printed objects to associate the object with its source 3D printer — in much the same way that a 2D color printer impresses its serial number and the print date/time on each document, using tiny yellow dots not visible to the viewer.

Crafting Personal Storefronts

Even if you don't have a 3D printer, you could create an online storefront to sell your own designs by taking advantage of services like Ponoko, Shapeways, and iMaterialize. These services have 3D printers of their own — and allow individuals to upload their own designs to be printed and shipped in a few days' time. These designs aren't limited to 3D-printed plastic kittens and the like — they can be fashioned with a great deal of artistic style and creative skill, as in Figure 6-5, which illustrates the online Ponoko storefront of mathematical artist Asher Nahmias, who goes by the name Dizingof.

Figure 6-5: The Ponoko online storefront for artist Asher Nahmias (Dizingof).

Many of the more mature online storefronts for 3D-printed goods are starting to provide their own tools for the design and creation of items to be sold, simplifying things for those hobbyists without strong CAD backgrounds.

Creating a unique design

To illustrate the power of services like Shapeways, Kirk created a "For Dummies" 3D-printed keychain fob by using one of Shapeways' tools to convert 2D artwork into a 3D model. He just followed these steps. (Note that every step was without cost until he ordered the final object for delivery.)

1. **Create the black-and-white text and graphic design using a free online word processor.**

2. **After you have the text and image the way you want them, save everything as an image on your hard drive.**

3. **Upload your image into Shapeways' 2D-to-3D design tool, selecting the thickness of the design.**

   You can create the final object here, but to give it a more interesting background and border, Kirk added a few extra steps. Consider these optional:

   a. *Export the STL file generated by Shapeways' tool, import it into the free TinkerCAD software from Autodesk, and add the details you see in Figure 6-6.*

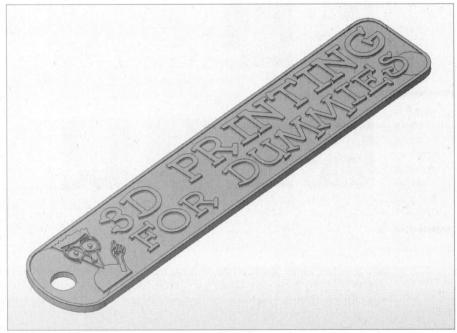

Figure 6-6: The "3D Printing For Dummies" keychain fob, ready for printing.

   b. *After adding a curved, raised border and a solid background to connect the picture and all of the letters, export the design as an STL back to your computer.*

4. **Wait patiently for the commercially printed version.**

   Kirk specified that his key-fob from Shapeways be printed in "Alumide," which is a nice-looking mixture of plastic and flakes of aluminum. The object was delivered about two weeks later. (See Figure 6-7.)

Fabricating a unique product on demand

After Kirk was happy with the model he created in the preceding section, he uploaded it into his Shapeways collection so that it could be ordered. He also shared it publically on his KKHausman storefront, where it can be ordered by anyone at prices ranging from $4 USD (white plastic) to $85 USD (polished silver). (See Figure 6-8.)

Obviously, Kirk did not have to print the local version of the key-fob — and certainly doesn't expect that anyone would actually buy a copy of this somewhat plain design, much less one made from polished silver. However, the same process could be used to create your own designs for sale, using nothing more than your own creative drive and free online tools. You can control the type of materials that can be ordered and the prices for each. For this example, he selected all the available material options for an item this small, and added $1 to the raw production cost, as an example of the marketplace functionality. Your own designs can be much more elaborate and priced accordingly, without ever having to create a physical object yourself to get started.

The example key-fob took about 15 minutes to complete because Kirk added details beyond the simple text and graphic image. If you simply wanted to create custom placecards with your business logo for a table at your next board meeting, you could just put in the text and use default options to create each card in a couple of minutes. It takes a couple of weeks to receive these items, but that time is shortening as the online vendors increase the number of printers they have available for custom fabrication. New materials such as ceramics and precious metals (like gold and titanium) are also being added all the time to enhance the options available.

Services such as Shapeways and Ponoko offer another way to make money using 3D printing — whether by direct printing of a creator's objects or by creating items sold by their designers to the public at large, for profit. As with other DIY source sites such as Etsy, these vendors profit from their investment in high-end commercial 3D printers that are still well beyond the means of the average citizen at home.

Because this equipment is available, individual designers can create new boutique industries entirely online — from design to the ordering page to the fabrication system — until the created object is shipped and delivered to the consumer as a finished product. Design of 3D-printed objects is only in its infancy as a new trade, built atop two sets of skills:

- Technical skills with 3D-modelling software
- Artistic skills to fabricate designs that interest the consumer in ways not possible with mass-manufactured "this year's model" goods

This new model of manufacturing allows the design to be customized for every order; it does not rely on warehouses filled with bulk items or intercontinental shipping of those goods from another country where labor is less expensive. Additive manufacturing is an early example of the potential for transformative business evolution beyond traditional mass manufacturing. Understandably, this potential is creating some concern in countries whose major export is cheap labor for making bulk goods. We discuss the potential for 3D printing to revolutionize manufacturing as an element of the "Third Industrial Revolution" in greater detail in Chapter 7.

Creating Impossible Objects

There are certainly less expensive techniques for traditional mass manu-facture of a standard plastic product like the keychain fob we used as an example. That advantage disappears, however, as the product becomes more complex. If (say) a name tag were to include a 3D physical representation of each person's facial features next to their name for security purposes and ease of identification, the cost of production would increase dramatically for traditional manufactured equivalents (if they could be produced at all). At the extreme end of personalization and customization, some structures are simply "impossible" to fabricate at a reasonable cost.

3D-printed robotic toys are already being sold as products — for example, the delightfully interactive Makie doll — but this concept is not limited to small-production shops. Disney is already employing 3D-printing systems to create custom Disney Princess dolls with your daughter's own face atop Belle's or Cinderella's gown if you visit the 3D-scanning studio at one of their theme parks. Disney is also using 3D printing to embed light pipes directly into solid objects, creating custom lighting for their exhibits that utilizes power-efficient LED lights in place of traditional Edison bulbs or fluorescent coils — illumination with an improved coverage of the area tailored to its specific use and layout.

Figure 6-9 shows three of the Printed Optics designs from Disney's research labs, each of which can create a unique pattern of light and dark within a space based on its unique needs. Saving these designs in a computer means a new light can simply be printed out when needed — or an old fixture can be repurposed to suit a new display by changing only the light-pipe array.

Figure 6-9:
Disney's new lighting designs use 3D-printed light pipes.

Image courtesy of Karl Willis/Disney

This is another example of the transformative potential in 3D printing, where re-use of existing objects can still mean a design custom fit to the new purpose — or where only the changed components need to be replaced, while costly durable elements can continue in use until they cease to function. In Disney's case, the LED illuminators are rated for up to 20 years of continuous use, greatly reducing the power and bulb-replacement costs over the lifetime of a display.

By translating traditional omnidirectional illumination into unique designs for light, Disney obviously cuts its operating costs and improves the visual appeal of its displays. But these designs can be converted into products that can be sold to others for profit as well, creating a new industry around each new product's digital designs.

Building New Tools

Another industry that demonstrates the new potential in 3D printing involves the creation of new tools — both to design objects and to fabricate existing designs — made possible in this amazing new arena of options. 3D printers need to be able to accommodate the materials and environments in which they work. A 3D printer using lunar soil in an airless environment, for example, will require a few changes from the traditional practice of mass fabrication of bricks and cinderblock for traditional construction, as would a submersible 3D printing tool able to repair damaged submarine components during underwater operations, or a 3D bioprinter designed to repair living tissues within the body itself. But the software tools that drive these new printers will also need to be updated to merge techniques from animation modeling, mathematical structural analysis, and many other disciplines into applications that can realize the amazing potential in these new tools under development.

Moving beyond solid blocks

When Kirk started learning technical drafting, he used traditional tools — a pencil and his trusty French curve on a portable drafting bench — which he still keeps around to show his CAD students when they complain about how hard it is to learn solid-modeling techniques. CAD software has evolved to two-finger manipulation on a tablet (as we show you earlier in the book), and yet the final results are attractive enough that Kirk's 7-year-old's creations adorn her walls. Some cleanup is needed to address support for overhangs and inner geometries that would result in loose components rattling around in an internal void, but these are practical matters created because most CAD software today is intended to create solid objects.

Certainly the objects may have penetrations and voids, and can even include multiple components of assemblies to be fashioned into the final shape. However, most CAD programs still design objects with a definite volume and boundary areas, which results in relatively solid materials in the final form. 3D-printed materials are being designed with different material types and structures throughout the entire object — created in a single pass, without assembly of sub-components in the final stages of manufacturing.

To address this potential, new tools are needed that can create objects whose internal solidity and porosity vary to create drainage channels or to provide lower weight with the same structural strength as their solid counterparts. This is a familiar design because nature has been creating bones this way for some time — and it must work, or birds would not be able to fly so easily. New software applications like the Within Medical designer (see Figure 6-10) are being developed to allow a hybrid mixture of solid and porous elements in a 3D-printed design; other variations are being developed to handle transitions between different materials and the varying material densities throughout objects.

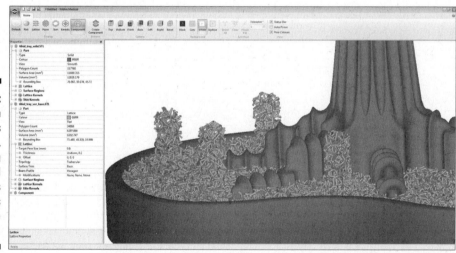

Figure 6-10: Within Medical's CAD design, illustrating solid and porous elements for a bone implant.

Image courtesy of Within Technologies

These tools are creating new industries as their capabilities become realized and new applications are found in a production environment. The products that emerge are more akin to organic designs than solid-block objects. Autodesk has already mentioned its interest in the developing field of bioprinting, and is already investigating the techniques an application will need in order to build tissues and complete organs from living cellular material. From racecars to NASA habitations in space, 3D-printed fabrication offers new production capabilities and resource efficiencies that will have an impact on multiple industries. No wonder so many new opportunities for software designers are beginning to flourish in this space.

Creating the tool that will create the tool

Making tools to make other tools is a time-honored activity. When Kirk teaches classes in traditional blacksmithing — using a coal fire, a glowing bit of metal, an anvil, and a sledgehammer — he often takes students through the phases of creating their own first sets of tongs and other tools necessary for blacksmithing. As a youth in Kentucky, he learned to smelt iron from ore, and to convert blocks of that iron into forged shapes. He used one such shape, together with wood from a tree harvested from family property, to create a black-powder "long rifle" that would have been at home in Daniel Boone's home. It remains a functional firearm accurate enough to hunt food with; as such, it's a "living history" example of building the tools to build other tools and self-sourcing some of the materials.

Fast-forward the technology to the 21st century: When Kirk teaches students about additive manufacturing, he shows them how to create their own 3D printers. The approach is similar to what you find in the end chapters of this book. Starting in Chapter 11, you get a look at how to build your own 3D printer from simple kits available today. Of course, if you have the time and inclination, you can self-source all the components and materials needed to build one from scratch. The current level of 3D printing is closely akin to the early days of industrial design when it was possible to make your own tools and start working.

The creation of new printer designs is another way that 3D printing is being commodified today. An explosion of commercial alternatives is providing increasingly larger build areas and improved material options to meet the swell of new applications being sought to meet the manufacturing needs of military, medical, and space technologies. In addition to commercial products, basic Fab@Home and RepRap open-source designs have evolved into hundreds of different clone and derivative designs.

One of the best-known designs is the MakerBot, developed by Bre Pettis, Adam Mayer, and Zack Smith, who also include the co-founder of the popular 3D-model repository ThingiVerse. The original MakerBot CupCake design was based on open-source RepRap systems, but has since evolved through several rounds of open-source derivatives into a "prosumer"-level, closed-source product: Replicator 2/2X. This commercial 3D printer is the current envy of many schools and fab labs. Makerbot was recently sold to Stratasys, returning one of the most popular FDM/FFF printer designs to the company that held the original patents on FDM additive manufacturing.

If you visit crowdfunding sites such as Kickstarter, IndieGoGo, or RocketHub, you'll see new designs and configurations of 3D printers constantly evolving — from the SLA-based Form 1 (see Figure 6-11) to the latest iterations of RepRap printer variants with ever-lower costs, lower part counts, and increased size as hobbyists take the basic open-source hardware design and iterate increasingly sophisticated alternatives.

Figure 6-11:
The Form 1
SLA printer
that was
successfully
crowd-
funded on
Kickstarter,
raising
almost $3
million USD
in 30 days.

Image courtesy of FormLabs

Creating your own design, open-source or otherwise, and then selling kits of pre-selected components — or even pre-assembled and tuned models — is another popular way to commodify 3D printing. Future opportunities in this area are only expected to explode as the fundamental patents on several types of additive manufacturing start to expire in 2014.

Chapter 7

Understanding 3D Printing's Effect on Traditional Lines of Business

*A*s we say in Chapter 1, the transformative potential of additive manufacturing is so great it may one day bring about a third Industrial Revolution, one in which local production will displace the complicated and resource-intensive traditional manufacturing process. This chapter discusses the potential disruptions resulting from this evolution — and its likely impact on not only traditional manufacturing, but also personal individualized manufacturing, and even biological elements of the human body.

Transforming Production

In addition to its ability to use sustainable alternative materials like PLA instead of traditional petrochemical-based materials, additive manufacturing could also repatriate manufacturing tasks currently outsourced to locations that offer lower-cost mass production. Such a shift, in turn, may well impact the industries involved in the transportation and storage of mass product quantities — and reduce the environmental impact of cargo transportation. Manufacturing in less industrialized settings may also result in less environmental impact — and lessen the need for regulation.

The fundamental technologies behind additive manufacturing may also transform the materials (and quantities thereof) used in the production of goods.

This could affect industries that currently supply parts to existing production lines: As we become more capable of the low-impact (green) manufacture of structural members — with complex interior designs like a bird's wing bone instead of a solid mass of steel or aluminum — such a change in product may also trigger a change in process, along these lines:

- Reduced quantity of material needed for the same end result.
- Improved potential for re-use of recycled source materials.
- Stronger, lighter products created closer to their markets.

The resulting energy savings would be passed along to industries that currently supply fuel and energy to drive the traditional manufacture of goods. One result: an environmentally friendly impact on second-order consumption (reduced resource requirements due to the changes made possible rather than as a direct result of using 3D-printed products.)

Displacing the production line

The potential presented in additive manufacturing as it matures suggests a fundamental transformation in the production of material goods. Supporters like to discuss the possibilities inherent in ad-hoc personalized manufacturing at the consumer level, whereas critics argue about the damage any transition away from traditional mass-manufacturing, storage, and distribution would make to existing economies. Who is right? We address examples of disruption to traditional manufacturing processed and the economies founded on mass manufacturing later in Chapter 16.

These concerns follow the same fears that buggy-whip makers and farriers faced when mechanization replaced the need for horse-drawn carts, when hand-spinners were replaced by automated thread makers, when coopers faced the rapid production capacity of injection-molded barrels, or when automated looms transformed textile production capabilities — all examples of this same shift during earlier transformational stages in the first and second Industrial Revolutions.

The mobility of manufacturing to place production in close proximity to consumers offers a mechanism to eliminate the need for mass production of bulk goods that would then have to be shipped and stored in a fuel-hungry post-Peak Oil economy a decade from now. With the potential already developing to print everything from engine parts to whole houses by moving production directly to the consumers' sites, many cargo container ships will be put out of business if the "3D Industrial Revolution" takes off and reaches a fraction of the promise in its potential.

3D printing, crowdfunding, robotics, ad-hoc media content, and a host of other technologies — taken together — will not only alter the course of production but fundamentally shatter traditional manufacturing practices and related industries such as advertising and marketing.

When you consider the capability to print entire houses as well as the materials therein, you can see how this transformation could affect even something as prosaic as industries that currently move and store household goods, at the most extreme end simply re-creating everything at the new location. The same company could reclaim materials used in the previous building and furnishings — a form of full recycling that would impact all industries that presently store goods or ship furnishings to the new house.

Similarly, this would impact those trades that would traditionally build the destination building and store the furniture before selling new models to consumers, along with companies that would manage the property during its transition to new ownership, all the way down to the lawn service that would provide care during the lack of tenancy. The new way of doing business will be very disruptive to traditional practices across all levels of industry, but it will also open up wholly new opportunities for consumers and producers in the new industrial age.

Many of the world's largest economic powers stand to be displaced in the face of this latest Third Industrial Revolution and will certainly move to prevent its transformation as long as possible. This opposition can already be seen in early arguments suggesting that all 3D printers should be registered with the government on the grounds of the danger they present to the public in terms of 3D-printed firearms or mis-manufactured components placed into service causing horrible injuries or death.

However, controlling this technology won't be so easy. The RepRap platform, for example, can fabricate using many different sources of materials. Kirk's students have been able to build functional 3D printers using scrap parts from old discarded electronic garbage (stepper motors, switches and rails from old ink-jet printers, electronics built from chip-level Arduino microcontroller boards and motor driver RAMPS open source designs). And PLA filament has been successfully formed from tapioca. When garbage + natural plant materials = 3D printers, the concept of forced registration and control of this remarkable technology proves to be difficult or even impossible.

In medical and engineering settings, the success of additive manufacturing has been thoroughly proven. Consider the magnificent reconstruction of the Saturn V's colossal rocket motors by NASA scientists. This technology was designed to provide heavy-lift capability for the Orion's space launch system that will replace the retired space shuttle for manned exploration of the Moon and Mars. 3D printing is preparing the vehicles that will carry our future astronauts, and 3D printing will provide them with the tools and possibly even the food they will need during their journeys. In medicine, 3D printing may soon provide replacement parts for our bodies. And the military is finding many uses for 3D-printed, in-the-field rapid prototypes. Trying to stuff this genie back into its bottle should be very nearly impossible, with such a tremendous global force of inventors finding ever-more-capable solutions to expand the capacity that additive manufacturing offers.

The path from here, however, will not be without its impediments. Many in the world depend on things remaining the way they have always been. But as the past Industrial Revolutions have shown, the easier, less costly and more efficient solutions will win out. Perhaps future generations will hear of our own equivalent to John Henry or study about the time before we could build replacement organs in school biology class as they wonder how we ever managed to live without the marvels they enjoy.

Abbreviating the manufacturing chain

Traditional manufacturing involves a sequence of events that take place in scattered locations. A cellphone's lithium battery offers an example:

1. Collect basic resources such as iron and lithium.

2. Transport the materials to locations where materials for individual components can be created, such as steel or intercalated lithium compound.

3. Transport the materials to sites for processing and finishing into sub-assemblies such as batteries.

4. Transport the sub-assemblies to locations that will fabricate finished products such as cellphones.

5. Transport the finished product for consumer packaging.

6. Transport the packaged product, often internationally, to consuming locations.

Thus, when you shop for the newest cellphone model at a store near your home, you're on the far end of a long chain of events. The manufacturing cycle looks different for an equivalent product of additive manufacturing:

1. Collect basic resources.

2. Create needed materials from collected resources.

3. Transport materials to a fabrication site in each town or region.

4. Have individual customers select product options before manufacture.

5. Use the data files that define the product design to fabricate a specific model of the final product that includes the chosen options.

In addition, recycling earlier products as feed stock for the production of complex, multi-material new designs would reduce cost to consumers and encourage the recovery of materials that would otherwise end up in ever-expanding landfill disposal sites.

Providing local fabrication

Some goods such as coat hooks and children's party favors can already be produced easily at home using a consumer-grade 3D printer. A walk through the local mall will show you many other products that can be made at home today — plastic eyeglasses, jewelry boxes, and cellphone cases. And because making these items at home means you can customize them as you like, the result would reflect greater variation than this years' production models in simple white or black provide.

Research is already showing that thousands of dollars can be saved by individual use of consumer-grade 3D printers to produce small plastic items at home. For more durable or complex designs, it seems likely that a dedicated fabrication facility would be needed to handle specialized and expensive materials, using more advanced additive manufacturing equipment. In the United States, the United Parcel Service (UPS) is currently developing additive manufacturing services such as these, intended for deployment at their distribution centers. The idea is to fabricate items locally and then deliver them to consumers, without need of traditional manufacturing and distribution chains. The U.S. military services are developing additive manufacturing centers that fit into shipping cargo containers, able to be dropped in support of warfighting personnel. We may soon see more mobile fabrication centers travelling ahead of events to prepare personalized items for sale or traveling in the wake of storms to provide items useful in recovery.

Researchers are currently exploring ways to use natural materials to fabricate protective structures for just such need. Markus Kayser at MIT built his original Solar Sinter to make use of the abundant sunlight and natural sand available in Egypt to fashion durable items and prototype structures. NASA and the ESA are exploring automated systems that will build shelters on the moon, but those same technologies can be applied here on Earth with equal ease because the models cost almost nothing to duplicate from one computer to the next.

Eliminating traditional release cycles

Globally, the transition between seasons imposes a cycle of goods alternately suitable to warm and cool weather. Similarly, massive corporate marketing efforts transform durable goods into the next cycle's models in support of new purchasable goods to ensure a continued influx of capital to sustain the manufacturing organizations. Some cycles provide actual improvements and innovations beyond prior models; others are more akin to purely "cosmetic" changes. As cycles of change are repeated, components for repair become scarce and demand an increasingly higher cost per item in order to maintain operational capability of the original design. Automobiles exhibit this trend over many years. For example, components for a vintage collectable such as a WWII-era Willis Jeep are increasingly unavailable except through specialty providers that charge high prices in keeping with item scarcity.

Through additive manufacturing, a representative model of each component can be designed (or input from original manufacturing diagrams) to allow the creation of new parts for a half-century-old vehicle without requiring its replacement with this year's model. Customers could specify new features as 3D-printed add-ons to include some of this year's latest innovations, even in last year's model. This threatens the traditional manufacturers of durable goods because it risks the elimination of "this year's model" as a calculable revenue stream based on the planned obsolescence of repair components that currently use materials subject to known rates of degradation by wear and corrosion. A replacement part created by additive manufacturing can (for example) just as easily replace aluminum or brass components with titanium or tungsten versions that last for many decades with only minimal wear.

Although manufacturers could simply refuse to share their 3D models for replacements to create an artificial scarcity, it is already possible to simply scan worn out parts, strengthen them or customize as desired, and print replacements directly without needing the original designs. This concept should soon be simply a factor of the distant past, although demand for raw materials to create those stronger titanium or tungsten equivalents will certainly influence the markets of the future. Some consumers might prefer a low-cost plastic or recycled aluminum part to a long-term truly durable equivalent simply to release that titanium for other purposes.

Challenging Intellectual Property Laws

It's all a matter of perspective: Bringing manufacturing back to locations close to where the products are consumed is generally seen as a good idea by those in the industrialized world, but for people living in the developing world, whose employment is based on low-cost manufacturing in the traditional setting, it's a threat to their livelihoods. Similarly, threats to intellectual property (IP) rights and protections create a number of criticisms — particularly among those whose fortunes are attached to intellectual property. If your income is based on control of your own personal creations and designs — or on the creations and designs of other individuals — then you take threats to intellectual property very seriously indeed.

Threatening IP protections

The U.S.A., the E.U., and other members of the World Intellectual Property Organization (WIPO) provide legal protections under patents for both *utility* (functionality) and *design* (ornamental design of a functional item). These protections last for a period of years from the time they're issued. During this term, designers can prevent the unlicensed use of their registered intellectual property designs in products for sale; manufacturers must pay a licensing fee.

Current U.S. utility patents model those of the WIPO and the World Trade Organization (WTO) through the Trade-Related Aspects of Intellectual Property Rights (TRIPS) agreement: A 20-year protective term from the date of filing is in force, provided that certain fees are paid properly. Design patents cover only the ornamental aspects of the product, are protected for only 14 years, and may be invalidated if the design has a functional use (for example, a chandelier shaped like a gear could lose its design-patent protection because the function of the gear might be covered under a different utility patent, or might already exist as prior art).

Design patents provide protection against the duplication of a particular object's physical form, but are intended to encourage competition through the development of derivative designs that can then be patented by their creators in turn. And the grant of a patent requires that the work be original and non-obvious, so examples of previous designs can invalidate a design claim if it can be shown that the design has been in public use or already exists as *prior art*: a photo or scaled drawing that describes the same design.

Physical designs like the alien cube from the movie *Super 8*, or other non-functional movie props (like Kirk's prized model of the Oscillation Overthruster prop from the movie *Buckaroo Banzai* that was later used in a number of "Star Trek" TV episodes — see Figure 7-1) may also be protected under copyright, which protects non-functional designs from being copied for sale to protect their artistic value. The difficulty for IP owners is that designs like this can be copied using nothing more than photographs (as shown in Figure 7-2) which can be taken from a distance without the owner even being aware of the duplication.

Figure 7-1:
A resin
cast of a
movie prop
from "Star
Trek" and
the movie
*Buckaroo
Banzai*,
together
with two
smaller
3D-printed
copies.

Figure 7-2:
A 3D-model
capture of
my movie
prop,
using free
photogram-
metry and
multiple pho-
tographs; no
specialized
equipment
for scanning
was used.

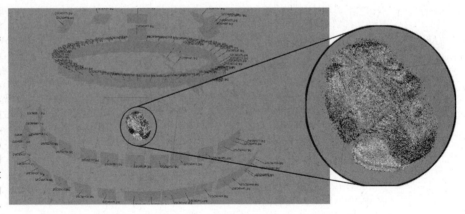

This presents a challenge for manufacturers, whose next-year body design for a new car could be captured by a photographer, transmitted to a fabrication facility, and made available as a 3D-printed overlay for last year's model before the new version is even in the manufacturer's showrooms for sale. Obviously, I would not sell copies of my prop's model, but knock-off vendors take advantage of minimal changes to create commercially transferrable variations that approximate the patented designs.

Because additive manufacturing allows individuals to copy or create new items with a "look and feel" similar to that of patented designs, it's encouraging a reformation of existing patent laws. Until the laws change, however, the technology will continue to cause trouble. The plastic tank model shown in Figure 7-3, for instance, is Thomas Valenty's personal design for a model used in playing the Warhammer board game, originally created by Games Workshop. This is not a direct copy of an existing model, but is designed with a similar "look and feel." Valenty's posting of his model online resulted in a challenge by Games Workshop, who claimed Valenty's 3D model file violated their intellectual property rights (that is, if someone downloaded Valenty's design, they would not need to buy the official object from Games Workshop). The ThingiVerse repository received a takedown notice on the basis of protections under the Digital Millennium Copyright Act (DMCA) that is better known for suits against illegal file-sharing of music and video files. This takedown notice was intended to eliminate the possibility of someone downloading a copy of the design — not the physical object but only its virtual representation — which could then be used to create an object for personal use.

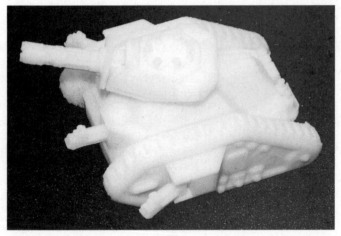

Figure 7-3: A 3D-printed copy of Thomas Valenty's personally-designed game "tank" model for Warhammer gameplay.

Assigning legal liability

As of the writing of this text, individuals can still make items for their own use without having to retain a lawyer and pay for a full search of all IP registrations to identify potential conflicts. This is true of patented designs. You can write your own operating system, which can look like a commercial design as long as you do not distribute it to others or you can duplicate the trademarked shape of protected soda bottles for your personal use at home. So, now that an individual without significant design skills can create at home a look-alike replacement component for an older car that might still be protected intellectual property, there's potential IP trouble. The legal system is trying to come to terms with how to protect the designers' right to make a profit from their designs and individuals' right to make their own personal items without an impossible level of cost and legal review. The same applies to potentially dangerous tool and weapon designs. The question is when personal use becomes something more.

If a component or other product fails to function properly, often the result is recalls and replacements in the world of traditional manufacturing. Consumers who create exact copies of such items may have unwittingly taken on the liability for any damage or harm resulting from their use. If you use a 3D-printed vacuum cleaner in the next few years, produced at a local fabrication site of the sort that UPS envisions, and the handle fails and causes injury, where does the legal liability lie? Is it the original designer's fault? Is it the fault of the manufacturer who might have employed different materials? Is it the fault of the owner who paid for the replacement part, who might not even have known it was not an official factory-manufactured replacement? Our traditional insurance policies and other legal factors of liability will need to be updated in the years ahead to reflect the amazing innovations that are before us.

Leveraging Expired Patents

Patents protect designs for a number of years, but what happens when they run out? Items that old are no longer protected by intellectual property controls preventing their duplication. Any object older than the term of patent — or released from patent due to discovered prior art or failure to pay the applicable fees — can be produced by any manufacturer for sale. In fact, the United States Patent Office (USPTO) is currently providing a body of 3D-printable objects courtesy of a lawyer, Martin Galese, who has been converting expired patents into 3D-printable objects that you can download from Thing-I-Verse to print for yourself or order from his storefront at Shapeways. Figure 7-4 shows two of his designs: a flower vase from 1895 (U.S. Pat. No. 165,456 by Samuel Vanstone) and a wristwatch stand from 1979 (U.S. Pat. No. 4,293,943 by Victor Avery).

Figure 7-4: Two of Martin Galese's designs — a flower vase and a wristwatch stand — created from expired patents.

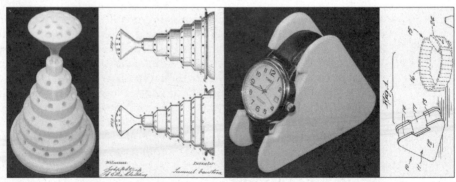

Currently, the U.S. Patent Office has illustrated diagrams of over 8 million patents granted since the Patent Act of 1790 allowed for citizens to apply for a patent. The vast majority of these are already past their term of patent, and available for reproduction, with similar pools of designs held as expired intellectual property throughout the world. If the current laws are retained, there is nothing to stop entrepreneurs from bringing back many collectables and offering 3D-printed reproductions for sale. If the files that define 3D models of designs become protected under *copyright* law instead of patent law, however, then their use could be delayed for centuries. (Copyright protection lasts until 70 years after the author's death; advanced geriatric care and new medical procedures could extend human life well past the century mark before the 70-year countdown even begins.)

Rare items are rare only because they are no longer being manufactured. Obviously, then, collectors of rare items depend on their investment's value being protected and want to ensure it stays out of manufacture. A 1971 factory-original Plymouth Hemi 'Cuda was recently offered for sale at $2 million USD. If a 3D-printed '71 'Cuda became available, collectors would surely try to print one! However, owners of the remaining few original cars might feel their investment threatened if someone were to take the original copyrighted designs for these amazing pieces of machinery and use them to start manufacturing 3D-printed copies because patent control over that particular intellectual property had long since expired.

Innovating around intellectual property

Additive manufacturing is still in its infancy — and many of the designs for rapid fabricators themselves are still under patent protection. The expiration of patents on two early modeling techniques — stereo lithography and fused deposition — opened the way for the development of the many open-source RepRap variations, as well as the new boutique production of home printers like the Form 1. Fundamental patents covering laser-sintered granular-bound fabrication will expire in 2014. This and other expiring patents will open the potential for many new commercial and hobbyist systems. Eventually this development will bring down the price of creating 3D-printed objects of metal and other materials — which will offer a new range of opportunities for creating and commoditizing such objects.

However, not all intellectual property controls have been holding back the floodgates — patent protections have actually encouraged new development in the arena of 3D printing. Entirely new opportunities result. When (for example) 3D Systems held all production rights for stereolithographic fabrication, another company sought alternate ways to use photo polymerization without relying on a liquid pool for fabrication of the developing object.

Objet (now combined with Stratasys) developed the photopolymer PolyJet technology from ink-jet printing capabilities, allowing the application of thin films of liquid plastic that could be rapidly hardened by UV light.

This photopolymer process is much easier to manage without the large vats of liquid plastic needed for SLA fabrication, but each technique still provides its own advantages. Where some of the largest and most precise 3D printers use variations of stereolithographic and multi-photon lithographic fabrication shown in Chapter 2, the PolyJet alternative allows a mixing of different types of liquid plastics. The process is similar to the way 2D printers can mix colored inks to create full-color photo reproductions. As a result, Objet's printers can create objects whose physical properties vary from one point to another, even throughout the object itself, to allow flexibility in one area, a higher frictional surface in another, or variations in transparency and color for aesthetic or functional purposes.

Protecting intellectual property rights

Without the barrier created by 3D Systems's control of the original SLA patents, the PolyJet alternative might not have become available for much longer. As the earliest additive manufacturing technologies come out of patent control — and new technologies are developed — new opportunities will emerge for the transformation of manufacturing and the production of entirely new products.

As with the music and motion picture industries, new technologies create a threat to the intellectual property of established companies. Schemes are already being developed to provide some type of Digital Rights Management (DRM) that will restrict 3D models to control what types of materials they are licensed for (say, plastic and glass but not metals) or to restrict the number of copies that can be produced from a single 3D design file. As long as self-built 3D printers are available, however, mandatory DRM controls are likely to remain absent for home production systems. Commercial vendors might be forced to comply with some type of DRM solution, with complex algorithms scanning each model to see if it violates someone else's intellectual property or includes items restricted from fabrication.

To make this possible, it will first be necessary to develop a database of all protected intellectual property designs — and then create a search engine that can be linked to a 3D printer's software to approve or deny the fabrication of a particular design. Aside from potential attacks on such a service from people who support open-source design, not much will prevent an operator from bypassing a designer's controls on the type of materials that can be used, replacing (say) an aluminum powder cartridge with a gold powder cartridge — regardless of whether the designer ever intended a solid gold version of the object.

Imposing Ethical Controls

Some objects are protected by virtue of their use, such as firearms or high-security keys for handcuffs and other protected locks. New systems promise to protect against the creation of 3D-printable firearms by identifying characteristic components, which could run into problems when they block the fabrication of any tube that is 9mm or 10mm or any other diameter matching firearm ammunition. Just as with DRM, as long as self-created 3D printers are available, any software controls can be easily bypassed to allow the fabrication of protected designs.

Figure 7-5 shows the Liberator, the first 3D-printed functional firearm. (Note that we have modified the firearm from its original design files in various ways to render it inoperative for educational purposes.) These weapons present a difficulty for law enforcement because although their designs are intended to comply with current U.S. laws for legal firearms, they could be modified to be undetectable by current security scanners.

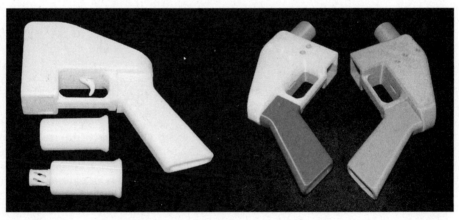

Figure 7-5:
The 3D-printed Liberator firearm, as modified for the purpose of educating law enforcement with a non-functioning model.

In addition to 3D-printed weapons, it is equally possible to create other controlled designs such as high-security keys for handcuffs and other secure locks. (See Figure 7-6.) Because these functional keys are made entirely of plastic, they could easily be carried through security metal scanners by criminals. Students at MIT recently created 3D-printable models of the controlled key blanks used by Schrade's Primus high-security locks. The uncut key blanks cannot normally be acquired by civilians. Researchers have been able to duplicate physical keys using photographs from up to 200 feet away, needing only the blanks to create fully functional keys capable of bypassing traditional physical security controls in government, medical, and detention facilities.

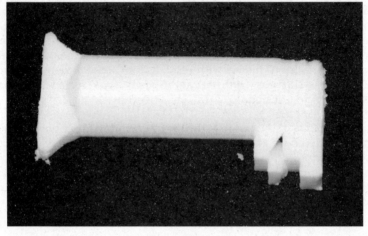

Figure 7-6: A 3D-printed high-security key used by German police handcuffs.

As 3D-printable drugs become available, or (for that matter) 3D-printable body tissues and organs, ethical controls will encounter difficulties with this new form of manufacturing. Where we once were concerned with athletes doping their blood, we may someday have to find ways to identify custom body modifications that allow all manner of extreme physical feats.

Software alone will not provide a technical method of control in the ethical or unethical uses of products that were once simply impossible but which are now becoming more than possible. The medical field may present us with more than just 3D-printed tissues for reconstructive surgery and medical treatments in a few decades. Legal controls such as patents are already facing challenges when applied to biological organisms; digitally fabricated viruses and other such materials are entirely possible, and will present a whole new spectrum of difficulties in their application, liability, and legal controls.

Chapter 8

Reviewing 3D Printing Research

*A*dditive manufacturing applications already suggest fundamentally transformative potential across many different elements of manufacturing and production. The technology's true potential, however, is still being discovered. Research continues on the applications of translating virtual electronic models into physical solid form in a variety of fields. This chapter reviews current research into the next generation of additive manufacturing techniques, materials, and technologies.

Building Fundamental Technologies

New discoveries take time to develop into their mature form. The discovery that magnetism could be created at will by passing an electrical field through a loop of wire opened up whole new possibilities in electricity and electronics — and these, in turn, led to technologies such as computers, cellphones, and most of the modern world itself. The emergence of automation transformed manufacturing; now the combination of computers, robotics, and many other disciplines allows us to fabricate small plastic objects at home with the same ease as we previously printed out recipes on our home inkjet and laser printers. As researchers continue to expand the capabilities of 3D printers, they create new tools that can lead to new capabilities we can't even imagine now. Here, however, are some that we can.

Crafting educational tools

Any new tool provides only limited value until its operator has been trained in its proper use, so opportunities are emerging for teachers who will educate future operators of additive manufacturing systems. Many schools are starting to develop programs around 3D printing and its remarkable potential. In these programs, new innovations and their applications are being tested — from 3D-printed foods at Cornell to printed plastic boats at the University of Washington. Obtaining a personal 3D printer is inexpensive and easy when the tool can make the tool: A single 3D printer in a school can be used to create more 3D printers so that they become more available to educators and students.

In order to develop the next generation of scientists and engineers, the DARPA-sponsored MENTOR program started placing commercial-grade 3D printers in select high schools around the U.S.A. Kirk's own *SOLID Learning* program includes K-12 primary schools in the United States, the United Kingdom, Australia, and South Africa, where he has been developing strategies for teachers to incorporate 3D-printed materials and tools into their existing curriculum to enhance student learning.

The advantages of having 3D printers in school don't stop there. Teachers often have difficulty with maintaining enough necessary equipment in a given class, especially as student population shifts from one year to the next. Using a 3D printer, teachers can create lab equipment and classroom examples to assist in several different courses — from solar-powered water-electrolysis systems to 3D-printed models of artworks or animal bones.

In addition to no-kill "dissectible" animal models and replicas of ancient cultural artifacts, mathematical and aerospace designs can be tested in the lab — often using tools such as a wind tunnel that was itself 3D-printed into existence. Kirk recently created 3D molds of animal footprints that teachers could fill with common liquid rubber and silicone compounds to create stamps, as illustrated in Figure 8-1.

By building RepRap printers that use stepper motors from surplus 2D printers and other basic items from local suppliers, students learn basic mechanical and electrical controls, robotic feedback systems, and computer drafting and 3D modeling. They learn about the properties of various materials and the advantages of sustainable development.

Figure 8-1:
3D-printed animal foot molds, starting with a scanned animal's foot and concluding with an ink footprint.

Expanding 3D printing options

From the first 3D printer solidifying objects in a vat of liquid photopolymer to today's latest two-photon lithography systems, the level of resolution and detail in the printed product has improved hundreds of times. Even the liquid photopolymer printer has improved: New innovations such as the micro-lattice lithographic system are currently being developed by researchers at HRL Laboratories to provide new capabilities for photopolymers.

As we discuss in Chapter 7, intellectual property controls on the basic SLA patent caused Objet to develop the PolyJet. Expect this process to continue; other companies are now driving ahead with new systems capable of lower-cost operation, greater speed, greater build volume, and a wider range of materials. Researchers are constantly developing new strategies for performing the same task of depositing materials one layer at a time to solidify a virtual model into physical form. Even the basic self-REPlicating RAPid prototyping (RepRap) system designed by Dr. Bowyer has seen many iterations derived from the original Cartesian system that drove motors in X-, Y-, and Z-axis movements. Today's Delta and Polar systems reduce the overall complexity (and cost) of 3D printers. Quentin Harley, a South African designer, is currently evolving his Polar-style "Morgan" RepRap (shown in Figure 8-2), trying to reduce the cost of its creation to less than $100 USD.

Figure 8-2:
The
low-cost
Morgan
RepRap.

Image courtesy of Quentin Harley

As each new researcher and designer examines and updates the basic forms of 3D printers, and as original patents expire, a tremendous expansion in capability occurs. So far, only the preliminary patents on SLA and FDM fabrication have expired, but patents on fundamental sintering systems expire in 2014. The expected result is many new opportunities in consumer-level 3D printers — and considerable current research is trying to prepare for that time. An early example of the expected struggle over intellectual property is the 3D Systems legal challenge to the FormLabs release of the Form1 SLA printer — a function similar to a derivative patent still held by 3D Systems. One difficulty for many innovators in 3D printing comes in the form of costly patent searches to protect garage-level inventors from the unintended duplication of derivative patents — not only for the objects printed, but for the devices that print them.

3D-printed electronics

Of all potential developments, fully 3D-printed electronics are of significant interest in both commercial and hobbyist applications. Researchers at the University of Warwick have created conductive PCL-based filament by mixing carbon black into melted plastic before it's extruded as filament; they call the result *carbomorph*. Carbomorph can be used to print circuits directly into objects, eliminating the need for wires and conduits in traditionally-manufactured electronic devices. Carbomorph's physical properties also allow it to be integrated into other objects and 3D-printable materials, creating sensors directly within the object itself. This type of design will change how we manage repairs in much the same way monolithic computer motherboards changed desktop PCs, resulting in a "replace it if it breaks" mentality. However, the protection provided by integrating electronics directly into a component should allow it to last longer than its earlier wire-connected component-based ancestor.

Creating Functional Designs

Disney is examining ways to integrate electronics into 3D-printed objects to create the next generation of toys, as with the chess pieces shown in Figure 8-3, which can display a current board position or one planned by a computer adversary.

Figure 8-3: Examples of Disney's integrated electronics in inter-active chess pieces.

Image courtesy of Karl Willis/Disney

Today's 3D-printed electronic devices provide only light pipes for displays and integrated circuit paths, but research continues to explore increasingly more complex fabrication techniques that could soon allow a whole device and its electronics to be printed from a single design file and used immediately. Imagine 3D-printed batteries and photovoltaic panels providing power to 3D-printed circuitry and displays, controlled by 3D-printed sensors — all in the same solid form. Present-day working models direct from 3D printers are expanding well beyond the capabilities of the original nonfunctional rapid prototypes that additive manufacturing was developed to produce.

Drones, robots, and military applications

The U.S. military is currently trying to develop 3D printers that can create drones and robots, printing both not only structural elements and control electronics, but also micro-batteries and control surfaces. Once this capability is achieved, a single fabricator can be dropped in a forward area and used to fabricate multiple drones, unmanned submersibles, or terrestrial robots to gather intelligence and protect warfighters in hostile areas.

If this capability is expanded to include the fabrication of explosives, the same fabricator could churn out a stream of warfighting agents able to prosecute a war remotely — or entirely independently — guided by asynchronous programming done before deployment, without risk to the originating geopolitical agent's citizens. Coupled with advancing experiments in artificial intelligence, some researchers are concerned that a *Skynet*-like threat straight out of the *Terminator* movies could emerge without careful controls or as a result of enemy hacker compromise of the control systems.

Direct production of functional devices is already being studied with the University of Southampton's Low Orbit Helium Assisted Navigator (LOHAN) experimental high-altitude spaceplane prototype, following their previous 3D-printed Southampton University Laser-Sintered Aircraft (Sulsa), the first fully 3D-printed scale-model aircraft. Airbus and other commercial airline companies are also looking into the potential for directly fabricating entire full-scale aircraft, employing a massively expanded 3D printer to minimize weight and use less aluminum while providing the same structural strength, and reduce the amount of post-production assembly required.

Von Neumann machines

Self-replicating nonorganic life forms were originally described by mathematician John von Neumann in the 1940s, but the first mention of the concept of machines building machines in literature extends back into the early 1800s. Von Neumann's ideas have found their way into many artistic creations — including the popular television series *Stargate,* whose principal antagonists include the Replicators formed from basic building blocks (Figure 8-4 shows a copy of the prop), able to harvest local resources to create more copies of themselves.

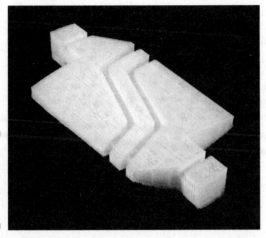

Figure 8-4:
A 3D-printed prop of the Replicator block.

Although these are only fictional creations and no self-replicating robots exist today, the RepRap 3D printer design can print many of the materials needed to fabricate a second 3D printer. That capability is an early step toward self-replication. If later self-replicating robots could gather their own materials from the environment, researchers are concerned that a nanotechnology-manufacturing weapon could inadvertently convert all material into a basic "gray goo" composed of nothing more than nanofactories trying to create more nanofactories. Researchers are currently trying to create automated fabrication factories to gather raw materials from seawater or lunar soil, while protecting against even the possibility of a runaway expansion and a theoretical "gray goo" end-of-the-world scenario. Potential uses for nanoassemblies and nanotechnology are discussed in greater detail in *Nanotechnology For Dummies* by Earl Boysen, Nancy C. Muir, and Desiree Dudley.

Expanding Material Selection

We cover many of the different currently-available materials in Chapter 4, but the number of materials is in constant flux as researchers create new or hybrid materials to provide additional capabilities through 3D printing. The conductive "carbomorph" is an example of a hybrid composite material made from melted thermoplastic mixed with carbon black to create a composite material that can be extruded using standard ABS settings on a standard 3D printer but that will also conduct electricity.

Other options include different colors of filament or filament with metallic glitter, thermal color-changing or glow-in-the-dark pigments and dyes. Other researchers, such as German researcher Kai Parthy, are adding to the materials available to consumer-level printers. One example that uses composite materials is LayWoo-d3, a material that looks like wood and can be machined like wood for finishing. Further consumer-level examples include LayBrick — a material that resembles sandstone, intended for architectural modeling — and BendLay, a translucent and flexible filament for light pipes.

A recent development in 3D printing materials is so-called "4D printing." No, the process doesn't actually create theoretical multi-dimensional objects like the tesseract (shown in the standard three dimensions in Figure 8-5). In 4D printing — according to its developers at MIT — materials are arranged during fabrication so that a reactive material is placed alongside a flexible material to create a fused "sandwich" of the two. After fabrication is complete, warming up the reactive material causes the printed object to deform or change its shape — much like adding water to a compressed soda straw wrapper makes it expand away from the droplet. In other words, the object is printed using three physical dimensions but is only fully expressed across a period of time (time, according to Einstein, being the fourth dimension).

Figure 8-5:
A 3D model of a theoretical 4D cube called a tesseract.

Providing for Long Space Voyages

The U.S. National Aeronautics and Space Administration (NASA) is researching technologies that will support manned exploration beyond the earth's atmosphere — including a special FDM 3D printer being sent to the International Space Station. Further space applications include

- ✔ Printers that use electron beams to melt wire instead of blown metal granules for use in near-vacuum environments.

- ✔ 3D-printed nozzles and other components of spacecraft.

- ✔ 3D printers capable of fabricating living areas for explorers using nothing more than local materials and power from sunlight (see Figure 8-6).

- ✔ Long-duration foodstuffs that can be printed into solid form from powders and water.

- ✔ Bioprinters capable of producing everything from edible meat for astronauts' protein needs to body tissues and organs for advanced medical care during extended voyages far from the nearest tissue donors back on Earth.

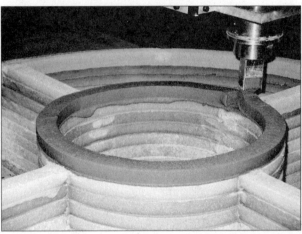

Figure 8-6:
A prototype for a multi-chambered lunar habitation module.

Image courtesy of Contour Crafting

Whether repairs involve the vessel or its inhabitants, or even their shelter far from home, NASA is investing in research to provide astronauts with all the tools they'll need during their trip — even if a particular tool hasn't even been invented when they leave the Earth far behind. This avoids the need to take two of every possible tool in order to have a spare (just spares for the 3D Printer, many of which could be printed using another 3D Printer), making multi-partner international exploration much easier without incurring the difficulty of having only metric wrenches when an English measure is needed (or the contrary) to fix components fabricated in different countries.

In fact, NASA's research in this area hopes to eventually allow the mining of asteroids and other orbital bodies for fabrication of space vessels, space stations, and solar power plants entirely in space. Built to a large enough scale, this potential capability could provide power to ground stations from orbit, and even cast shadows to reduce the Earth's atmospheric temperatures. Thus additive manufacturing offers the potential to transform our world in ways we could not even consider when the first pass of an SLA laser solidified liquid into hard plastic.

Although many of these experiments suggest changes that can be made decades from now, researchers today are using additive manufacturing to test strategies for rejuvenation of the Earth's resources using designs such as the artificial reef shown in Figure 8-7. The reef is intended for fabrication using synthetic rock or concrete; it will be used to test colonization of the reef by natural coral and marine biodiversity over time. Such efforts may help repair natural reefs damaged by mankind.

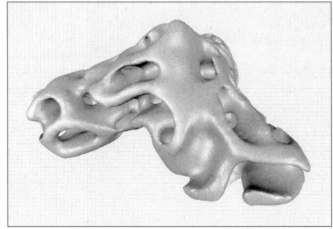

Figure 8-7:
A 3D
rendering
of a reef.

Creating Medical Opportunities

In addition to 3D-printed homes for living organisms — such as custom coverings for hermit crabs or new underwater parks where fish can swim and play — 3D printing is starting to make many new medical opportunities possible. A promising area is personalized manufacturing that uses non-bioreactive materials configured for use in biocompatible matrices.

The first medical applications of 3D printing were external appliances and prosthetics designed to improve the lives of their recipients, but newer implants such as jawbones and skull protective plates are already being used by doctors to assist those under their care. Just ahead, 3D printers will provide custom pharmacology for patients, mixing every day's dosage of different medicines to meet the particular needs of a patient's treatment and recovery protocols.

Perhaps the most incredible area of research into additive manufacturing is that of bioprinting or the creation of living tissues and organs from carefully layered cells allowed to grow into the desired form. Present-day patients in need of organs may pass away without a compatible match being found, while many others must endure a lifetime of anti-rejection drugs to maintain the closest match that can be found. Bioprinted structures could be made from an individual's own cells, eliminating issues of availability and rejection, together with ethical and religious concerns over transplant of body parts, usually from a deceased donor.

Researchers are currently developing techniques for organ replacement that incorporate 3D printing. Using small orthoscopic-type incisions — through which the failed organ can be removed and the new organ constructed within the patient's body to reduce secondary injury from the surgery itself — could reduce surgical risk and speed recovery time following an operation. The first simple tissues were layered without structure, but tiny blood vessels have been successfully 3D-printed by using sugar frameworks around which the cells can bind together. More recently, complex organs such as the liver have entered testing after being fabricated from donor cells in layered configurations that provide the necessary complex filter needed for life. The full promise of these technologies is still ahead, but 3D-printed stents (expanding tubes that hold open constricted blood vessels) and simple artificial structures to treat conditions of the trachea and kidneys are already being tested in patients today.

The field of bioprinting is experiencing tremendous changes almost daily, with researchers vying to capture key patents that will drive the development of surgical products for decades. This competition is strong, even now: Several labs that originally expressed interest in having their technologies illustrated in this book had to back out and request removal of details and photographs from the manuscript to avoid competitors' duplication of potential intellectual property. Researchers in the United States, the European Union, Japan, China, and many other areas are racing to be first to patent a 3D-printed heart and other such achievements. This is one area unlikely to see many open-source designs for quite some time.

Part IV
Employing Personal 3D Printing Devices

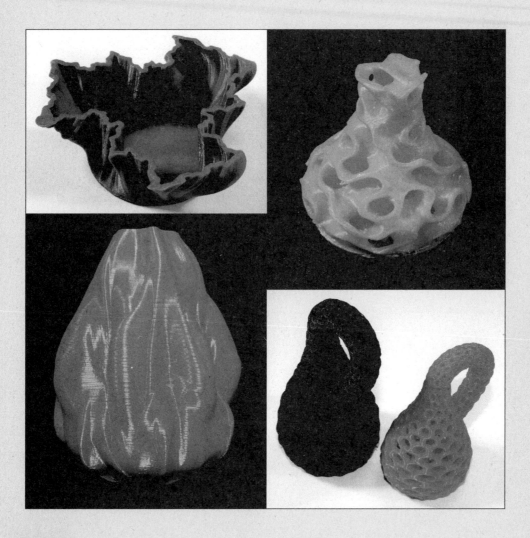

Find out how to create a 3D object in TinkerCAD at www.dummies.com/extras/3dprinting.

In this part...

- ✔ Explore examples of artistic creation made possible by 3D printers.

- ✔ See how individuals make use of this exciting technology in both home and small business settings.

- ✔ Review the considerations you should make before deciding on a 3D printer, whether you plan to simply purchase one or decide to forge ahead and build one of your own.

- ✔ Take a look at the different types of coordinate systems in available 3D printers.

Chapter 9

Exploring 3D-Printed Artwork

Additive manufacturing offers many new techniques for creating interlocking components or objects with complex interior structures, and it's no surprise that creative minds find them attractive. These techniques allow artists to create designs or structures too complicated to be created through traditional means. This chapter provides a window into some of the many different types of artistic creations made possible through 3D printing — from personal designs only a few centimeters in length to large, multi-story sculptures for outdoor display. The artists discussed here have graciously allowed us to include illustrations of their designs, and many have shared them for download by others — where possible, we indicate their sources for you here so you can try out some of these works after you build your own 3D printer in the chapters ahead.

Adorning the Body

Among the first uses for 3D-printed adornment are personalized jewelry and plastic-based clothing — matching both design and visual appeal to individual taste and preference; the customer selects the virtual model as well as the material used to fabricate its physical form. In Chapter 6, I discuss the commercial storefronts of artist Asher Nemias (Dizingof), at which he offers his mathematically-inspired designs for sale through Ponoko in gold, silver, and other materials.

Figure 9-1 illustrates another storefront shared by multiple designers on Cubify, where both physical objects and some virtual 3D models can be purchased for download for local fabrication. Here a number of fashion items — from shoes to 3D-printed clothing — can be obtained and then customized. Commercial vendors are also using the same technologies to design custom-fit athletic apparel for competitors, reducing the weight of items or adding features not available from off-the-shelf traditionally-manufactured alternatives. Because a runner's shoes can now be 3D-printed with cleats and structural elements placed according to an athlete's individual physical kinematics (the way their bodies move), shoes can be reduced to a minimal weight and perfectly fit to the athlete's body measurements to provide a fractional competitive advantage at the highest end of performance.

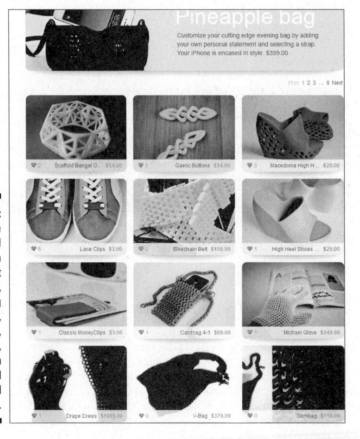

Figure 9-1:
The 3D-printed Fashion storefront at Cubify, illustrating bracelets, hairclips, shoes, and even 3D-printed clothing and handbags.

Personalizing Our Environment

Where once it might have been possible for a craftsman to customize tools for a blacksmith's forge or a carpenter's shop, today's craftspeople and artists can take advantage of additive manufacturing to customize their tools to fit different body dimensions and personal preferences.

Figure 9-2 shows several 3D-printed guitar bodies created by Olaf Diegel, who can personalize a fully functional electric guitar body to suit a performer's arm and finger length as well as any personal aesthetic preference. These items can be created to match a band's style or any marketing efforts to promote the band's music.

Figure 9-2:
Examples of
Olaf Diegel's
custom
3D-printed
guitar
bodies
for fully
functional
electric
instruments.

Also, abstract information can be fabricated in solid form to personalize our environment. Using 3D-printing systems we can create custom-curved, biologically-inspired shapes for dwellings and outdoor statues — such as the treelike form designed by the Francis Bitonti Studios (see Figure 9-3).

Figure 9-3:
Outdoor
3D-printed
artistic
statue
designs
from the
Francis
Bitonti
Studio.

Today, we can leverage 3D printing to customize our toys, or tools, and even our environment while the future of this amazing technology offers the potential to customize our bodies as well. Once the field of bioprinting matures, replacement body parts may become the focus of entirely new trades and services. One day we may be able to print replacements for failing organs or even improvements for muscles or limbs. When performers can transform their appearance to fit a particular role or athletes can add new muscles and connective tissues as easily as they customize running shoes, our legal system will also have to develop new methods of regulation and identity management to meet those new capabilities.

Returning to Personal Creation

In past eras, stone was chiseled or wood was carved by craftsmen to build individual creations unique in form and function. Mass manufacturing replaced this time-intensive process by fabricating large numbers of goods fast enough to serve a massively expanding population — but at the cost of small features common in earlier designs. Many older buildings illustrate this development: Gargoyles and other decorative features adorn their walls, even in locations not easily visible to passers-by. Today's architectural slab-construction is undoubtedly faster, but those small details have been discarded as unnecessary affectations. With the development of 3D printers, we can return to a less "slab-fab" world and return artistic expression to our designs. We might even return to the old ways, using 3D printers to fabricate replacement gargoyles to sit atop our building's rooflines, restoring and preserving the unique artistry of each in the face of demolition and slab-sided modern "construction" in their place.

Figure 9-4 shows vases produced using tie-dyed nylon filament. These are based on Richard's own designs and others shared on ThingiVerse, but the choices of local fabricators make each vase unique in its individual form and color. As we can integrate more of our personal nature and preferences into selections for new creations, we create a much more unique environment surrounding us, changing the face of today's mass-produced, one-size-fits-all world.

Figure 9-4:
Richard's tie-dyed nylon vases, created using RepRap printers like those we discuss in Chapter 11.

It is possible that even more unique changes may be integrated into our mechanisms, such as the delightful experimental design for a research submarine shown in Figure 9-5. The Octopod, the creative design of Sean Charlesworth, is a biomimetic idea for an underwater recovery and salvage vehicle, inspired by the animal that performs a similar type of exploration in nature. Borrowing from nature allows new designs to take advantage of generations of specialization, affording new qualities not present in traditional alternatives.

Sean designed a unique iris door to allow diver egress from the Octopod submarine, which he then shared in the form of a 3D-printable gift box as Thing #31855 on ThingiVerse. Kirk printed the copy shown in Figure 9-6 for his daughter to hold earrings and other small items, using filament colors she selected to match her room's decor.

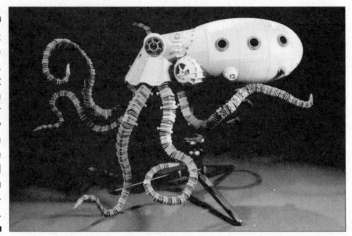

Image courtesy of Sean Charlesworth/Charlesworth Dynamics

Figure 9-5:
The Octopod, a concept for an underwater recovery and salvage vehicle designed by Sean Charlesworth.

Figure 9-6:
Kirk's daughter's iris box, designed by Sean Charlesworth (Count-Spatula) and shared on ThingiVerse.

Visualizing the Abstract

One of the magnificent aspects of 3D printing as a medium for artistic expression is that it allows very abstract ideas to be represented in solid form. Often difficult concepts become easier to understand than simple descriptions and flat photographs would allow.

Mathematical models are amazingly detailed and fluid in their representation. Designs like those of Asher Namias and Stijn van der Linden (see Figure 9-7) can transform simple equations into elegant works of art.

Figure 9-7: Mathematically-inspired 3D-printable objects from designers Stijn van der Linden (Virtox) and Asher Namias (Dizingof) originally obtained from ThingiVerse.

Sharing Can Go Too Far

Figure 9-7 illustrates a current issue regarding open-source designs shared for fabrication by others. The partial Julia Vase shown in the upper left remains available as Thing #126567 under the Creative Commons license with a requirement for Attribution in its display. (Stijn van der Linden is also known as Virtox on the repository.) The other designs of the gyroid vase, lava vase, and Klein bottles are no longer shared by their designer (Asher Namias, known as Dizingof) who was using a similar CC license requiring Attribution for their display when he shared his remarkable designs for download — which is how I was able to print these for my classes.

Asher discovered that his work was being used to illustrate a number of commercial 3D printers' capabilities to reproduce the intricate and fluid forms of these mathematically-inspired models — but the vendors included no visible attribution to identify the objects' source designer, as was required. As a result, these designs can still be purchased as solid objects through Mr. Namias's online marketplaces but are no longer available for download and local fabrication by the public. As 3D printers become more common, this is a scenario that may become all too commonplace as our laws come to terms with the concept of objects only represented as electronic data.

Mathematical models are also used by the Sugar Lab to create amazing edible creations formed from granular sugars (see Figure 9-8). These are magnificent examples of new options available for personalization as additive manufacturing options for materials expand into new areas. Not only successful 3D printers but also even scrap filament left over from failed prints and discarded supports can become works of art.

3D-printable objects that can be easily shared offer ways for artists to engage with the public in the creation of "crowdsourced" art such as the PrintToPeer effort created by artist Jeff de Boer. This Canadian artist is known for his 3D-printed designs inspired by armor such as chain, scale, and plate mail. He has created a site to facilitate his artwork, where individuals can create their own personalized scale designs and then print out copies to be shipped to the artist.

Figure 9-9 shows the design Kirk created based on the logo from this book's cover, which he then downloaded and printed using different colors and combinations of colors of plastic filament. These will be included in the final large artwork compiled from all contributors by Jeff de Boer, along with a few designed by Kirk's children and students that they decided to print for themselves. The design is also available at Shapeways.

Figure 9-8:
Edible math art, courtesy of the Sugar Lab.

After original patents for selective laser sintering expire in 2014, creating another hundred of these scales will not take weeks to print six at a time on the flat build plate, but instead can be accomplished in hours by printing stacks of them arranged horizontally within the three dimensional build volume. 3D-printed artistic creations and even business cards may become much more commonplace in the next few years as options for personalization provide a way to stand out from the crowd.

Kirk hands out samples of 3D-printed materials whenever possible, which has encouraged others to contact him to find out more about additive manufacturing and his SOLID Learning educational program. The word is getting around. Kirk recently had a university dean call him over to show him a remarkable 3D-printed movie prop from *Raiders of the Lost Ark* (see Figure 9-10) — which Kirk had originally printed some time ago as an example for a workshop, using a fan's design shared as Thing #118125 on ThingiVerse.

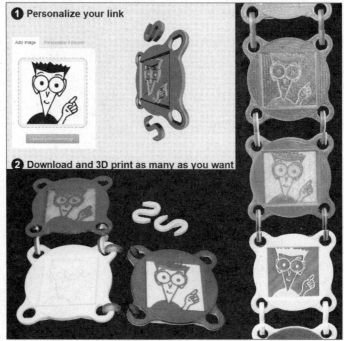

Figure 9-9:
PrintToPeer scales using the For Dummies design from this book's cover.

Figure 9-10:
A copy of the movie prop from *Raiders of the Lost Ark,* printed from a model shared on Thing-I-Verse by its designer (MacGyver).

Art may also serve a purpose without losing its artistic value, so we encourage you to design whatever your ideas suggest and collect 3D models you enjoy. Print copies of these and hand them out whenever possible to spread the word about the changes that are coming through the expanding development of additive manufacturing in its various forms. If you want someone to call you for more information, simply include your name and contact information directly in the object you print. It costs no more to create an object with an "engraved" text message than it does to print the original solid object itself.

Chapter 10

Considering Consumer-Level 3D Printers

*T*o this point in the book, we have examined many different types of additive manufacturing and the application of these technologies in current and near-future settings across many different venues. This chapter examines the types of 3D printers you can obtain or build for yourself now, for the price of a home appliance.

Commercial systems have many materials and fabrication techniques still under intellectual property protection, but the earliest types of additive manufacturing such as stereolithography (SLA), fused freeform fabrication (FFF), and fused deposition modeling (FDM) have passed into the public domain. FFF/FDM 3D printers are growing in number; vendors such as Microsoft carry the popular MakerBot Replicator 2 in their stores, and the Staples office supply locations offer both the Cube printer and the proprietary plastic-filament cartridges it requires to operate.

In the coming chapters, we will examine the construction of self-REPlicating RAPid prototyping (RepRap) 3D printers that you can purchase fully assembled, as a kit of components, or even build from common parts using nothing more than your own "sweat equity" and crafting skills. The RepRap platform has been reformed into a number of different configurations and can be used with both melted-thermoplastic extrusion or paste/gel extruders for food or bioprinting capabilities.

Examining Cartesian 3D Printers

The very first consumer-level 3D printer variation (the RepRap *Darwin,* shown in Figure 10-1) used FFF/FDM to fashion objects from melted thermoplastic that had been first formed into filament. The filament could be fed steadily into the extruder's "hot end," which melted the plastic as it was added, one layer at a time, to the solid object being formed. This process is sometimes referred to as *growing* the new object, although this is not a biological process in current RepRap systems.

The structure of the Darwin printer (and many of its derivatives) resembles that of a commercial overhead crane, moving the extruder in a rigid framework above the build plate that lowers one layer at a time as the object is constructed. In its simplest form, the extruder applies melted thermoplastic within an area defined by X-, Y- and Z-axis Cartesian coordinates (see Figure 10-2).

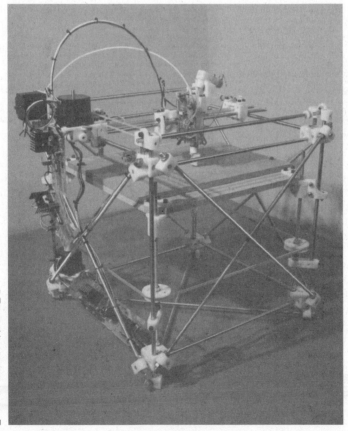

Figure 10-1: The first consumer-level RepRap 3D Printer, the Darwin.

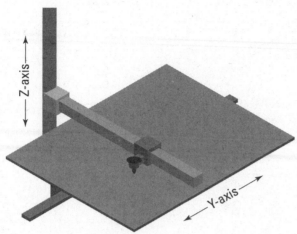

The Cartesian coordinate system carries the name of its source, the French mathematician and philosopher, René Descartes. His system is used to describe any location in a three-dimensional space by measuring the distance in three dimensions from an origin point. For a 3D printer, that origin point represents the home location of the extruder and build plate.

The example shown in Figure 10-2 is like the Mendel Max design we show you in Chapters 11-15: It involves an extruder moving in the X-axis along a rigid frame that is elevated in the Z-axis one layer at a time, while a motor performs the Y-axis movement by sliding the build plate itself below the extruder. Like the original Darwin, other Cartesian designs may move the extruder into a rigid gantry that provides both X-axis and Y-axis movements, while the build plate itself is only lowered one layer's height at a time and does not otherwise move. This is the same strategy used by Polar 3D printers, which we discuss later in this chapter.

Whether the build plate is lowered or the extruder framework raised, the overall volume that is available to Cartesian format printers is that of a rectangular box limited by the framework's maximum span along each axis, as illustrated in Figure 10-3. Cartesian systems can be easily scaled up to larger volumes by extending and reinforcing the framing and upgrading to larger, more powerful motors and motor controllers.

Oversized FFF/FDM thermoplastic-extrusion printers are often equipped with larger extruder nozzles, limiting individual layer resolution in favor of faster print jobs overall.

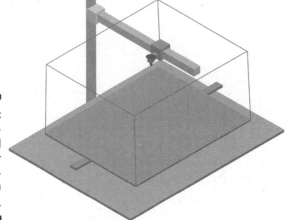

Any objects that exceed the build volume's capacity can be scaled down to fit in the available space or their design can be cut into pieces for assembly after fabrication. Many different techniques can be used to link separated parts from clips and spaces for magnets to threaded holes for screw assembly like the ones shown in Figure 10-4. Even traditional adhesives and resins can be used to link 3D-printed components together to achieve assemblies larger than the build volume of an available printer.

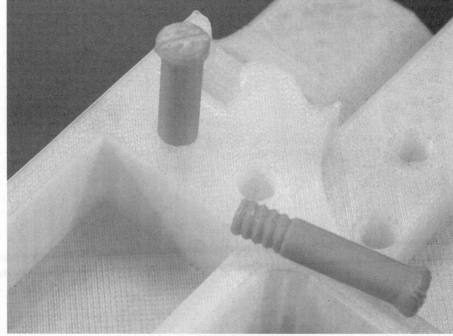

Figure 10-4:
Components of this non-functional 3D-printed firearm are held together with 3D-printed screws that match threads built into the model itself.

Exploring Delta Options

Another strategy used to create 3D-printed objects is based on the techniques used for delta-style robots (which move in 3D space by moving connections along separate parallel frame components). With this technique, movement relies on multiple frames attached via linkages to a rigid central extruder (as detailed in Figure 10-5). By moving each end of the frames, the (X, Y, Z) position of the extruder can be calculated mathematically by the printer's control electronics.

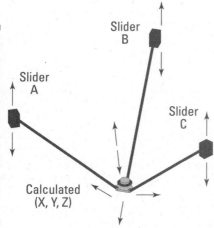

Figure 10-5: As the frame sliders in a delta printer move up and down, the extruder is moved in all three axes of motion.

Examples of delta-format printers include the Rostock Max we will build in Chapters 11–15 and Richard's own 3DR design shown in Figure 10-6. (Richard's UK-colored printer is an open-source RepRap design shared via GitHub and available from his personal RichRap blog.) Delta printers rely on simpler frameworks than their Cartesian cousins because the electronics provide all three movements along X-, Y- and Z-axes; the transit uses the same motors. There are no separate systems for moving the extruder and build plate independently within a rigid framework.

Figure 10-6:
The delta-style 3DR printer designed by Richard Horne.

Because FFF/FDM printers rely on the adhesion of layers of melted thermoplastic to hold down successive layers, rather than gravity, some designs can even be operated upside down without changing the print quality. This is being explored by NASA in microgravity, using a FFF/FDM printer on the International Space Station in orbit around the Earth.

Delta-style printers are described by some as "fun to watch" because they are always in motion, regardless of whether the extruder is being raised or lowered, transferred along a flat plane, or being transferred between any two locations in three-dimensional space. The length of the linkages between the sliders and the extruder mount limit the build volume, which at its highest point must still fit below the extruder and within the support framework. Although technically a triangular space, the build volume for most delta-style printers is represented by a tall cylinder above the build plate, as shown in Figure 10-7. Objects can be built so long as all elements fit within the transparent cylindrical volume. This assumes a linkage that allows access beyond the triangular edge, but many designs provide a slightly smaller build volume to reduce mechanical components needed for the slider's linkages.

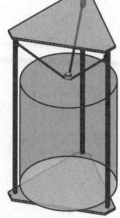

Figure 10-7: The possible build volume for a delta-style 3D printer.

A delta-style printer doesn't rely on its framework to support the increasing weight of the printed object, so it can be made from lightweight metals such as aluminum or locally available structural materials such as bamboo. Like all RepRaps, delta-style printers can be equipped with FFF/FDM thermoplastic hot-end extruders (like the one shown in Figure 10-8) or with gel or paste extruders for other purposes. The figure shows a standard *J-head*-style FFF/FDM extruder hot-end, which would be fed plastic filament incrementally by the extruder's stepper motor. The thicker wires provide power to the heating element; the smaller wires report temperature measurement back to the electronics from a small thermocouple. Both sets of wires are secured within the hot end by using polyimide adhesive tape originally designed for spacesuits.

Based on the weight of the extruder and the print material, delta-style printers can be controlled by toothed belts, lightweight chains, or even braided fishing line to connect each slider with its associated motor.

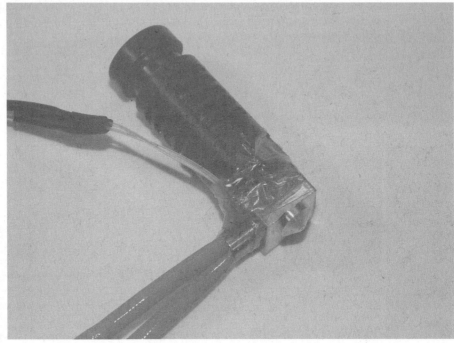

Figure 10-8:
A standard
J-head-style
FFF/FDM
extruder
hot end.

Understanding Polar Fabrication

A third technique for moving the extruder within a three-dimensional volume involves rotating either the build plate or the extruder's support around a central point to build a single layer. This type of design, based on the *polar* coordinate system described by Greek astronomers and astrologers, relies on rotation around a fixed *pole* (like the Cartesian system) and measurement of the distance along a radius or *ray* from that pole at an angle theta (θ) to represent the measure of rotation.

Knowing the pole's location, the angle theta, and the measure of the radius from an axis running through that pole, any point in a flat plane can be defined using the polar coordinate system.

Figure 10-9 illustrates what a true polar 3D printer looks like — using a rotating build plate over which the extruder would be manipulated in its position from the center and height above the build plate — but full rotation of the object results in distortion due to adhesive drag of the melted thermoplastic as the build plate revolves around the pole. Other alternatives place the extruder's framework through the center of the build plate, but this arrangement requires more complex mechanical connections and leveling is more difficult.

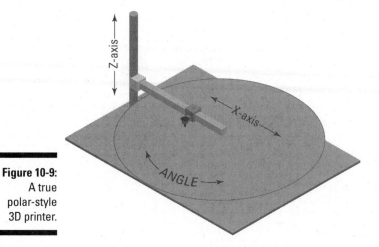

Figure 10-9:
A true
polar-style
3D printer.

A recent effort for the Gada Prize involves a polar-style system used in SCARA robots, which perform the same type of movement using a multi-part arm rotating around a common pole (see Figure 10-10). By creating a four-segment linked parallelogram, both the ray length and angle can be controlled from the central pole by varying the angle that each inner segment follows. The SCARA-designed 3D printer was designed by South African engineer Quentin Harley, who named the RepRap Morgan.

Figure 10-10:
The Morgan
has a
SCARA-
robotic
extruder
movement
that uses
a two-
segment
arm.

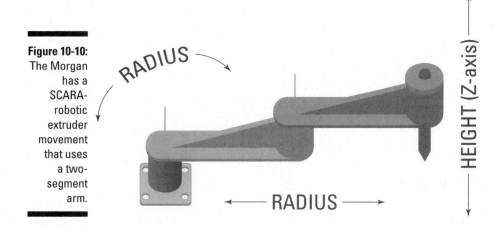

By using an articulated arm and a stable build plate, this design avoids the difficulties of a true polar system because the object only needs to drop one layer at a time — like some Cartesian systems without the need to operate in a full circular path around the pole. Because the object being printed only drops downwards and does not rotate, there is no twisting force on the object, so no torque is transferred due to the cohesion of melted thermoplastic.

To reduce the complexity of mechanical support elements, the SCARA polar design only uses part of the possible full circle around the central pole. Its build volume is typically limited to a half-circle or less, leaving room for structural support to either side of the build plate (as shown in Figure 10-11). Objects can be built so long as all elements fit within the transparent hollow partial cylinder's volume.

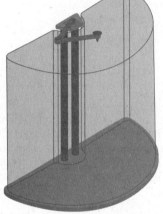

Figure 10-11:
The possible build volume for a SCARA-polar 3D printer.

Living in South Africa, Harley has made it possible to construct a Morgan RepRap using a wide variety of local materials even when a hardware store is not easily found. He's currently trying to reduce costs to fall below $100 USD for a full 3D printer's construction, although at the time of this writing it still remains just over that mark, including the electronics. Some of the non-printable components (called *vitamins*) for the RepRap Morgan — such as rollerskate bearings, stepper motors, and control electronics — must still be acquired from vendors. Even so, the RepRap community is continually trying to create 3D-printable and hand-crafted alternatives to these items as well.

Building Emerging Alternatives

In addition to FFF/FDM variations of the popular open-source RepRap printer, many affordable consumer-grade alternatives are available — from the open-source Fab@Home paste or gel-extrusion design to the proprietary

Form1 stereolithography (SLA) system. Community-designed open-source hardware and software designs become part of many different consumer-level designs, as we discuss in Chapter 11.

As more patents on the fundamental intellectual property for additive manufacturing expire, many alternatives will already have been developed. Legions of hobbyist designers are following the example set down by the founder of the open-source RepRap design, Adrian Bowyer (an engineer, mathematician, and former academic at the University of Bath in the United Kingdom). While fundamental laser-sintering patents are set to expire shortly, open-source alternatives to other (more proprietary) designs that use granular binding are already being explored. An example is the Pwdr 1 printer shown in Figure 10-12.

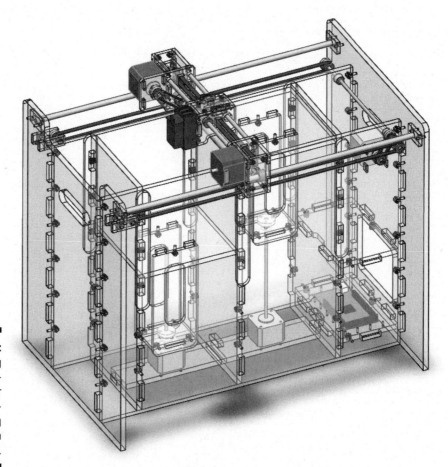

Figure 10-12:
A rendering of the open-source Pwdr granular-binding 3D printer in development.

The Pwdr's open-source design is based on common inkjet printers, applying a liquid binder to fine granular powder held in one hopper and transferred using a roller to create each successive layer in the build chamber on the other side. Because the patents behind this design are still held as protected intellectual property, a Pwdr kit or printer cannot yet be sold to consumers, but its designers are working to perfect a design that can be created by individual hobbyists as soon as patent restrictions expire.

Chapter 11

Deciding on a RepRap of Your Own

. . . .

. . . .

*R*epRap is a wonderful machine that can replicate itself. It's an inexpensive 3D printer that can print most of its own components. For beginners in the world of 3D printing, it's a great place to start. Over the course of the next few chapters, we show you how to make your own RepRap 3D printer.

The first step in making your own RepRap 3D printer is selecting a design. For anyone new to the wonderful world of self-manufacturing, this can be one of the hardest steps. RepRap has hundreds of machines and many bewildering variations on designs, so where do you start and what's the best design for you?

In this chapter we first explore a number of available RepRap 3D printers, and attempt to work out what machine design is right for you.

We also explore the different materials you can use in a home 3D printer, and discuss the individual parts of a 3D printer which is essential knowledge if you decide to build up a machine from a kit.

Evaluating Your 3D-Printing Needs

When selecting a design for your first 3D printer, it's good to first determine what you plan to do with it. Ask yourself, "What do I need a 3D printer for? And what am I expecting a 3D printer to do for me?" Often the reply is "I don't need it for anything in particular, I just want one." This answer is absolutely fine. Let's face it — 3D printers are an exciting new technology and are well worth exploring just for the fun of it.

Another common reply is "I want to print 3D-printer parts and sell them." This answer is one a lot of people use to justify investing the time and money in a machine that can naturally make more machines. One word of caution here: It will take a little time before you are able to achieve results good enough to sell, but it's a fine goal that will drive you forward and the very one that's already helped spread RepRap to every corner of the world.

Do I want a RepRap or another 3D printer?

Next you should work out whether you actually just want any 3D printer or specifically a RepRap. This distinction is important. Due to the demand for 3D printers, many companies have built on the RepRap technology to produce machine designs that can be traditionally mass-manufactured. It's ironic that the success of a low-cost self-replicating machine now makes it hard enough for manufacturers to keep up with demand that some companies choose to mass-produce parts. This leads to a few issues for the customer; one is that if you can't reprint parts for your machine, it's harder to upgrade, repair, or self-replicate.

These issues are obviously not a problem if all you want is a 3D printer and have little interest in RepRap's self-replicating nature. There are many machines available that will fit the bill, and almost all of them started from a RepRap branch or using its core technology. Some still class themselves as RepRaps, whereas others aim to hide those origins.

The one thing that keeps RepRap on top is the fact it can upgrade itself. Other printers that are made up of mostly laser-cut parts, pre-fabricated frames, or custom injection-molded parts will still be able to print the parts for a RepRap, even if they can't print parts to replicate themselves. In this respect RepRap technology becomes ever more fertile and other machines become sterile and risk constant obsolescence. So it's easy to see that every 3D printer manufactured during the last 30 years can help RepRap grow bigger and better; even the mass-manufactured machines of recent years contribute to the overall goals of the project.

I won't tell you *not* to buy a non-RepRap machine. Only think about what you need a 3D printer for and whether the benefits of RepRap outweigh those of the other options available.

RepRap is an open-community project, and its technology forms the basis for almost all new home 3D printers. But RepRap stays vibrant and ahead of the game by its diversity and by the sheer number of users and developers found in its community.

One of the core benefits of RepRap is the control it offers you. Changes, upgrades, and enhancements are made to RepRap on a daily basis by individuals and companies all around the world. With RepRap, almost any improvement or enhancement you can imagine has already been implemented by one developer or another, someone who has probably made that improvement available to you.

This doesn't just go for machine-based improvements, either: You can also find upgrades for software and machine firmware (software running on the electronics of the printer). These updates can help you avoid a lot of frustrations. Many consumer printer manufacturers, for example, fix the settings of their printers so you can print only with a specified material or at specified speed and quality settings. With a RepRap printer, you can print with simple settings or you can alter virtually any single aspect of the machine. This flexibility becomes really important when you're trying to create adventurous objects or wanting to print with new or unusual materials.

Not everyone will want this much control, of course, but pretty much anyone can appreciate the freedom this flexibility offers: With RepRap, you're not limited by arbitrary manufacturer settings. You're limited only by your own imagination.

Do I buy a ready-built 3D printer or use a kit?

Should you buy a 3D printer or a kit? To answer this, go back to your reasons for needing a 3D printer in the first place: If you want to use it as a tool, and the output is the only important factor, then a commercial machine fully built, with backup, support, and training available may be the way to go. This route is more costly and (as mentioned earlier) will somewhat limit what you can do with the machine. It's also harder to get online community support, because the commercial models are not the machines most people are using, upgrading, and tinkering with. Thus fewer people will have a desire to assist you, and to be fair, that's now the job of the company that sold you the commercial closed-source machine.

I always recommend building from a kit or (if you're feeling more adventurous) sourcing all the parts yourself. It's the best option at this stage of the game. These machines are still highly mechanical, so parts will wear out, components will require careful calibration, and over the life of your 3D printer, you'll run into all sorts of problems that interfere with your printing. Consider, however; that these same issues will occur with any 3D printer, no matter the cost. This is just the nature of the technology. This is why it's better to have built up your own machine and to understand exactly how these parts work together to function as a 3D printer. When you've built your machine, you're in a much better position to repair and maintain it. And it's not as hard as you may think.

Don't be too worried. Building up a 3D printer from a kit is really not as hard as it sounds. Almost all kits have completely ready-built electronics and wiring, so your job is only to assemble the mechanical framework, measure and mount parts with nuts and bolts, and then plug in all the connections into the electronics control board. If you do all this carefully and according to the instructions, it can be a highly rewarding experience.

The RepRap community now extends to every corner of the world, and comes together in many different ways. For anyone seeking advice, the very best way is to join a local group of like-minded individuals. It's a lot to take in and a steep learning curve, but well worth the effort. In no time at all you'll be confident with the technology and could be designing your own modifications for the RepRap community.

Open, Closed, and Licensing

RepRap is an open-source project — from the very start it had to be, since trying to limit or stop a machine that can duplicate a significant proportion of itself is almost an impossible task. The open nature of RepRap provides a huge benefit for sharing amongst the wider community of makers, designers, and users. This open aspect does not limit the project to being a hobby or restrict its use over closed-source machines. It does the exact opposite as long as you pay attention to the licenses used.

Despite the fact that RepRap is open-source, the use of almost all RepRap technology is still being provided to you under a license. This is worth keeping in mind — it could be highly important if you intend to make a business out of 3D printing or of building upon other people's work in this field.

A typical hardware or software license details what you are allowed to do with the files being made available. The core of the RepRap project falls under the Gnu_General_Public_License. On the whole, this means the files are free of charge and anyone can use them.

The Gnu Public License was designed around open-source software; using Gnu for hardware projects is possible but not ideal. This limitation is due to the fact that hardware projects have a physical presence that can be shown out of context from the original project or re-used without obvious acknowledgment to the original.

Therefore, many of the hardware elements for RepRap along with the associated 3D designs or supporting electronics are now licensed under a Creative_Commons_License. For example, the very heart of most RepRap 3D printers is an Arduino electronics control board; these fantastic modular sets of electronics are used for all sorts of control projects and industrial tasks all around the world.

Arduino controllers are open-source hardware and software, licensed for use with the Creative Commons_Attribution_Share-Alike_license. This arrangement allows for both personal and commercial use, but you must share the files in the same way Arduino does and also give credit attribution to Arduino with the documentation of your design or changes.

A typical Creative Commons license uses a simple set of icons as a logo to indicate what type it is and what you can or can't do with it legally. The Creative Commons (CC) license shown in Figure 11-1, for example, allows you to copy, distribute, or transmit the work; to adapt the work; and also to make commercial use of the work it covers.

Figure 11-1:
A typical
Creative
Commons
License
icon.

In the logo, the icon of the little person in a circle means that this is provided on the condition that you attribute the work in the manner specified by the author or licensor — you must also not do this attribution in a way that suggests or implies that the author has endorsed you or the use of your work.

The SA icon means *share alike,* so all derivative work must be shared under the same license; in this case, the derivative work can also be used commercially. For example, you would not be allowed to take this work, build upon it, and then change it to a non-commercial license to stop others from building upon it.

Another common example of how this license works could be the original design of a 3D model: In this respect, the designer may want to make the files available for individuals to use but may also want to restrict the model's use for commercial benefit and might even not allow derivative work based on the design. This arrangement still allows you to download the 3D model, print it out, and use it, but it's licensed only for your own personal use.

The logo in Figure 11-2 specifies that work can be shared but is not licensed for commercial use (NC) and also does not allow any derivatives (ND). You are still required to attribute the work to the creator or licensor when you share it.

Figure 11-2:
Another
Creative
Commons
icon
example,
with more
restrictions
on commer-
cial use.

If you obtain a 3D model under this license, you're not allowed to sell a 3D-printed version of the model, to modify the design for you to re-publish, or to sell the model's design files.

You *can* print out the model and have it on display, as long as you ask permission from the author and make the author aware if the design or print of the model is helping you sell something else, such as (for example) a 3D printer that has printed the licensed model. When you do so, however, it's of the utmost importance to provide attribution to the designer, to display the licensed name of the model, and to show the license. You are then complying with the license terms and the designer will get credit for the design, all of which is visible to anyone who sees the printed object on display.

When you don't provide attribution, the license system breaks down, and the designer whose work has been used this way is less likely to share the next design (or be very happy) with you.

It's good to be aware of how anything is being licensed to you, regardless of whether you've paid for it. Even if it's being given for free, you may still have legal restrictions on how you may use it.

Selecting a 3D Printer Design

When selecting a 3D printer design, don't disregard some of the more common RepRap 3D printers that already exist. These established designs should not be considered old or out of date just because they're not at the very cutting edge; consider them as stable ways to get started, a sensible choice, a springboard for further adventures into this new industrial revolution. All of the 3D printers discussed here are based on established technology and their use is widespread in the community. Any of them would be an excellent first choice for your first 3D printer.

RepRap designs

The very nature of RepRap is based on survival of the fittest, so many designs, changes, and upgrades fall from use or are superseded by evolutionary changes as users and other developers take them onboard. Watching a RepRap design grow and change, and even sometimes die out, is one of the joys of an open-source hardware platform. The following list describes the most common designs for RepRap 3D printers, in approximate chronological order, but as always, these designs are subject to constant upgrade and innovation:

- **Mendel:** The original Mendel printer was designed by Ed Sells at the University of Bath in the UK. After the original Darwin started replicating at various universities around the world, Mendel set a new standard for RepRap printers that is still strong and used today in many derivative machines. The Mendel concept is Cartesian, much like existing 2D printers or plotters in its operation. As described in Chapter 10, most Cartesian-based machines move the print bed back and forth along the Y axis, move the printer carriage from side to side on the X axis, and lift or lower the entire X-axis and printing carriage on the Z axis (usually with two motors, one on each side). The original Mendel printer is now considered overly complex to build, but modern versions of the Mendel have become popular and account for a high proportion of the RepRap 3D printers built by users.

- **Prusa Mendel:** The most widely constructed and used RepRap 3D printer is the Prusa Mendel and its many derivatives. (A modified Prusa Mendel appears in Figure 11-3.) This machine, designed by Josef Prusa, was a simplified version of the original Mendel design. The Prusa version, due to its simplicity, proved to be highly popular. Version 2 of the Prusa Mendel is still built today and is still highly recommended as an excellent first machine.

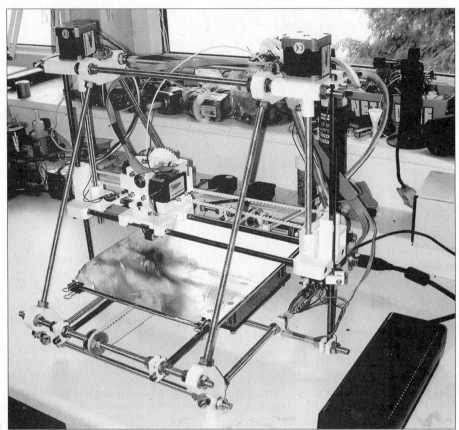

Figure 11-3:
Prusa V2 -
RepRap 3D
printer.

- **Mendel90:** (See Figure 11-4.) This is a variant on the Mendel design that uses a rigid frame, usually laser-cut wood, and plastic acrylic sheet or laminated Di-bond material as the main structural elements (rather than the traditional RepRap threaded rods used on the Prusa machines). It uses almost all 3D-printed parts, apart from the main structural frame, which is often manufactured of an aluminum-and-plastic di-bond laminate. Mendel90 was designed by Chris Palmer. Also known as Nophead, Chris is one of the original RepRap team members who shares a vast amount of RepRap and 3D-printing information available on his Hydraraptor Blog (at `http://hydraraptor.blogspot.com/`). This is an essential read for anyone wanting to really understand the history, challenges, success, and failures of 3D printing at home.

Figure 11-4:
A Mendel90
RepRap 3D
printer.

Image courtesy of Alan Ryder

✔ **Prusa i3:** The Prusa i3 has a hybrid design, combining elements from Mendel90, Wallace, and others to make a simple-to-build high-quality home 3D printer. Version 3, known as *i3,* is a revised version of Mendel, similar in concept to Mendel90 but using a rigid central wooden, acrylic, or aluminum frame and threaded rods that support the moving bed on the Y axis. (See Figure 11-5.) The Z motors are also positioned at the base as per Mendel90, as this provides Z axis movement with a flexible coupler, resulting in ultra-smooth sides to your prints. Over-constraint on the Z axis vertical movement on previous V2 designs often produced z-wobble which would appear as bands or grooves on the side of a printed object. We look at this machine in more detail in Chapter 12.

✔ **Huxley:** Huxley can be considered a miniaturized version of the Mendel that uses mainly smaller-geometry components — 6mm rods for the frame, rather than 8mm, and smaller printed parts. The build area is smaller, but more than enough for many applications. It's also wonderfully portable in its design. The first Huxley machine was also designed by Ed Sells at the University of Bath. Huxley was an unofficial project until it was unveiled to Adrian Bowyer and then published as an official RepRap printer. It was not as popular to start with as its bigger brother Mendel, mainly because many people were trying to build their very first 3D printers, and so opted for the more mature Prusa Mendel design. The Huxley was redesigned by Jean-Marc Giacalone as the eMaker Huxley and sold fast, quickly becoming one of the most popular kits available.

Figure 11-5:
The Prusa i3
3D printer.

✔ **Wallace/Printrbot:** Both Wallace (see Figure 11-6) and the Printrbot share a similar configuration. Only Wallace, however, can be considered a true RepRap because its parts are still produced by printing. The Printrbot's ability to self-replicate was more limited since it required the use of a wooden laser-cut framework. Even so, this approach allowed the production of very low-cost kits and ready-built machines, some specifically designed for educational purposes.

The open-source Printrbot Jr V2 printer designed by Brook Drumm, for instance, is built on RepRap technology and constructed from laser-cut plywood. Due to its mass-manufactured laser-cut frame, it's one of the least expensive ways to get a home 3D printer. Its superior motion elements also improve its printed output. (See Figure 11-7.)

Figure 11-6:
A RepRap
Wallace
printer
designed
by Rich
Cameron as
a RepRap
3D-printable
version of
the Printrbot
style of
minimal
design.

The Printrbot cannot print another Printrbot. Its intricate, interlocking, laser-cut framework is designed to be routed by CNC machines or a laser cutter; it cannot be easily reproduced by hand. Wallace, on the other hand, can replicate much of its own structural framework and only requires a simple bed cut square. That's the difference with the RepRap concept: Get the printer to produce the complex parts and allow almost anyone to easily make the remaining parts using standard tools.

Home 3D-printer kits

If RepRap 3D printers are not to your liking, a whole host of home 3D-printer kits are now available and many, like the Printrbot, replace the use of 3D-printed parts with machined, laser-cut, or stamped-out parts. Whether you want a kit with a lot of ready-made 3D-printer parts or a kit

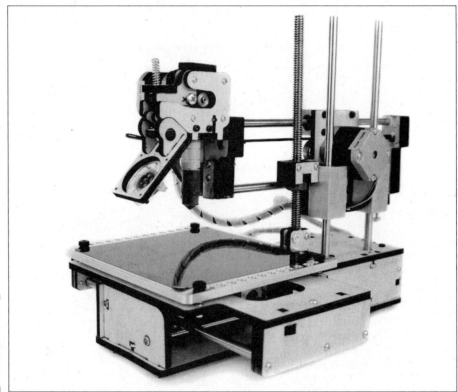

Figure 11-7:
The open-
source
Printrbot Jr
V2 printer.

with few of them comes down to budget and to personal preference. The kits all share the same RepRap electronics, firmware, and software slicing programs; all can achieve similar high-quality print results with a little care and tuning.

In Chapter 13 we look at RepRap-based printers that use both 3D-printed parts and threaded rod along with those that also incorporate laser-cut or machined frames. We also cover Cartesian with MendelMax V2 and Prusa i3 printers, and Delta models with the RostockMax and 3DR designs.

There are endless variants of Cartesian-based 3D printers. The 3D printers in the list that follows can all provide excellent printed objects; all are available in kit form or individual components can be self-sourced using guides and construction manuals for advice.

The following list describes more of the popular home 3D printers that are available as kits:

✔ **MendelMax V2:** This machine has evolved through a number of versions, originally using many 3D printed parts to now having many parts laser-cut or machined. The V2 model is covered in Chapter 12.

✔ **Ultimaker:** This 3D printer, again based on RepRap technology, was one of the first kit machines to be sold. (See Figure 11-8.) It uses laser-cut wooden panels to make a box frame and has a configuration similar to the early RepRap Darwin: The print bed moves only up and down and a lightweight print head moves in the X and Y axes. But the Ultimaker is no Darwin; it's a very fast printer that introduces the use of a *Bowden fed extruder*. This method of plastic extrusion moves the mass of the motor and filament-drive system to a static position on the machine; the filament being extruded then enters a slippery PTFE (Teflon)-based tube that does not allow the filament to bend, buckle, or compress. At the other end of this tube (usually about 500mm long) is the moving print head and hot-end that melts the incoming filament being pushed by the remote extruder. This setup allows the (now very light) print head to move very fast indeed, so faster printing and potentially higher accuracy can be achieved. We explore Bowden fed extruders in more detail in the sections that follow.

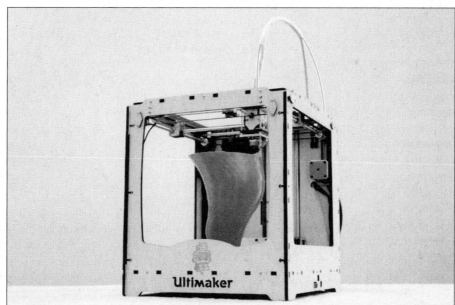

Figure 11-8:
The
Ultimaker
3D printer.

✔ **The Tantillus:** This 3D printer was originally designed as a fully print-able machine. Tantillus is a lot like a miniature Ultimaker. Original versions not using the laser-cut frame have the highest percentage of printed components used in any RepRap printer. The case frame construction was originally fully 3D-printed. This design had one of the highest proportions of 3D-printed components of any RepRap. Another version, using a laser-cut acrylic case, was designed for an easier DIY kit and successful crowdfunding campaign by its creator Sublime. One of its unique features is the use of high-strength fishing line instead of belts to provide the X and Y motion, resulting in a fast-moving machine and high-quality prints. (See Figure 11-9.)

Figure 11-9:
The Tantillus
3D printer.

Almost all home 3D printers have about the same level of quality and speed, so don't get too hung up on the exact model to choose for your first machine. This is especially true with a RepRap; you will be able to upgrade and evolve the design or print out most parts for another or future model!

The experimental designs

At any given time, the RepRap community has thousands of experimental modifications going on all around the world. Every now and again, a totally new branch sprouts out. These new or vastly different machines usually attract a lot of attention and may require other developers to help refine them into something that can be used by the many other users in the community.

Color Plate 1: This bowl is made of natural granular sand sintered layer-by-layer using only the sun's heat to fuse powder into solid form.

Image courtesy of MIT's Markus Kayser.

Color Plate 2: Neptune's form is finely detailed in this stereolitho-graphic (SLA) figurine only a few inches in height.

Image courtesy of FormLabs.

Color Plate 3: This 3D printed articulated gown was created by wrapping a mathematically inspired design around the precise body dimensions of model Dita von Teese.

Photo courtesy of Francis Bitonti Studios.

Color Plate 4: This artist's rendering illustrates a future 3D printed construction site building habitations on the moon one layer at a time using sintered lunar soil.

Image courtesy of Contour Crafting.

Color Plate 5: An artistic reimagining of table flatware made possible through 3D printing.

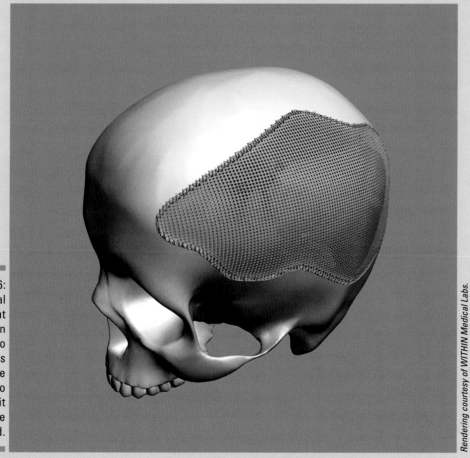

Color Plate 6: This cranial cap implant has been custom fit to the recipient's existing bone structure so that it will fit perfectly once installed.

Color Plate 7: An acetabular titanium implant for an artificial hip bone replacement, whose complex 3D printed internal structure allows bone to grow into the implant to provide a more effective bonding than possible using traditional implants.

Photo courtesy of WITHIN Medical Labs.

Color Plate 8: An artist's rendering of a future lunar construction site being created by a next-generation of the SinterHab robot, as imagined by NASA's JPL and the European Space Agency.

Rendering courtesy of NASA and the Jet Propulsion Laboratory.

Color Plate 9: This example of a 3D Printed light pipe replacement for the Edison-style light bulb offers a glimpse into future efficient custom illumination options.

Color Plate 10: These 3D printed chess pieces include integrated electronics and fiber optic light pipes to display each piece's position on the board.

Color Plate 11: These examples of 3D printed guitar bodies allow each artist to express their own unique style and preferences as imagined by the artist.

Photos courtesy of Olaf Diegel.

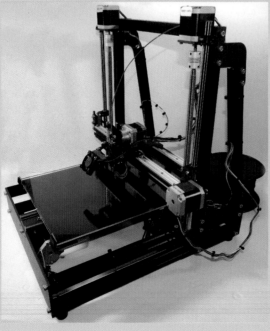

Color Plate 12: In the last section of the book, we discuss building your own RepRap like this Cartesian-style MendelMax 3D printer.

Kit provided courtesy of Maxbots and the Makers Tool Works.

Color Plate 13: Two examples of Richard's 3DR Delta-style printers illustrate the flexibility possible in open source RepRap concept, with colorful components (created using another 3D printer) together with common hardware such as steel rods and bearings, extruded aluminum framing, and braided fishing line to move the individual sliders.

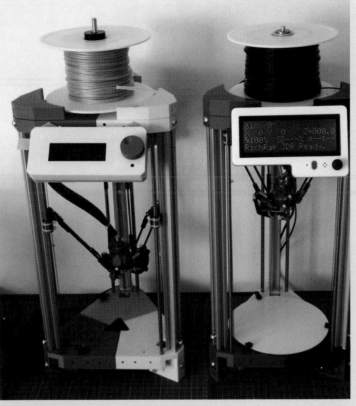

Color Plate 14: A beautiful example of edible 3D printed art formed from granulated sugar bound into geometric shapes.

Color Plate 15: A beautiful outdoor 3D printed biologically-inspired artistic statue, intended to be printed in metal for long-term display and enjoyment.

Color Plate 16: An artist's vision of a planned 3D printed lunar colony, as envisioned by NASA's SinterHab group and the European Space Agency.

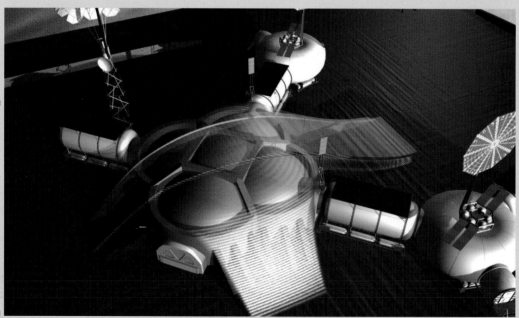

Color Plate 17: Filament for printers like the RepRap come in many different types of materials such as nylon, PLA, and ABS plastic, available in a rainbow of colors and opacity.

Color Plate 18: Multi-dimensional objects like this 3D-printed tesseract are impossible to represent in 2D flat photographs.

Color Plate 19: Many colors of material can be combined during 3D printing to suit individual taste and preference, as shown in this range of smartphone cases.

Color Plate 20: Colored filament can even be mixed across different layers to create unique works of art, as this 3D printed frog illustrates.

Color Plate 21: Even the discarded plastic filament can be used by some 3D printing enthusiasts to craft art in its own right, as this melted assortment of thermoplastic scraps demonstrates.

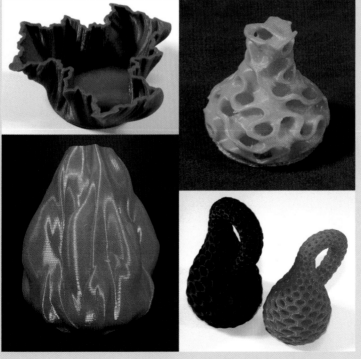

Color Plate 22: Many different artistic styles can be produced using 3D printers, as in the case of these mathematically-inspired objects whose base 3D designs were shared by designers such as Asher Namias (@Dizingof).

Color Plate 23: Some types of plastic filament like nylon can be dyed using common textile coloring agents, allowing the creation of completely unique objects like these multicolored vases.

Color Plate 24: By mixing different types of materials using multi-filament extruders, transparent and opaque materials can be blended to create amazing works of art like these pastel vases.

Color Plate 25: Artists are not limited to single objects, but can build more complex designs from smaller 3D printed components like this biologically-inspired submersible design intended for underwater salvage.

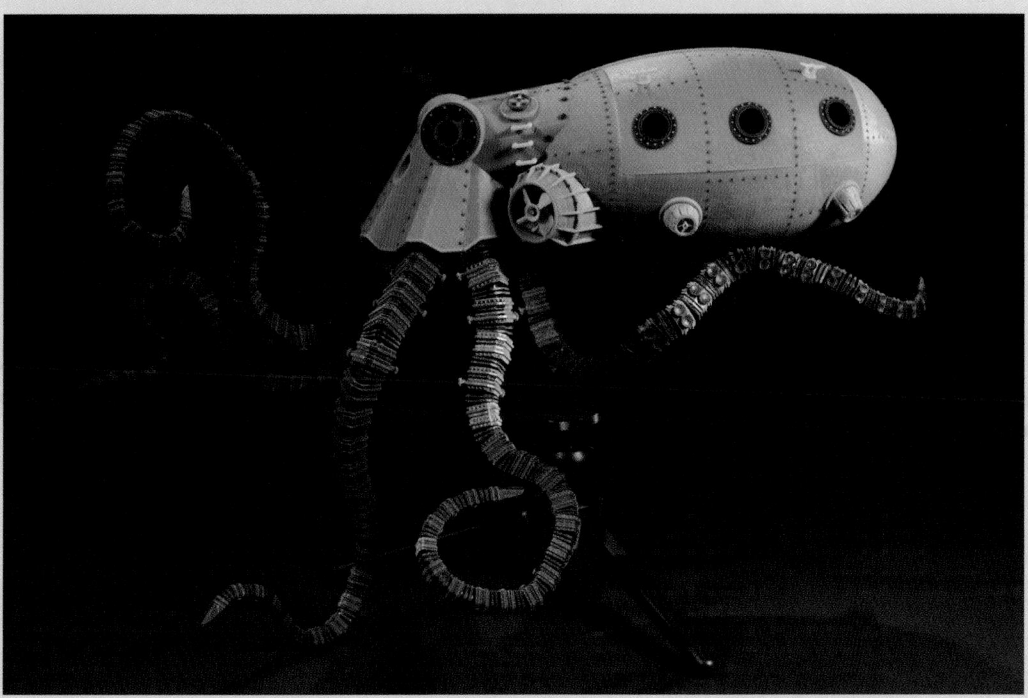

Photo courtesy of artist Sean Charlesworth.

Color Plate 26: Multi-filament extruders can also be used to create single-print objects that varying in composition within interlocking features, as this delightful dragon demonstrates by holding its Valentine's Day gift.

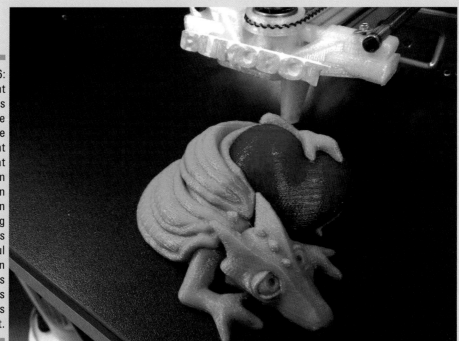

Color Plate 27: Objects designed for 3D printing must take into account the capabilities and limitations in the type of printer being used, as in the case of these FDM/FFF extruded filament bridges spanning the open funnel below. In granular binding, sintering, and liquid photopolymer systems, spare unused material supports the solidified object during construction.

Color Plate 28: 3D printing allows exploration and sharing of public works too fragile or too rare to risk otherwise. Museums can capture a 3D model of a famous work of art, which can then be printed out at another location for display or printed in different scales to have objects that visitors can touch and handle without risk to the original.

Color Plate 29: Complexity creates no additional work in additive manufacturing, so complex internal structures can provide the same level of physical strength with a reduced amount of material, providing ecologically sound and lighter-weight alternatives to traditional cast manufacturing. This 3D printed heat exchanger includes a spiral fluid channel within the lightweight metal form.

Image courtesy of WITHIN Medical labs.

Color Plate 30: Personalization no longer requires extensive additional effort in creating a new design. 3D printed objects can be customized down to the specific facial features on a plastic model as shown in these printed reclining figures.

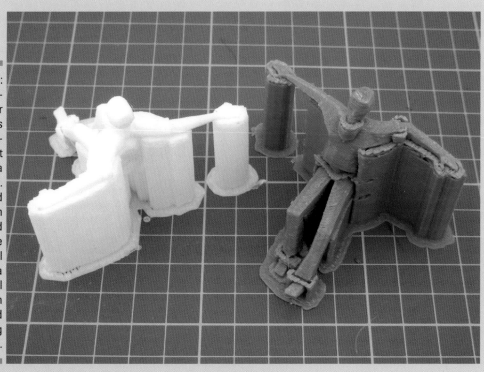

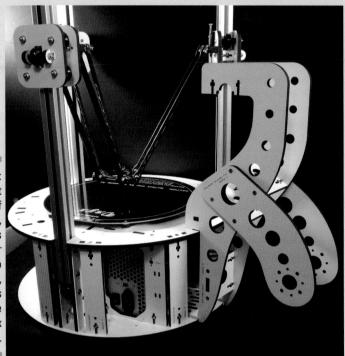

Color Plate 31: In the last section of the book, we discuss building your own RepRap 3D printer, like this Delta-style RostockMax model.

Kit provided courtesy of SeeMeCNC.

Color Plate 32: These Dummies Guy tiles were included along with thousands of tiles from other creators in the "Linked" sculpture, an attempt to create the world's largest collaborative sculpture by artist Jeff de Boer and the PrintToPeer group.

Such innovations are some of the most exciting new developments. It's not always the aim in RepRap to keep on making things ever faster and more accurately; some of the most challenging design issues come from thinking about using lower-cost materials that may be more accessible to more people in the world. Other innovators seek a new arrangement to occupy less desk space but still print large objects.

All the designs we've looked at so far use the Cartesian coordinate positioning system. The next wave of popular home 3D printers use the delta triangulation-based coordinate system, as described in Chapter 10.

Many of the most successful branches of delta 3D-printer designs come from a concept machine called the Rostock and advanced design called the Kossel, designed by Johann C. Rocholl, who has also further developed the delta firmware branch of Marlin that is used on many RepRap Delta printers.

The following are the most popular delta 3D-printer designs:

✔ **RostockMax:** This design is inspired by the original Rostock, but employs a laser-cut frame and makes innovative use of bearings that run on aluminum extrusions to provide the linear motion of the machine. (See Figure 11-10.) It's also one of the bigger machines, capable of printing models of significant size. We look at the RostockMax kit in more detail in Chapter 12,

✔ **3DR:** Richard designed an alternative delta printer, which uses mainly 3D-printed parts for the structure of the machine. We compare the assembly of the 3DR to the Rostock Max 3D delta printer in Chapter 12.

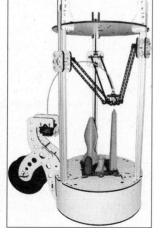

Figure 11-10:
A Rostock Max 3D delta printer; designed by SeeMeCNC.

Most RepRap printers can be scaled to different sizes, so don't assume the stated build area of a machine is the maximum it can be. Typically a building envelope of 200 cubic millimeters is standard, but RepRap machines can be scaled up to many times this size. Non-RepRap printers are usually limited by the size of the laser-cut frame, which is often not so easy for the individual builder to scale.

Further machine arrangements

As mentioned in Chapter 10, many other mechanical configurations can be used to position a printhead in 3D space. Other projects under the RepRap banner are using a SCARA-based system — this concept employs a component like the lower part of a human arm, jointed and extending in and out while pivoting around a fixed point. Stewart platforms, polar printers, robot arms, and full bi-ped systems are all other examples of the many forms a 3D-printing machine can take.

Choosing Print Media

With most home 3D printers, you have a wide choice of materials to choose from and an even wider range you can use in paste form if you use the appropriate style of extruder.

Thermoplastic

Home 3D printers mainly use thermoplastic as the material of choice for manufacture of objects.

It's possible to use almost all types of thermoplastic, but melt temperature and toxicity are critical factors in material choice. Make sure your work area has all necessary safety measures. Good ventilation should be used with all 3D printing, especially in a home environment. Charcoal-filtered fans as used with soldering stations are a good addition.

This section lists some common types of thermoplastic. Your 3D printer will normally use PLA or ABS, but be aware that many more and interesting materials are being experimented with; many have been designed to provide a specific purpose or aspect (such as temperature, strength, flexibility, and optical clarity).

When a thermoplastic is processed for use in a 3D printer, it's usually produced in a factory using specialized plastic extruding equipment and 100% new material. The material, when extruded as a tightly controlled plastic "wire" (round in cross-section), is called *filament*. 3D-printing filament is commonly available in standard diameters of 3mm and (more recently) 1.75mm.

The origins of 3D-printing filament came from the automotive plastic-welding industry. For years, in the early days of home 3D printing, standard spools of 3mm plastic-welding "wire" were used. These days, plastic extrusion companies all over the world manufacture dedicated filament for the 3D-printing industry. This is critical as the tight tolerance of 0.1mm diameter and having true round filament are of great importance to ensure high quality printed parts.

Although many suppliers use all-new materials in their filament, the use of recycled plastic or *regrind* is a fine goal for 3D printing. Many people believe that one day we will be able to recycle old plastic milk cartons and packaging to use in 3D printers. Many projects such as the Filabot are working on a way to manufacture your own filament. Presently, however, creating regrind is a slow and complicated process. At the moment, it's much easier to buy ready-made filament on the roll.

Other, less common thermoplastic materials include nylon, and *laybrick,* a plastic- and chalk-filled material useful for architectural models. Another option is *laywood*, a 40-percent-wood-fiber blended PLA (about which more in a moment). Laywood can be painted, drilled, tapped, and sanded in much the same way you'd work woods such as MDF. (Figure 11-11 shows laybrick and Figure 11-12 shows laywood.)

PLA / PHA plastic

PLA (PolyLactic Acid) is one of the most common types of 3D-printing filament. PLA plastic is manufactured from cornstarch; during the process, the lactic acid is polymerized; the resulting thermoplastic has been used in industry for many years. PLA is commonly used as sweet wrappers, coffee jar lids, and many other products.

PLA can be recycled and will start to break down when exposed to industrial composting facilities. Because PLA is a non-petrochemical plastic (not formed from oil), it's regarded as an eco-friendly choice.

PLA has a low *glass transition temperature* of 60 degrees C; this is the point at which the material starts to turn from a solid to a liquid. The glass transition point is also the temperature used by a 3D printer's heated bed to hold a

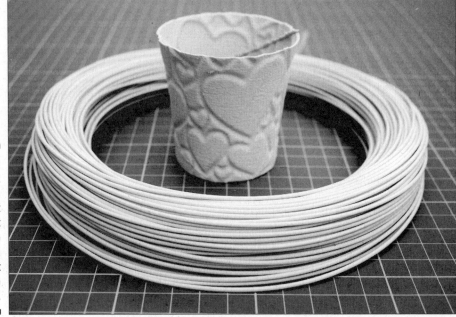

Figure 11-11:
Laybrick material is quite soft when first printed, like chewing gum, but hardens like chalk.

Figure 11-12:
Temperature can alter the color of laywood material, giving it a lighter or darker shade, or even woodgrain effects.

model in a stable state while it's being 3D-printed. This is critical to keep the part from disconnecting from the build platform during a print and also to minimize the warping effect caused by accumulated layers of melted plastic. (See Figure 11-13.)

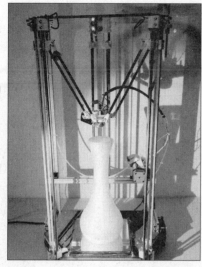

Figure 11-13:
Large objects like this vase can be produced in PLA plastic without significant warping.

Another critical temperature to know for 3D printing is the *useful melting point*. For PLA, that's around 160 degrees Centigrade. A temperature of between 160 and 210 degrees C is often used for 3D printing of PLA. Much higher and the plastic will be too runny for 3D printing; at that point, it also starts to break down.

With PLA, fans are also often used to help cool the print layers during a print. This may sound like a bad idea, but for some small prints being done very quickly it's usually the only way to ensure that a layer is cool enough to allow the next layer to be added. Otherwise you end up with a plastic blob rather than the object you had in mind. Fans can also minimize the curling of an object's printed edges; often the result is a better overall surface quality. PLA filament can come in various grades of hardness and softness.

Melting PLA produces a sweet smell — something like cotton candy or popcorn — which makes it well suited for printing in a home environment.

PHA (polyhydroxyalkanoates) is similar to PLA but made by the bacterial fermentation of sugar (rather than the cornstarch used in PLA). The formation of lactic acid is not required, so the manufacturing process is more straightforward. PHA is still in the early stages of use in industry, and has one unfortunate side effect: It can smell like manure when breaking down.

PLA / PHA in natural form is semi-translucent; however, it can be altered with pigments into a wide range of translucent and opaque colors. (See Figure 11-14.)

Figure 11-14: PLA filament can come in a wide variety of colors and effects, including glow-in-the-dark, metallic, and fluorescent.

Some color pigments can have various effects on the extrusion temperature, and whether the object being printed will stick to the 3D printer's build surface. It's always a good idea to use uncolored natural or white material when first using your 3D printer.

A heated build platform is not essential when using PLA. If you expect to do your print jobs at room temperature, you can use a cast acrylic platform or various types of tapes and adhesives to print smaller parts successfully. For objects measuring around 130mm or more, however, a heated platform is recommended.

Some sources of low-cost filaments have been known to produce filament that contains materials other than the plastic you were expecting. If this material is just an additive or another type of thermoplastic, the resulting filament can just be unpleasant to work with. However, if the other material can't be melted or won't pass through the extruder nozzle, it can totally jam up your whole 3D printer. Be especially careful when using filaments of black material, because contaminates or even rejected batches or materials can be hidden that way. Always buy from a high-quality source.

ABS

ABS (acrylonitrile butadiene styrene) is another common choice for 3D printing. Being oil-based, it's not eco-friendly like PLA, but it has an advantage of having a much higher glass transition temperature. So, for parts and objects that are going to be subject to temperatures up to 100 degrees C, ABS is an ideal choice.

A heated build platform is essential for printing with ABS; a minimum temperature of 100 degrees C is required for the platform and around 240 degrees C for the extruding nozzle.

Natural ABS is an off-white color, but it can be processed to be clear or colored during its manufacture, using techniques similar to those for PLA.

Avoid fan cooling if you're working with materials such as ABS. A fan or even a breeze that cools ABS too fast will make the plastic layers warp upward, knocking the printed object off the print bed before the process is finished. Result: an awful mess.

Not all ABS is the same. It's manufactured from a blend of three chemicals, mixed in varying proportions to affect the properties of the finished plastic. ABS from different suppliers can act very differently; some requires more (or less) heat to extrude, some will be softer, and some is more brittle. ABS has a lot more variation than PLA.

Paste

Paste materials can be used on 3D printers that use a modified extruder, usually a syringe or other type of cylinder. Such extruders press out the paste material in much the same way you press out cake icing from a piping bag. Because many types of pastes are available, syringes are often chosen for being food-safe; however, you shouldn't re-use these syringes for different materials or try to use a normal thermoplastic extruder!

All sorts of food-based materials can be used in a 3D printer with an appropriate extruder, but the paste must have the consistency of toothpaste so layers can be built up on top of each other. Frosting, marzipan, cookie dough mix, and masa are all ideal candidates for 3D printing. Chocolate is a much more complex material for 3D printing, but it is possible to print chocolate items at home. If you pay close attention to temperature and cooling methods, you can provide some wonderful possibilities for decoration and customization of cakes and treats for loved ones and friends.

In addition to all sorts of foods, almost any other material in paste form can be used as a 3D-printing material. Cements, fast-setting resins, ceramics, and even precious-metal clays can allow you to produce traditional artistic objects from solid materials. (See Figure 11-15.) We look at the paste extruder in greater detail in Chapter 14.

Figure 11-15:
Fine porcelain clay can be printed with a paste extruder, and even fired afterwards in normal kilns to produce ceramics.

Identifying Components

Like the very early home computers, many home 3D printers now come in kit form. Although the parts are relatively straightforward to assemble, the build can be a little daunting before you start to visualize how all these components come together to produce a finished machine and then how these parts act together to form a working 3D printer. Not to worry; read on.

Structural framework

The framework of a RepRap 3D printer is usually a common material that can be found in many countries around the world; this is one of the ways RepRap is making 3D printing more accessible to more people. Common threaded rods, very often M8 or M10 size, are often used as the framework. Some printer kits use laser-cut wooden or aluminum plates as part or the entire frame. In some designs, extruded aluminum tubes (often used for industrial racks or production equipment) can provide a strong and lightweight framework for a 3D printer.

The extruder

The extruder or *hot-end* of a 3D printer is one of the most critical parts to ensure good quality and reliable printing. The last thing you want, after 7 hours of a 8-hour print, is for the extruder drive to strip the filament or the hot-end to jam. These issues will stop the flow of plastic and ruin your printed object. If you have too many of these problems, your new 3D printer will spend most of its time turned off or in a constant state of "being fixed."

The most common type of hot-end has an aluminum or brass nozzle with a small hole (typically 0.4 or 0.5mm in size) at the end. This is where the molten plastic is extruded on to your build platform layer after layer. Brass is often used as it's easier to machine, wears well, and provides adequate heat conduction. Brass is also more forgiving: If it's a separate screw-in nozzle end, brass means you are less likely to damage it. Aluminum transfers heat faster and can improve print speed, but Aluminum hot-ends transfer are less common.

Although nozzle holes of 0.5mm are common, smaller holes (down to around 0.2mm) allow for a finer level of detail. However, the smaller nozzle holes have a major downside — they increase print times dramatically, often up to 10+ hours, even for small objects. On the other hand, nozzles having a 0.6mm or 0.8mm nozzle hole size will allow much faster print times, usually with only a small loss of overall detail, for most types of 3D printing. You can still retain a good level of vertical detail, even with a bigger nozzle hole, by printing lower layer heights. Models that are printed as a single outside wall, such as a cup or a pot, often benefit from a bigger nozzle to add strength and wall thickness to the object.

The extruder nozzle is screwed into a heating block, and often these two parts are integrated together and machined as one part. The heating block contains a heating element, this can be a vitreous enamel resistor, a length of nichrome wire or a *cartridge heater*. A cartridge heater is usually a safer form of heating the plastic. A temperature sensor, usually a thermistor, is also required to provide a closed-loop sensing system the electronics can use to control exact heating of the material being extruded to within a few degrees.

Another critical aspect that every hot-end needs is a way to isolate the heating block from the incoming filament feed. This is fundamental, and if not carefully designed and accurately made will result in many problems with materials jamming. This section of the hot-end is called the *thermal break* and commonly made from a high-temperature plastic; usually PTFE (Teflon) and PEEK (another very high temperature thermoplastic). PTFE is used because it has a very low friction against the incoming filament, which is really important: As soon as the filament starts to reach its glass transition temperature, it starts to act more like rubber — in particular it starts to grip against the walls of the cool-end. The cold-end is holding the heating block in place and this material is an insulator it impedes the transfer of heat. It's still critical to keep the cold-end as cool as possible, so one common technique is to use a small fan to blow cool air against the cold-end and help keep a good thermal isolation between cold-end and hot-end.

There are many different types of RepRap hot-ends. Each performs much the same job but some designs are better suited to particular types of machines. The most common hot-ends include the following (see Figure 11-16):

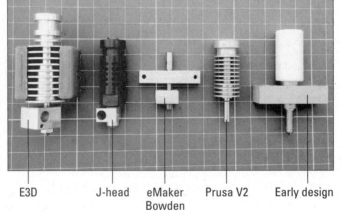

Figure 11-16: Many different types of RepRap hot-ends.

E3D   J-head   eMaker Bowden   Prusa V2   Early design

✔ **E3D:** This nozzle is designed for both high-temperature materials and a very low degree of ooze, so it is excellent for accurate and fine printing.

✔ **J-head:** A good all-around design, limited in temperature to below 250 degrees Centigrade because of the materials used. The J-head nozzle has more parts than the newer stainless-steel designs, but it's easy to use and service. (See the assembled and exploded views of this nozzle in Figure 11-17.)

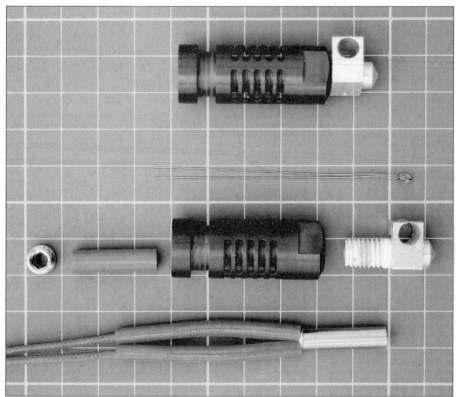

Figure 11-17:
The J-head
nozzle is
a great
all-around
choice.

- ✔ **eMaker Bowden:** This is the hot-end used on the small Huxley printer.

- ✔ **Prusa V2:** A stainless-steel barrel with aluminum cooling fins, this nozzle can reach extremely high temperatures if desired.

- ✔ **Early RepRap hot-end design:** This hot-end is less used these days because its white PTFE thermal break often failed due to jamming or to operating at too high a temperature.

Stainless steel is increasingly popular as the cold-end isolation for newer hot-ends. Stainless steel can withstand much higher temperatures than PEEK and PTFE, and so it can extrude thermoplastic materials with melting points higher than 250 degrees C, such as polycarbonate, (used in bulletproof glass). Even PEEK can be extruded, allowing you to print the cold-end insulator for another hot-end.

Build plate

The build plate of your 3D printer can be made from any of various materials. Because many 3D printers move the build plate backward and forward on the Y axis, it's desirable to make the build plate and any heating elements as lightweight as possible so the Y axis can move and accelerate quickly.

The *build plate* is normally a flat surface of wood or aluminum, often with a printed circuit board (PCB) fixed on top. The PCB acts as a heating element when powered by the 3D printer's electronics. Also required are thermal insulation and a way to level the build plate mechanically. With a heated build plate, you can print with a wider range of materials, but heating the build plate does add another level of complexity to the printing process and the electronics then require a much more powerful power supply.

Many 3D printers make use of the fact you can print PLA without a heated build surface. This lower temperature keeps down the overall cost and power requirements of a 3D printer, but limits you to printing with a smaller range of materials. You can almost always add a heated bed later if you find that your project requires it.

Instead of printing objects directly onto the heating PCB, having a smooth surface to print onto, usually a sheet of glass, is a good idea. When printing with PLA, the material sticks directly onto clean glass if heated to 60 degrees C; when the print is completed, the parts will pop off the glass when it cools down.

If you are not using a heated surface with PLA, the very best material to use is 3M Blue Painter's Tape for Multi-Surfaces (Part number 2090). Covering the printing area with this tape will allow many prints to be completed before you have to cover the build plate with new tape.

A plain cast-acrylic build surface can also be used for PLA, but be very careful to fully calibrate the hot-end nozzle's distance from the acrylic: If the nozzle is too close, the printed object will be almost impossible to remove from the surface after printing.

ABS has the opposite problem: It can have trouble sticking to the build plate. For success with ABS printing, the surface must be heated to 100 degrees C. In addition, you have to add a layer (usually of Kapton tape) to the heated glass plate to control how the ABS object sticks to the build plate. (PET tape can also be used for this purpose.) If you are still having problems getting your ABS parts to stick, then a thinned-down solution of ABS and acetone painted onto the extra layer (whether glass, Kapton, or PET) will add bonding strength.

Finding good materials for the print surface is an ongoing task in home 3D printing. No one single surface has been found suitable for all thermoplastic filaments. Thus, many users opt to fix the glass plate onto the PCB heater plate with office bulldog clips, which allows quick removal of build plates and exchange with other materials if necessary. (See Figure 11-18.)

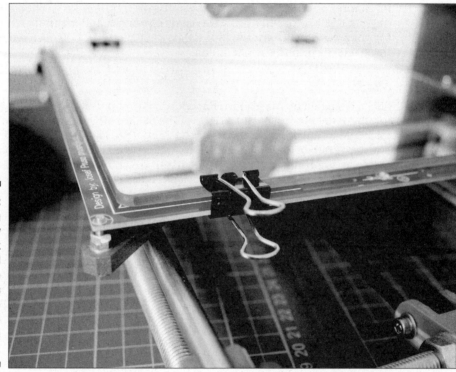

Figure 11-18: Bulldog clips allow for quick removal and secure the mirror-glass plate to the heating PCB while printing.

Printing with nylon requires the use of a cellulose-based printing surface. Tufnol, wood, or cardboard are often used successfully.

Control electronics

The electronics of your 3D printer will most commonly be based on the open-source Arduino platform. We look at various RepRap electronics, including their modular parts and connections, in Chapter 13.

The program running on the electronics for a 3D printer is called the *firmware*. It's quite normal for you to be required to change key settings in this firmware and upload these changes to the electronics.

Software

Another critical part of 3D printing is the software used to design, output (or convert), repair, and then process 3D models into code that can be understood by the 3D printer.

In Chapter 15, we take a look at the software required for producing 3D objects and explore the software used to process and manipulate 3D models for your RepRap 3D printer. In the following sections, however, we describe a few basic 3D printing applications.

Slic3r

Slic3r, designed by Alessandro Ranellucci, is an open-source conversion tool for 3D-model processing for printing. The Slic3r software can be downloaded for PC, Mac, and Linux at www.slic3r.org. (See Figure 11-19.) Slic3r is in a constant state of upgrade, which makes it an ideal choice for the rapid developments in 3D printing. Many enhancements are constantly proposed and produced by the community; check back often to find out what's new or improved.

Figure 11-19:
Slic3r.

The main task for any 3D print-slicing program is to cut up a model into fine layers all geometrically and dimensionally correct and plan paths for the extruded material used on each layer. When the print-slicing program does its job correctly, the 3D printer's firmware processes this data and controls the movement of the printer's components to print out the finished model.

The slicing program also analyzes the model for printability, and can then decide whether additional commands are needed — whether to print extra material to help support a bridge, for example. Further, if you select to use support material, the slicer will do best to add the required breakaway support material without your needing to change the model. Thus a slicing program must apply some intelligence to slicing a model; providing overhangs of material and sections of bridging may require changing the perimeter outlines of the object or detecting when solid layers that go in a specific direction must bridge a gap in an object to keep the print strong and appealing in its final appearance.

RepRap 3D printers use a control language called *G-code*, as do the full commercial 3D printers that cost upwards of $50,000. G-code is an industry standard set of commands and codes used to script the path that a 3D printer (or even a CNC milling machine) uses to produce a 3D object. Thus all the software tools used for RepRap can also be used for high-end machines. The difference with RepRap is that the further development of G-code is highly dynamic; new codes and commands can easily be added to the G-code set as the technology develops further. Many different slicing programs exist for 3D printing, but Slic3r is a favorite with RepRap users all over the world. Other slicing programs you may wish to investigate include Cura, Repetier host, and Kisslicer.

Netfabb

Netfabb is a very powerful commercial software package that is ideal for many aspects of 3D file manipulation. It's not open-source, but a basic version that's still amazingly functional is available for free download from www.netfabb.com.

RepRap users favor Netfabb basic for checking model files prior to sending them to the slicing program. Netfabb allows you to rotate, scale, and modify (or fix) your object models. Loading a model into Netfabb before loading it into Slic3r enables you to ensure that the model looks 3D-printable, that it is in the correct orientation, and that it will print out at the size you expect and require.

Netfabb basic is available for Windows, Mac, and Linux. A cloud-based version is also available and is often even better at fixing issues with 3D model meshes that have errors or refuse to slice correctly.

Professional versions along with specific packages of Netfabb tailored for different 3D printers (including the Ultimaker) are available to buy.

Pronterface

Pronterface is an open-source RepRap user interface for controlling your 3D printer and sending G-code files off to print. The complete Printrun package of software was developed by Kliment Yanev and is widely used in the RepRap home 3D-printing community.

The Printrun package is available for Windows, Mac, and Linux from `http://koti.kapsi.fi/~kliment/printrun/`.

Pronterface is an essential program for the easy use of your 3D printer. In Chapter 15, we use Pronterface to control, set up, and help calibrate your 3D printer, so it's well worth downloading in preparation.

Pronterface can also be linked with Slic3r. Doing so allows you to load model files and run background slicing into G-code with Slic3r from the set profiles you've already defined.

Repetier-Host

Repetier-Host is an alternative slicing engine and control panel for your 3D printer. It's similar to Pronterface and Slic3r in function, and can be linked to Slic3r.

Repetier-Host is available for Windows, Mac, and Linux, and can be downloaded here: `http://www.repetier.com/download/`.

ReplicatorG

ReplicatorG is another well-established open-source package for both model slicing and 3D printer control. It has been widely used by some closed-source manufacturers of 3D printers, but has yet to attain wide popularity with RepRap users and developers.

ReplicatorG is available for Windows, Mac, and Linux, and can be downloaded from `http://replicat.org/`.

Part V
Creating a RepRap 3D Printer

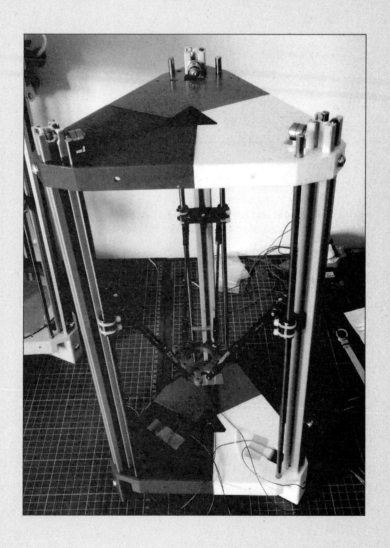

In this part...

- Select, design, and assemble your own RepRap-style 3D printer using either do-it-yourself kits or by sourcing all of the components and electronics yourself using the fantastic RepRap open source hardware designs.

- Assemble and calibrate your own 3D printer using common hardware components and a little "elbow grease."

- Find out how to print in multiple colors.

- See how to maintain your extruder and how to keep your RepRap upgraded.

Chapter 12

Assembling Structural Elements

*I*n this chapter, we discuss where to locate suitable materials or buy a 3D printer kit. We look at building up the frames of both Delta- and Cartesian-style 3D printers. We show you how the machine motion and sensing operations work, and prepare for wiring and incorporating the electronics discussed in Chapter 13.

Although this chapter covers a lot of ground, it should not be considered a full build guide for a specific printer. Instead, it should further assist you in selecting the most suitable machine to build for yourself.

Locating Materials

For a new user, one of the most daunting things about RepRap is collecting the raw materials required to build up the 3D printer, and then trying to identify whether what you've found is suitable to use.

As previously discussed, building up your own 3D printer is well worth the effort. Buying one already assembled may sound like a good idea, but in reality, you'll need to understand how the machine works to keep it up and running in the longer term.

Kits

A kit of ready to use parts can be one of the best ways to start with RepRap 3D printing. You should get all the parts you require, cut to size and ready to assemble. A poor kit includes unlabeled and unnumbered parts all mixed together, and includes no instructions or guidance about what to do next. A good RepRap kit will include labeled bags of individual parts or fixings; a really great kit will even include the tools you require to assemble the machine — usually open-end wrenches or Allen keys. (See Figure 12-1.) It's also likely that the kit will include a link to online build instructions, or to a section of the RepRap forum or Wiki where you can find out more about your kit and its assembly.

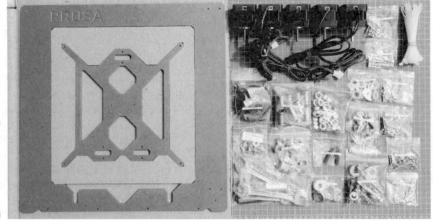

Figure 12-1:
An
impressive
3D-printing
kit.

It's worth taking time looking for a RepRap kit; these come from all sorts of individuals and 3D-printing startup companies, and can have a very wide range of qualities and technical support backing them up. Ask questions about the kit you're looking at; see how long each vendor takes to respond, and whether they provide helpful advice or reassure you with their knowledge on the subject. If you don't like the reply, move on.

A good kit vendor is open about the materials used in the kit, and usually can point you to all the open-source information you need about the design. Some vendors are helpful even to the point of giving you a full list of materials for the kit, so you could make one (or many) yourself.

A poor kit vendor, on the other hand, aims to hide this information from you. He may just state that the kit is for a particular type of RepRap printer, try to convince you that it's a special version, or may omit specific details about the contents of the kit. If the vendor is not forthcoming with detailed information, move on to another supplier.

Kits can vary greatly in quality. Before you buy, know what to look out for from kit suppliers and ask questions if the information is not provided. Some of the questions you might ask include the following:

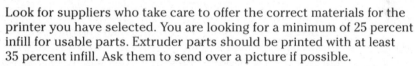

- ✔ **What materials have been used to produce the 3D-printed parts?** and **What is the fill density of the printed parts?** It's good to know the material; some kit suppliers may choose to provide some specific parts made of ABS if they require a higher temperature on the machine than PLA parts. In almost all cases, there is nothing wrong with using PLA for the machine construction; in fact, if the 3D printer design you have selected is using 3D-printed gears to drive the extruder or the motion of the machine, these *should* be made from PLA — they'll have a much longer wear life than gears made of ABS.

  Look for suppliers who take care to offer the correct materials for the printer you have selected. You are looking for a minimum of 25 percent infill for usable parts. Extruder parts should be printed with at least 35 percent infill. Ask them to send over a picture if possible.

- ✔ **What electronics are being provided? Are they a RepRap standard or a custom development from the supplier?** Electronics may not be provided in the kit at all; it's quite common for electronics to be bought separately from the mechanical kit.

- ✔ **Is the kit based on a recent release of the RepRap 3D printer you're considering?**

- ✔ **If the kit has laser-cut parts, what material is being used, and how thick is it?** Check with other sources and suppliers: Are they are cutting corners with reduced thickness or flimsier materials?

- ✔ **Are the linear rails provided in the kit stainless steel or just basic carbon steel?** It's well worth paying a little more for stainless steel; parts made of it wear better and don't tend to produce as much black oil residue over the rods and bearings.

- ✔ **What motors are provided with the kit?** Make sure they are true bipolar 4-wire motors; ask what their current rating is. Another thing to check with the motors that will save you time is whether they have cables with connectors already fitted onto the ends. Most commonly, NEMA17 motors are used for RepRap kits; these have a stated current rating depending on the overall length of the motor body. You are looking for a minimum of 1.2 amperes (A). A more powerful motor will be rated at 1.7A; the maximum rating for a NEMA17 motor is around 2.5A.

- ✔ **Are plastic parts included?** Some kit suppliers may not provide the 3D-printed plastic parts; so do check to see whether that's a separate option.

If you are buying a smaller 3D printer such as the Huxley, it's normal to have smaller NEMA14 motors supplied. These should operate correctly for the lighter-weight machines, but bigger machines will often require bigger motors to move the heavier axis quickly — most commonly, NEMA 17 motors for home 3D printers. Much bigger NEMA 23 and 34 motors are often used for CNC milling machines and other subtractive manufacturing machines, and thermoplastic extruders almost always require a NEMA 17-sized motor to operate well and quickly.

Self-sourcing

Self-sourcing all the parts — that is, finding what you need on your own — can be good when you want to build more than one 3D printer, or if a group of individual users plans to build the same printer together.

It's often the case that if you try to buy parts for just one printer, it will cost you as much (or even more) as buying a ready-made kit of parts. This is exactly why a good kit supplier will provide you all the information needed for you to buy or identify all the parts required for the RepRap printer you're interested in. The information is already out there online anyway. Going to the trouble, time, and extra risks of sourcing all the individual parts yourself can save significant cost when you are building with a group of friends or at a local hackerspace or fab-lab. If you are only building one printer and you decide to self-source, you will often need to buy more components than you really require, or you'll have to pay significantly more for just the small number you need. Also, you may end up paying significant fees in delivery and duty charges to get hold of all the parts from around the world. Finally, be aware that it's not uncommon to find poor quality components or substitute parts that you were not expecting or that don't fit your machine build. This is why it's often better for individuals to buy a complete kit from a single supplier than to self-source.

If this is your first 3D printer, of if you don't fancy spending a lot of time ordering many different parts from a lot of different suppliers, a kit is the best way to start out.

Printing your own

Of course, when you have a working 3D printer, the whole job of making another one for yourself or a friend is almost totally under your control. Even upgrades and spare parts for your own 3D printer are straightforward to print out.

RepRap printers are becoming self-reliant and more printable all the time. This unique aspect of RepRap technology makes it one of the most rewarding parts of owning a 3D printer you can modify, upgrade, and repair yourself, without relying on overpriced spare parts.

It's becoming more commonplace that someone with a 3D printer is not far from you and closer all the time. Many such people are willing to print out a set of parts for a reasonable cost or trade for other materials or services. In fact, one of the most common ways to justify the cost of owning a RepRap 3D printer is the capability to print off a few good sets of parts to sell or trade.

You can also use professional 3D-printing services and online print shops to get a set of RepRap machine parts printed out, but that's going to cost a lot more than using another RepRap to produce your parts for you.

eBay

It's always an option to turn to eBay or other online marketplaces; you can find out a lot of information from eBay sellers about printed parts, available machine designs, and the selling prices of all such items. The main word of warning is that the quality of 3D-printed parts offered on eBay is uneven: Some will be of unusable quality; others may just allow you to get up and running but needing replacement soon after you get them. Fortunately, there are a lot of good suppliers selling on eBay as well, so do your homework: Ask around in the RepRap community. Someone will be able to recommend and direct you to a reputable source of printed parts and machine kits.

Obtaining the Printed Parts for Machine Assembly

Later in this chapter, we begin building an example Prusa i3 3D printer. We start with the frame assembly and in subsequent chapters assemble all the other parts of the printer.

Kits for the laser-cut aluminum frame along with all the other mechanical parts are available from a wide number of sources. However, you can also buy or source your own set of printed parts if you wish to print your own. Or you can ask a friend with a 3D printer to produce a set for you. The master files can be found on Josef Prusa's github archive here — `https://github.com/josefprusa/Prusa3-vanilla`. The parts you'll need to begin construction are outlined in Tables 12-1 and 12-2.

Table 12-1	Printed Parts Required for the Lower Y-Axis Frame Assembly	
Part	**Details**	**Quantity**
Y Corner parts	Used with the M8 and M10 threaded rods to form the structural base of the Y axis	4 – one on each corner
Y Motor mount	Inserted onto the threaded rods to mount the Y motor	1
Y Idler mount	Inserted onto the threaded rods to mount the Y belt drive idler bearings	1
Y belt clamp	Used to clamp the Y drive belt tightly to the moving Y axis	1

Table 12-2	Mechanical Parts Required for the Lower Y-Axis Assembly		
Part	**Description**	**Type**	**Quantity**
Threaded rod	M8 rods 210mm long	Rod – Steel or stainless	4
Threaded rod	M10 rods 380mm long	Rod – Steel or stainless	2
Smooth rod	350mm smooth M8 rods used for motion of the Y axis	Smooth rod – Steel or stainless	2
Linear bearing	LM8UU linear bearings for Y axis motion	Motion	3
M8 nut	M8 size plain or locknut type	Fastener	22
M10 nut	M10 size plain or locknut type	Fastener	12
M8 washer	M8 size plain washer	Fastener	22
M10 washer	M10 size plain washer	Fastener	22
Ball bearing	624ZZ Ball bearings for belt idler	Motion	2
M4 bolt	25mm M4 bolt for Idler	Fastener	1

Part	Description	Type	Quantity
M4 nut	M4 size plain or locknut type	Fastener	1
M4 washer	M4 size plain washer	Fastener	2
Tie-wraps	100mm long 3.2mm tie-wraps to secure linear bearings and smooth rods	Fastener	7
M3 bolts	20mm M3 bolts to secure heated bed onto Y axis	Fastener – ideally stainless steel	4
M3 nut	Plain M3 nuts to secure heated bed onto Y axis	Fastener – ideally stainless steel	4
M3 washer	Plain M3 washers to secure heated bed onto Y axis	Fastener – ideally stainless steel	4
Laser-cut Y axis plate	Various designs exist; check the version for compatibility with your linear bearings.	6mm Aluminum	1
M3 bolts	16mm M3 bolts to secure the motor onto the Y axis mount another two to secure the Y belt clamp	Fastener – ideally stainless steel	4
GT2 timing belt	One of the GT2 timing belts.	Motion	1
NEMA 17 motor	NEMA 17 motor 1.2A to 2.5A rated.	Motion	1
GT2 Gear	Fit onto the NEMA 17 motor	Motion	1

Understanding the Machine Motion

Okay, after you've obtained the parts for your RepRap 3D printer or even before, it's worth considering how the finished device is supposed to work before you put it together. The components you can use for machine motion cover a wide range of materials, dimensions, and specifications; here's where we look at some of the common and more experimental ways to achieve the linear movement that makes 3D printing happen.

Z-axis motion

The Vertical axis called the Z axis on a Cartesian machine is normally driven slowly and with a high resolution setting to achieve fine detail and precise printed layers.

Most machines have to lift the entire moving X carriage, including the extruder with motor and hot-end, to achieve vertical Z-axis movement. Often they use two stepper motors, one on each side of the machine. Both motors run from just one stepper-motor output; they must stay in sync with each other.

On most RepRap machines, the way a vertical Z carriage usually achieves this lift is with a simple threaded rod attached to the motor shaft: A normal nut is trapped in the 3D-printed Z carriage so when the motor rotates, the nut is driven up and down the threaded rod; do this on both sides of the machine and you achieve parallel lift. This arrangement automatically provides a fine resolution for your print layers because one complete rotation even for coarse M8 rods moves the carriage only 1.25mm up or down per rotation. This is a simple, low-cost way to achieve fine resolution of movement; the main drawback is that a standard nut and standard threaded rod are not optimized for all the motion that 3D printing requires. You have to carefully limit the speed at which you drive the motors or they'll stall or skip.

Fortunately, a slow vertical Z axis is not a major limiting factor for most types of 3D printing. The print head spends a lot more time moving in the X and Y axes to print each layer than it does moving in the vertical. Of course, this type of threaded-rod movement is not used for the X and Y axes of a 3D printer because the motion would be unacceptably slow.

As you read in the chapters that follow, it can be a good thing to enable a *Z lift* feature that makes the extruder carriage jump up every time the machine has to move to a new printing point. Z lift can help stop the print nozzle from accidently catching on a piece of already-printed plastic (which can knock the model out of alignment). You want to make your extruder do a Z lift as quickly as your Z axis will allow.

Many original RepRap machines used M8 (8mm) or equivalent imperial-sized threaded rods for the Z-axis. More common today are M6 or M5 rods, which provide finer layers and can still be driven fast enough for high-quality results. (The printer in Figure 12-2 uses an M5 threaded rod and a trapped M5 nut, and connection to the motor is made with a short section of vinyl tube to allow the threaded rod rotary motion. A solid connection to the motor can cause the threaded rod to fight with the smooth vertical rods, which can cause print layers to be out of alignment.)

Figure 12-2:
The vertical
Z-axis drive
on a Prusa
i3 printer
uses an M5
threaded
rod and a
trapped
M5 nut.

Other available products are specifically designed for this sort of linear movement; they can normally be turned much faster than the standard threaded-rod-based systems. They do, however, cost more and can be harder to source and mount in your 3D printer.

Figure 12-3 shows three different movement systems that could be used for the vertical Z-axis. On the left is an M8 threaded rod and M8 nut, along with a typical printed carriage to hold the M8 nut. In the middle is an ACME lead screw; this is machined for linear movement, and comes with a matching square nut. This nut would have to be housed in a 3D-printed carriage, in a way similar to the M8. On the right is a fully machined ball screw; this can achieve high-speed motion using a spiral of trapped ball bearings, and could also be used for other axis movement if desired. This is significantly more expensive than the other two.

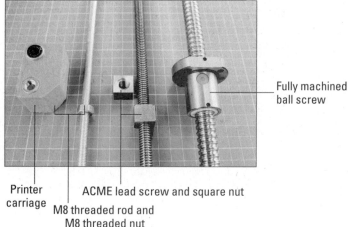

Figure 12-3:
Three
different
vertical
Z-axis
movement
systems.

Fully machined
ball screw

Printer
carriage

ACME lead screw and square nut

M8 threaded rod and
M8 threaded nut

X and Y axis motion

The X and Y motion of a 3D printer has to be as fast as possible; the faster you can position the print head at various points around the build plate, the faster you can produce 3D models. For this reason, we most commonly use precision timing belts and cogged drives connected directly to the motor shaft.

As with the Z axis, you still require a good level of resolution for these movements, so the belts we use are normally 5mm or 2.5mm tooth pitch; more recently, a 2mm version has become very popular. These timing belts have fine steel wires to stop the belt from stretching; they will wear out eventually but usually offer a good few years of printing.

Not so commonly used are line-based drive systems, which use high-strength braided fishing line wrapped around a printed spool attached to the motor shaft. The use of fishing line, popular on Delta-based printers, can have a number of benefits, including reduced noise and increased speed, and the line can usually be tightened to a greater degree than timing belts. They also have the added advantage of costing a lot less than timing belts.

Figure 12-4 shows a few drive systems used for X and Y movement. On the left is a printed spool with wraps of high-tensile braided fishing line, which is low-cost and can achieve very smooth and fast motion. The black GT-2.2mm timing belt in the middle is now a popular choice for many 3D-printer designs and kits. At the back, the white belts are 2.5mm pitch commonly used in Europe, along with matching aluminum pulleys.

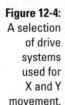

Figure 12-4:
A selection of drive systems used for X and Y movement.

2.5 mm tooth pitch timing belt

Printed spool wrapped with fishing line

GT-2.2 mm tooth pitch timing belt

Another important part of the movement system is the rails that the X, Y, or Z carriages travel along in a straight and flat plane. These smooth rods (or drill rods) are most often 8mm or 6mm in diameter, but depending on the size of machine, 10mm or bigger may be required. These rails are most often mounted alongside the threaded rod or timing belt. The carriage being moved slides along these smooth rods by the use of either linear bearings or bushings (which can be 3D-printed or made from brass).

Linear bearings are professionally made, and have a ring of small ball bearings inside an outer metal body; these bearings slide against the rod and provide a smooth motion. Although these bearings offer a long life, they do generate noise as they slide along. If a lower-noise solution is preferable, then the use of brass or 3D-printed bushings is ideal. Although bushings wear out much more quickly than linear bearings, at least replacement bushings can be 3D-printed for very little cost.

Figure 12-5 depicts rods and bearings for 3D printing. On the left is an 8mm stainless-steel smooth rod used in a Z axis assembly: A linear bearing fits into the 3D-printed Z carriage and slides up and down on the rod. On the right, a 6mm steel rod and 3D-printed PLA bushing provide a low-cost and perfectly acceptable alternative.

If you do decide to 3D-print bushings for your assembly that handles linear motion, be sure to use PLA as the bushing material. It's hard and will slide smoothly after bedding in. If you use ABS, the bushings will wear out almost immediately.

Many other types of professional rails and rods can also be used to control motion. An example appears later on in this chapter: The MendelMax uses linear rails for the X-axis and supported machined-smooth rods for the Y-axis.

Figure 12-5:
The rods and bearings used in a 3D printer allow the carriage or axis to slide smoothly along or up and down.

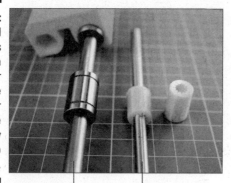

8 mm stainless-steel smooth rod and bearing

6 mm steel rod with a 3D-printed PLA bushing

The movement system for Delta-based 3D printers is basically the same as the X or Y axis of a Cartesian system, but all three axes (X, Y, and Z) are identical and travel vertically at three points of a triangle. The requirement for belt or line length tends to be twice as long in a Delta system due to the nature of the movement, which is often why fishing line is used. Along with the reduction in noise this can have considerable cost savings and also advantages of taking up less space.

Building the Frame Structure

Although the frame structure of a RepRap 3D printer can vary between designs and generations, they all perform the same function: to provide a strong, level, and accurate shell to which to attach all the other parts of the 3D printer. The following list describes the frame structure of four common RepRap designs:

✔ **Threaded rod (Prusa i3):** RepRap 3D printers started out by using threaded rods for the frame assembly, which allows for very accurate dimensioning with the strength and simplicity of 3D-printed parts.

The lower frame of a Prusa i3 printer is constructed from M8 and M10 threaded rods. (See Figure 12-6.) These can be accurately spaced and adjusted for a strong structure. In between is the Y idler timing belt mount, on which a bearing is mounted and around which the belt is threaded. On top, the 3D-printed parts in the channel will sit the M8 smooth rods for the Y axis and build plate to slide on.

Figure 12-6: The lower frame of a Prusa i3 printer.

Y idler timing belt mount

The Prusa i3 also makes use of two laser-cut parts for construction, one being the Y axis plate that will move forward and backward. (See Figure 12-7.) The other laser-cut part, the frame, needs to be accurately spaced apart for the movement to slide freely. Fortunately, threaded-rod construction is easy to adjust to get perfect spacing.

Figure 12-7:
The Y axis plate, made of 6mm-thick aluminum, simply requires 3 LM8UU linear bearings to be zip-tied on and a 3D-printed Y belt clamp bolted in place.

Figure 12-8 shows the finished Y-axis assembly, which now includes the motor, a GT-2 timing belt, and an idler pulley. One side of the belt is fixed to the laser-cut Y-axis plate; 8mm smooth rods are fixed onto the ends of the threaded-rod frame to allow movement.

Figure 12-8:
The finished Y-axis assembly.

✔ **Laser-cut and aluminum frames (MendelMax V2):** The MendelMax V2 design uses many laser-cut aluminum plates and standard 20mm extruded aluminum lengths to build up the main structure of the 3D printer. (See Figure 12-9.)

Bolts and trapped nuts are used to build up the frame. Careful measuring and alignment is still required. Once constructed, this sort of assembly produces a very heavy but solid frame. This is a more expensive way to construct a 3D printer, but has a more professional look.

Figure 12-9:
A
MendelMax
V2 frame.

✔ **Laser-cut wooden frames (RostockMax) Delta printer:** The RostockMax 3D printer uses almost all wooden laser-cut parts for its construction. (See Figure 12-10.) Only the vertical upright sections are aluminum extrusions. Cut channels in the wooden sections accept a standard nut, and bolts clamp each part together to form a solid structure. (See Figure 12-11.)

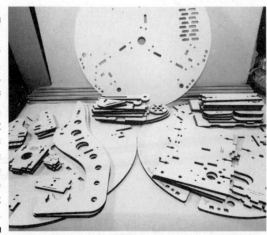

Figure 12-10:
A highly
precise
jigsaw
puzzle of
wooden
laser-cut
sections
forms the
frame
for the
RostockMax
3D printer.

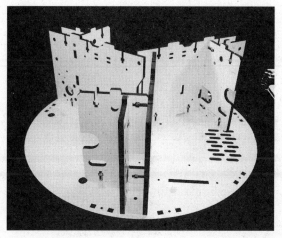

Figure 12-11:
The sections
are secured
together
with trapped
nuts and
bolts.

Electronics, power supplies, and wiring can all be mounted to specific sections of the wooden frame, achieving a neat and tidy look to the finished 3D printer. (See Figure 12-12.)

Figure 12-12:
During
assembly,
aluminum
extruded
sections
are fitted
to achieve
the vertical
height for
the Delta
printer.

✔ **3D-printed frame (3DR) Delta printer:** The 3DR Delta printer is a lot smaller than the RostockMax, but its frame is mainly constructed from a minimal set of 3D-printed parts that simply bolt together. (See Figure 12-13.)

Figure 12-13:
Three
identical
3D-printed
sections
have
vertical
upright
aluminum
sections
fitted and
can be
bolted
together.

At the top, another set of three identical parts can be printed in what-ever colors you choose. Electronics, wiring, and sensing components are also fitted onto the 3D-printed frame construction. (See Figure 12-14.) The result is a strong frame to which to fit the rest of the printer parts. (See Figure 12-15.)

Figure 12-14:
The three
motors
that drive
the printer
are also
attached
to the
3D-printed
parts.

Being mainly 3D-printed and able to print its own parts, the 3DR Delta printer is easy to change, evolve, or even scale up or down in whatever way required.

Figure 12-15:
A 3DR Delta printer frame.

Assembling the Prusa i3 Y Axis Frame

For our example build, the first part of construction is with the Y axis frame. The frame is made from four printed corners, with M8 and M10 threaded rods and nuts, and this forms a rectangle of smooth bars along which the Y axis can move back and forth, driven by a stepper motor.

To build the Y axis frame, follow these steps:

1. **Assemble the Y axis frame side:**

   a. Take one of the 380mm M10 threaded rods, and thread an M10 nut into approximately the middle of the rod. Slide two M10 washers and thread on another M10 nut to make a sandwich of washers in between the nuts, all in the middle. Do not tighten.

   b. Thread another M10 nut onto each end of the M10 rod about 45mm in.

   c. Slide an M10 washer onto each end, then fit the printed Y corner onto each end of the M10 rod. Check orientation of the Y printed piece: The M8 grooves to hold the smooth rods should be facing up and inwards.

   d. Slide an M10 washer onto each end of the rod up against the printed part.

   e. Thread an M10 nut on each end of the rod. Now you can hand-tighten the parts so the printed ends are secured by the M10 nuts and washers.

   f. Repeat the mirror image for the other Y axis side.

2. **Assemble the idler bearing mount:**

   a. Slide a M4 washer onto the 25mm M4 bolt and insert into one side of the idler mount, while holding two 624ZZ bearings in the middle of the mount. Push the bolt through.

   b. Slide another M4 washer on and secure with another M4 nut.

3. **Assemble the Y axis front and back frame sections:**

   a. Take two of the 210mm M8 threaded rods and thread on an M8 nut about 45mm onto one end of each rod, then slide an M8 washer onto the rod against the nut.

   b. Insert the ends of the M8 rods into the Y axis, printed corners-up, against the two M8 nuts and washers.

   c. Use another washer and M8 nut on each rod end to hand-secure the rod against the printed Y corner.

   d. Slide a nut and washer into the middle of each rod, then slide on the Y motor mount so it faces inwards.

   e. To secure the mount, use another two washers and nuts to sandwich the printed part; hand-tighten.

   f. Repeat steps a–e on the other end of the M10 rods.

   g. For this end we need to slide on the printed idler mount, again facing inwards. Repeat step e to secure the idler in the middle of the rods.

   h. You will need to add the third and fourth corners to the other ends of the rods using steps a–e.

4. **Measure and tighten the frame.**

At this point, your idler end should look like Figure 12-6, shown earlier.

Assembling the Moving Axis

After construction of the main frame, the next step is to start assembly of the moving axis systems. Cartesian 3D-printing designs often use very similar systems for movement. (Refer to Figures 12-6 and 12-7 to see the moving Y-axis assembly of a Prusa i3.) The moving Y axis of a MendelMax V2, for example, would have an assembly similar to that of a Prusa i3 (refer to Figures 12-6 and 12-7), except that instead of the Prusa i3's separate smooth rods and bearings, the MendelMax V2 uses a formed rail and linear bearing system. Likewise, the vertical Z-axis and X-axis assemblies of both the Prusa i3 and the MendelMax V2 use similar designs, but the MendelMax V2 doesn't use 3D-printed parts.

Figure 12-16 shows the X-axis and vertical Z-axis assemblies for a MendelMax V2. The MendexMax V2 uses plates for mounting, includes an ACME lead screw and positions the Z motor at the top, but is otherwise very similar to the Prusa i3 shown earlier in Figure 12-2.

Figure 12-16:
The X-axis and vertical Z-axis assemblies for a MendelMax V2 are similar to those of the Prusa i3.

The timing belt or fishing line drive needs to be secured to each of the platforms. This is usually achieved by gripping the line or clamping it with the carriage, pulling tightly, and then securing it with bolts or a simple zip-tie. (See Figure 12-17.)

Figure 12-17:
A GT-2 timing belt is secured to the Prusa i3 X carriage by wrapping zip-ties around the 3D-printed part and securing it.

Delta printers need to move with three carriages and a main platform. For a 3DR model, this is achieved by sliding each of the moving carriages up and down on smooth rods. (See Figure 12-18.) To enable the print head fitted on the main Delta platform to move around, the other ends of the universal joints have carriages fitted to each of the three sets of smooth rods. These move up and down, pushing the main carriage around in 3D space.

For the RostockMax, bearings run directly on the outside faces of the aluminum rails used for its construction.

Figure 12-18: A carriage fitted to a rod on a 3DR printer. These move up and down, pushing the main carriage around in 3D space.

The carriages themselves require the use of a universal joint so the main platform that holds the extruder hot-end can have a full range of movement around the printing platform. These universal joints can be 3D-printed, but just as printed PLA bushings tend to wear out fast, so would universal joints printed in PLA; they'd also move more loosely and less accurately as they wear out. To compensate for any loose-fitting joints, we often use a spring to pull the joints together; this reduces any slack in the mechanical system and improves the positional accuracy of movements. The 3D-printed main platform of a 3DR Delta printer has brass and nylon universal joints, which provide full movement and can position the printer's nozzle anywhere on the build platform. Springs are often fitted to remove any slack (known as *backlash*) from the joints. (See Figure 12-19.)

Once the carriages are fitted and timing belts or fishing line is connected, the motors can then control the movement of the main platform. (For a look at the completed movement assembly, refer to Figure 12-15.)

Assembling the Prusa i3 moving Y axis

For our example build, we continue with adding the moving elements to the basic frame above. Here we use linear bearings and smooth rods for the motion of the Y axis.

To assemble the moving Y axis, follow these steps:

1. **Fit the linear bearings to the laser-cut Y axis plate:**

    a. Place three LM8UU linear bearings onto the Y axis plate: They should sit into rectangular cutouts in the laser-cut plate.

    b. Secure these bearings with a single tie-wrap.

    c. Fit 20mm M3 bolts and M3 nuts into each corner of the Y axis plate. The bolt head should be on the underside along with the linear bearings.

2. **Assemble the smooth rods and Y belt clamp:**

    a. Fit the printed Y belt clamp with 2 x 20mm M3 bolts into the laser-cut plate on the same side as the linear bearings are secured.

    b. Very carefully slide the two 350mm smooth rods into the linear bearings. (One side has a single bearing and the other has two.)

At the end of this, your moving Y axis plate will look like that shown earlier in Figure 12-7.

3. **Fit the Y axis motor and Y axis plate to the frame:**

   a. Fit a NEMA17 motor onto the printed motor mount that's already been fitted to the frame; use two M3 x 16mm bolts to secure. Slide on a GT2 pulley onto the motor shaft and secure with a grub-screw.

   b. Place the smooth rods and moving axis assembly into the four printed corners. The cut-outs for them to sit into should be obvious. You may need to undo or slacken off the M10 threaded rod frame for them to fit.

   c. Use tie-wraps around each smooth rod end and the printer corners to secure.

   d. Turn the whole carriage over so the bed is facing down.

   e. Wrap the GT2 toothed belt around the idler bearing and along the underside of the frame towards the motor. Then wrap around the motor pulley and back into the middle.

   f. Secure the two ends to the printed belt clamp and fix them together with tie-wraps. Do not fully secure the tie-wraps at this point, as we will align and square up the frame before we tighten the belt.

4. **Align the frame and tighten the frame and the belt:**

   a. At this point everything is hand tight and can be slightly adjusted; the first step is to adjust the M10 rods so the smooth rods are securely fitted into their recess on the top of the printed frame corners. Tighten these, but don't tighten too much as you are compressing the printed part. We do not want these to break.

   b. Now align the M8 threaded rods so the smooth rods have a gap between them of 162mm at each end. It's important to get these parallel so the linear bearings can run smoothly along the rods and do not jam.

   c. Align the motor mount to the correct position along the threaded rods. This position varies depending on the style of the printed belt clamp; just make sure the GT2 belt is in-line at both ends.

   d. At the same time as the preceding step, adjust the idler mount position to achieve an in-line belt.

   e. Make sure everything is tight and check again that distances are matching on each side and on the front and back of the lower Y axis frame.

At the end of these steps, your moving Y axis should look like that shown earlier in Figure 12-8.

Assembling the Prusa i3 moving Z and X axes

The next step for our example build is to build up the second laser cut axis. This mounts both the vertical Z axis and the horizontal X axis. Tables 12-3 and 12-4 list the parts you'll need.

Table 12-3	Printed Parts Required for the Upper Z and X Axes Frame Assembly	
Part	*Details*	*Quantity*
X end idler	Used with the M8 smooth rods to make the X axis	1
X end motor mount	Used with the M8 smooth rods and motor to make the X axis	1
Z axis top left mount	Used to hold the vertical M8 smooth rods for the Z axis assembly	1
Z axis top right mount	Used to hold the vertical M8 smooth rods for the Z axis assembly	1
Z axis bottom left motor mount	Used to hold the vertical M8 smooth rods and the motor	1
Z axis bottom right motor mount	Used to hold the vertical M8 smooth rods for the Z axis assembly	1

Table 12-4	Mechanical Parts Required for the Upper X and Z Axes Assembly		
Part	*Description*	*Type*	*Quantity*
Threaded rod	M5 rods 245mm long – used for Z axis motion	Rod – Steel or stainless	4
Laser-cut X axis plate	The large pre-laser-cut aluminum frame	6mm Aluminum	1

(continued)

Table 12-4 *(continued)*

Part	Description	Type	Quantity
Smooth rod	320mm smooth M8 rods used for motion of the X axis	Smooth rod – Steel or stainless	2
Smooth rod	370mm smooth M8 rods used for motion of the Z axis	Smooth rod – Steel or stainless	2
Linear Bearing	LM8UU linear bearings for X and Z axis motion	Motion	7
Ball bearing	624ZZ ball bearings for X axis belt idler	Motion	1
M4 bolt	25mm M4 bolt for Idler	Fastener	1
M4 nut	M4 size plain or lock-nut type	Fastener	1
M4 washer	M4 size plain washer	Fastener	6
M5 nut	M4 size must be plain type as this is used for the Z motion	Fastener / for motion	2
M3 bolt	16mm M3 bolt for fitting	Fastener	16
M3 washer	M4 size plain washer	Fastener	6
NEMA 17 motor	NEMA 17 motor 1.2A to 2.5A rated.	Motion	3
GT2 gear	Fit onto the NEMA 17 motor for X axis	Motion	1
5mm flexible tube	Two 20mm sections of flexible 5mm tubing – used to couple motors to M5 threaded rods.	Motion	2
Tie-wraps	100mm long 3.2mm tie-wraps to secure linear bearings and drive belt.	Fastener	8

To perform the assembly, follow these steps:

1. **Assemble the X idler:**

   a. Slide the M4 25mm bolt with an M4 washer fitted into the X idler printed part.

   b. While sliding in the bolt, add an M4 washer, 624ZZ bearing, and another M4 washer to the inside of the X idler printed part.

   c. Fit an M4 washer and M4 nut onto the end of the M4 bolt.

   d. Push two of the LM8UU linear bearings into the idler mount. You may need to use some force to insert these, but be careful not to damage the plastic part.

2. **Prepare the X ends with linear bearings:**

   a. Push two of the LM8UU linear bearings into the X motor mount; as with the idler end, use caution when fitting.

   b. Slide two LM8UU linear bearings onto one of the 320mm M8 smooth rods; slide one more LM8UU linear bearing onto the other 320mm smooth rod.

   c. Fit the ends of the smooth rods into the X motor ends and X idler ends. Do this carefully they should be very tight and should be pushed all the way in.

3. **Fit the X and Z axes together. Use the following steps and Figure 12-2, shown earlier, for orientation:**

   a. Slide the two 370mm M8 smooth rods into the LM8UU linear bearings that were fitted into the X axis ends.

   b. Push fit the top left and top right printed mounts to the upper ends of the two 370mm M8 smooth rods.

   c. Push fit the bottom left and bottom right printed mounts to the lower ends of two 370mm M8 smooth rods.

4. **Fit the Z and X axes to the laser-cut frame:**

   a. Position the assembled axis over the laser-cut frame.

   b. Fix the top and bottom Z axis printed mounts to the laser-cut frame with 8 x M3 16mm bolts.

5. **Fit the X Carriage:**

   a. Place the printed X carriage onto the three linear bearings that were fitted to the horizontal X smooth rods earlier.

   b. Secure the carriage to the LM8UU linear bearings with six tie-wraps as shown in Figure 12-17.

6. **Fit the motor and drive belt used for motion of the X axis. Use the following steps and Figure 12-7 for orientation:**

   a. Fit a NEMA17 motor to the X motor mount using three 16mm M3 bolts.

   b. Slide a GT2 pulley onto the motor shaft and secure with grub-screw.

   c. Wrap the second GT2 drive belt around the GT2 pulley on the motor, guide this along towards the X carriage; the other end of the belt should wrap around the X idler bearing and also meet in the middle at the X carriage.

   b. Secure the belt tightly to the X carriage using tie-wraps as shown in Figure 12-17.

7. **Fit the vertical drive motors and the fine pitch M5 drive screws that are used for Z motion and lifting the X carriage up and down. Use the following steps and Figure 12-2 for orientation:**

   a. Fit a NEMA17 motor to the each lower Z motor mount using three 16mm M3 bolts.

   b. Thread one M5 plain nut onto each M5 threaded rod.

   c. Push 10mm of the flexible tube onto one end of each M5 threaded rod.

   d. Insert the 10mm of flexible tube onto the Z motor shaft. You will need to raise the X carriage or hold it out of the way while doing this.

   e. Finally, align the M5 threaded rod with the X axis motor mount and idler mount. The M5 nuts should push into the plastic mounts and the X axis will rest on these nuts.

Joining the Z, X, and Y axes all together

Now that you have the assembled Z/X axes and a separate assembled Y axis, you need to join both parts of the frames together, align everything, and tighten. The metal plate of the Z/X axes is fitted together with the set of M10 nuts and washers in the middle section of the Y axis, as detailed below:

1. **Slot the assembled Y axis into the middle of the vertical laser-cut Z/X frame and lower down so the M10 rods sit into the frame cut-outs.**

2. **Make sure one M10 nut and washer are on either side of the aluminum frame.**

3. **Measure each side of the M10 threaded rods and align the aluminum frame into the middle of the rod.**

   It is not essential at this point to have an exact middle point, as you will need to adjust this after we fit the extruder. When you are at the home position (0,0,0), the extruder nozzle is sitting in the front-left corner of the build plate. This distance should also be specific to the type of extruder and hot-end you choose to fit.

4. **Tighten you the M10 nuts secure enough so the frame won't fall apart while you wire up the electronics in the next chapter.**

Sensing the Home Position

For any 3D printer to understand where its print head is, it needs a reference point, called the *home position*. Before a 3D printer begins a print job, one of the very first actions it performs is to locate this home position. This is very important because the print head could be nearly anywhere in the space above the build platform. To ensure that the print head is at a known position, we use a sensor or switch fitted at the ends of each axis. The switch is triggered when the print head has reached home position. (See Figure 12-20.)

For Delta printers, the home position is at the very top of the machine. Thus the switches or sensors are usually fitted to the top frames on each of the three vertical arms in this design: When the carriages move up, they hit each sensor in turn and locate the home position. (See Figure 12-21.)

Figure 12-20:
A small micro-switch is fitted to the end of the Y-axis assembly on the MendelMax v2 so the 3D printer's electronics know when the axis has moved to the home position. A similar switch is required on each axis.

Figure 12-21:
The top underside of a 3DR Delta printer. At left, the small, white electronics board (one of three) senses home position magnetically. Here the main electronics control board is ready to wire.

When all the frame construction and moving axes systems are fitted together, the wiring of the electronics can begin. Again, it's not as complicated as it may sound. The electronics are modular and wiring is straightforward; when the wiring is complete, so is the home 3D printer. (See Figure 12-22.)

Figure 12-22:
The finished and assembled MendelMax V2 3D printer, ready for calibration.

Chapter 13

Understanding RepRap Control Electronics

In This Chapter

▶ Getting an overview of RepRap electronics

▶ Looking at modular components, sensors, and motors

▶ Examining RepRap wiring and connections

▶ Reviewing firmware configuration

The electronics and firmware running a RepRap 3D printer represent thousands of man-hours of development and refinement to achieve an operational machine. In this chapter, we explore common RepRap electronics, look at the firmware used to drive the electronics, and start to explain how all this comes together to make a 3D printer. We also look at wiring, upgrades, and optional parts, along with the sensors and motors that provide the all-important mechanical movement.

Overview of RepRap Electronics

Reliable and stable electronics — that's what you need for a 3D printer. It's at the very heart of the complex mechanical operation and must be dependable throughout the many hours it has to work while you're waiting for a complex print to finish.

RepRap electronics were born from the open-source Arduino project. Arduino is an industry-standard embedded control board that can be used for all sorts of applications from industrial control systems, robotics, and hobby electronics to quad-copter self-flying drones and wearable electronic devices. Electronics for RepRap normally take the form of a standard Arduino board and a cover "shield" (which contains the specific 3D printing electronics, drivers, and sensors) or a fully dedicated all-in-one set, still based on Arduino but customized specifically for RepRap and wider application in 3D printing.

Don't get too overwhelmed by the many different choices for RepRap electronics. They all perform essentially the same set of functions and can usually run similar firmware. They're all Arduino, and so are relatively common and compatible, varying mainly in features, and number of outputs. If you're looking beyond the standard electronics listed here, just check to ensure that the design supports modern firmware such as Marlin or Sprinter before you buy.

RAMPS

To date, the most common type of electronics used is a combination of the Arduino MEGA 1280 or 2560 standard control board and an open-source RepRap "shield" called RAMPS (RepRap Arduino Mega Pololu Shield), first conceived by Johnny Russell of Ultimachine. (See Figure 13-1.) The top of Figure 13-1 shows the RAMPS "shield" that plugs into the Arduino MEGA board shown later in this chapter.

Figure 13-1:
RepRap RAMPS and Arduino, a compact 3D-print controller with full functionality to add LCD screens, keyboards, and multiple extruders.

RAMBo

RAMBo (see Figure 13-2), an evolution of RAMPS electronics, uses an all-in-one format and has many new features. RAMBo is becoming popular with kit-builders and users, especially in the United States. On RAMBo, the stepper-motor driver devices come permanently fixed to the board rather than as separate modules. This lowers the cost, but if a driver device is damaged, the whole board can become useless. With separate motor-driver modules (as shown in the section that follows), you can replace a damaged module or upgrade to modules that offer finer step-resolution.

Figure 13-2:
RAMBo
combines
both the
Arduino
Mega and
a RAMPS
shield
into one
compact
control
board.

Sanguinololu

Sanguinololu (see Figure 13-3) is one of the original easy-to-build electronic sets for RepRap printers. Sanguinololu, as one of the smallest and lowest-cost electronic sets for RepRap, is ideally suited to hobby assembly. As shown earlier, it can be further expanded with a full graphic LCD display and memory-card slot to allow computer-free printing. It's still very popular; you can build it up at home from self-sourced components. Recent evolutions of this design include the Melzi board that is designed for mass manufacture using surface-mount components.

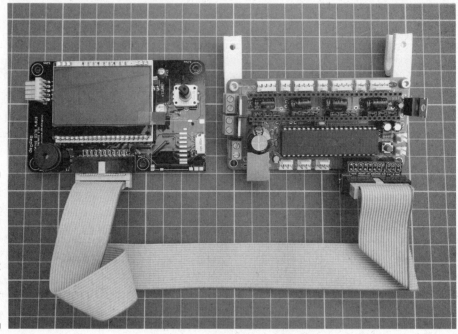

Figure 13-3:
Sanguin-
ololu, one
of the
smallest and
lowest-cost
electronic
sets for
RepRap.

Minitronics

Minitronics is an evolution of the Sanguinololu, this time with a focus on the minimum requirements necessary to run a single-extruder 3D printer. It has minimal expansion options, but is the most compact electronic package available for RepRap. The Minitronics board is tiny; everything is integrated. It can be mass-produced and has the lowest component cost, so it's an ideal choice for mass-market consumer-level 3D printers. (See Figure 13-4.)

Even though many RepRap electronics boards are becoming more integrated, generally it's still a good idea to consider using modular electronics. They can be upgraded or replaced if one part becomes faulty or damaged. It's quite possible you'll damage a motor driver at some point, so any electronic designs that have the drivers soldered down (instead of contained in a replaceable module) run the risk of being unrepairable.

RUMBA

RUMBA is another integrated board with many options for *future-proof* (easy-to-upgrade) expansion. It's a good choice for RepRap developers; its modular design allows for change and expansion, and can even drive up

Figure 13-4:
Minitronics
includes
only the
minimum
electronics
required
to run a 3D
printer.

to three separate extruders. (See Figure 13-5.) This controller makes use of stepper-motor modules in the same way as RAMPS. It also has an LCD display, memory-card modules, and thermocouple add-on boards to expand its functionality.

Elefu-RA V3

The Elefu electronics set is squarely aimed at both the developer (because it allows a lot of expansion and flexibility) and the novice. The power supply required for this board makes use of almost any industry-standard PC ATX unit: Simply plug your ATX into the board. All other connections are made via standard screw-terminals that are all clearly labeled on the board, which allows easy machine wiring with no need to crimp connectors or solder anything.

Expansion modules include an LCD board with memory card and rotary knob for navigating program settings and printing files without a computer connection. These expansion boards are also simply wired with screw-terminals. The Elefu design makes it clear and easy to wire up a 3D printer — and allows many expansion options, along with three separate extruders. It also makes use of modular motor drivers in the same way as RUMBA and RAMPS. (See Figure 13-6.)

Figure 13-5: RUMBA with an expansion adapter for a memory card to store model G-code, ready for printing.

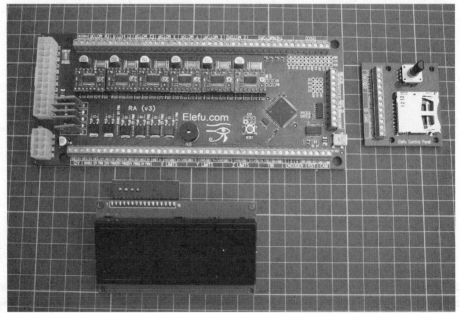

Figure 13-6: The Elefu design.

Megatronics

Megatronics is another integrated motherboard, highly capable of future expansion. It has three extruder options and is ideal for developers and for anyone who wants a machine with all the options. LCDs and keyboards can be added, and a memory-card slot comes as standard. (See Figure 13-7.)

Megatronics is the bigger brother of the Minitronics; it has capabilities similar to those of RUMBA, uses modular stepper-motor drivers, and can run with dual thermocouple temperature sensors — all standard. All the other electronics allow only thermistor sensing; although that's adequate for most users, thermocouples can handle much higher printing temperatures (over 300 degrees Celsius) so more exotic materials can be experimented with. Thermocouples can also be more accurate at temperature measurement and come pre-wired with high-temperature cable.

Figure 13-7:
The Mega-
tronics
integrated
mother-
board.

Adding Electronics to Your RepRap 3D Printer

We now have an assembled frame so we can start adding the electrical components to our example Prusa i3 build. We've already added some of the motors, so this section focuses on the sensors, heating elements, and the main electronics control board. The upcoming sections discuss these assemblies in more detail.

Preparing for electronics assembly

We divide the assembly of the printer electronics into five general stages, as follows:

1. Fitting the positional sensors to the frame.

2. Fitting the heated-bed to the Y carriage.

3. Preparing and fitting the main electronics board.

4. Preparing the power supply and connecting it to the electronics.

5. Connecting the motor and position-sensing wiring to the electronics.

The next few sections discuss these general steps in greater detail. It's also highly likely that your electronics kit will come with pre-wired components. The motors should have four-way connectors fitted; the position sensors will have three-way connectors,

A general list of the parts required for fitting these connectors (if your wires aren't already fitted with connectors) appears in Table 13-1; see Figure 13-15 for examples.

Table 13-1	**Parts Required for the Position-Sensing Operation**	
Part	*Details*	*Quantity*
Microswitch assembly	One sensor is fitted to each axis (X, Y, and Z) of the printer, at the home position 0,0,0.	3
Molex 3way 0.1″ crimp housing	Attach this if it is not already fitted to the wire ends of the microswitch assembly.	3
Crimp pins	Crimp these pins onto the wires and insert them into the connector.	9

Part	Details	Quantity
Tie-wraps	Use these wraps to secure each position sensor to the smooth rods of each axis.	3
Small screws	If you're fitting a positional sensor fixed to a printed circuit board, you may require screws; check your specific kit for details.	6

Fitting the positional sensors to the frame

At this stage, we fit the position sensors. The type of microswitch assembly used in the example build is similar to the model shown in Figure 12-20. Your kit may come with an optical or magnetic position sensor, as seen in Figure 12-21. All such components perform the same function. Figure 13-10 shows examples of position sensors.

1. **If the wires aren't fitted with connectors, crimp pins onto each wire and insert into the three-way housing.**

   You may have two or three connections, usually red for the +5V power, black for the ground connection, and white for the signal. Check the position of the electronics end-stop connectors before fitting into the connector housing. See Figure 13-15 for assistance.

2. **For our example build, we're using small microswitches; insert a tie-wrap into the two holes in each switch.**

   A position sensor can be a simple wired switch or fitted to a small printed circuit board (PCB), so fitting can be via a tie-wrap or screwed into one of the plastic printed parts.

3. **Place the switch on the smooth vertical rod of the Z axis on the left side of that machine; tighten the tie-wrap and cut the excess off.**

   This should be a tight fit, but also allow sliding up and down of the switch to position it at the correct height to ensure the printing nozzle home position is above the build bed. When the Z axis is driven down it will touch the switch and activate the electronics to stop at the set distance.

4. **Fit another switch in exactly the same way for the X carriage on one of the vertical 8mm smooth rods.**

5. **Fit another switch in exactly the same way for the Y carriage on one of the horizontal 8mm smooth rods, this time at the very back of the machine.**

   When the bed moves back to the home position, it will strike this switch and stop.

Fitting the heated-bed to the Y carriage

At this stage, we prepare to fit the heated-bed to the laser-cut Y axis. Table 13-2 lists the parts required for this procedure.

Table 13-2   Parts Required for Fitting the Heated-Bed

Part	Details	Quantity
Heated-bed printed circuit board	Model MK2a is most common, ready-wired and fitted with an LED indicator.	1
Wired thermistor	100k thermistor, ready-wired.	1
Kapton tape	High-temperature Kapton or PET tape for fixing thermistor to heated-bed printed circuit board.	100mm x 20mm tape
M3 nuts	These M3 nuts should be stainless steel if possible.	4
Insulation material	Various options are available.	1
Glass print surface	A standard 200mm x 200mm glass mirror tile, 4mm thick.	1

When you've gathered and laid out the required parts for assembly, follow these steps:

1. **Orient your heated-bed printed circuit board (PCB) so the electrical connections are at the front of the machine and the wires run under the PCB.**

2. **Turn the bed over so the wires are in front of you and are vertical relative to the printed circuit board.**

3. **Place the thermistor bead into the center of the MK2 heated-bed. You will see a small hole to insert it into.**

4. **Fit the thermistor bead level with the top surface of the heated-bed.**

5. **Fold the wires on the underside of the printed X carriage onto the three linear bearings that are fitted to the smooth rods of the horizontal X.**

6. **Tape down the wires of the thermistor with the high-temperature Kapton tape; also tape over the hole that the thermistor bead is sitting in.**

7. **Fold down the main power wires onto the bed facing away from you.**

8. **Tape both the heating wires and thermistor wires together to form a curved single set of cables facing back to the machine.**

You can now optionally fit some insulation material to the underside of the heating printed circuit board. This is a very good idea as it helps the bed heat up quicker and also minimizes heat loss and wasted power. Materials should have been provided in your kit, and can range from cork, metalized cardboard, fiberglass insulation, or a custom sheet of high temperature insulation. This is usually fitted with Kapton tape and also helps hold the cables away from the printed circuit board.

9. **Turn over the heated-bed printed circuit board so the LED is at the front and wires face backward on the underside.**

10. **Place the heated-bed onto the Y axis 20mm M3 posts fitted earlier.**

   The M3 nuts already fitted onto the posts now suspend the heated-bed at a set distance from the Y axis. We can fit four more M3 nuts to tighten down the heated-bed. By moving these nuts, we can alter the position of the heated-bed with respect to the Y axis so that it's flat at all corners, suspended at a set distance, and level.

   No need to level the bed just yet; doing so will be a required part of calibration later on, before the machine is ready to print.

Preparing and fitting the main electronics

At this stage, we prepare and fit a set of RAMPS electronics (refer to Figure 13-1) to the aluminum frame of the printer. Table 13-3 lists the required parts.

Don't fit any stepper drivers (see Figure 13-9) at this point.

Table 13-3	Parts Required for Fitting the Electronics	
Part	*Details*	*Quantity*
Arduino MEGA electronics control board	Model 1280 or 2560.	1
RAMPS	Model version 1.3 or greater. A ready-made RAMPS "shield" for the Arduino board.	1
M3 bolts	M3 x 20mm bolts.	4
M3 plastic stand-offs	These parts, around 10mm long, are for spacing the electronics away from the aluminum frame.	4
Tie-wraps	Optional tie-wraps secure the RAMPS shield to the Arduino MEGA.	4

When you've gathered and laid out the required parts, follow these steps:

1. **Fit the M3 bolts into the four holes of the Arduino MEGA control board.**

2. **On the back side of the board, slide the four spacers onto the bolts.**

   Now you can match up the mounting points on the back side of the vertical aluminum frame. These M3 tapped holes are specifically designed and spaced for the Arduino MEGA board. It can be fitted in only one orientation.

3. **Screw down the MEGA board to the frame.**

   Make sure you use spacers to hold the circuit board away from the aluminum frame; otherwise the board will short out on the metal.

4. **Fit your RAMPS shield onto the mating pins of the Arduino MEGA board.**

   The pins can only fit one way; before you push these parts together, check carefully to ensure that none of the pins are bent.

5. **Orient the heated-bed printed circuit board so that the electrical connections are at the front of the machine and the wires run under the circuit board.**

   You now have the electronics mounted, and can optionally fit some tie-wraps around the boards to secure them together.

Preparing the power supply and connecting to the electronics

Here's where we show examples of power supplies and wire gauges as a guide; check to be sure you've been supplied with good instructions for using and fitting your specific power supply. Table 13-4 lists the required parts.

All power supplies are different, so please check carefully the instructions supplied with your kit.

Table 13-4   Parts Required for Fitting the Power Supply

Part	Details	Quantity
+12V DC Power supply	For a machine with a heated-bed, you usually need a 200W (or higher-wattage) DC power supply running at +12V.	1
Power wiring loom	A four-way ready-made power loom rated at 11A+ for connecting to RAMPS.	1

Part	Details	Quantity
Ferrules	For termination of the power supply wires into the screw-terminal inputs of RAMPS.	4
Fitting screws or tie-wraps	The power supply is usually remotely mounted apart from the 3D printer, but it's a good idea to keep cables tidy by using tie-wraps.	As required

At this stage, we discuss the general connections you have to make to the RAMPS electronics. See Figure 13-12 for an example of the power supply we are fitting to our example build, and Figure 13-16 for example wiring types commonly used in 3D printers. If you need to connect up the wiring loom to your power supply, do that now. The general steps are as follows:

1. **Check the connections and power rating of your power supply.**

   You should have two positive and two ground connections coming from your power supply, The connections from your power supply should be rated at 11A+ for the heated-bed connection and 5A+ for the motor and other components.

2. **Check the four RAMPS screw-terminal connections for power input.**

   These connections are labeled: Two are positive and two are negative (GND). The screw terminal at the bottom-left corner of the RAMPS printed circuit board on the power input is a ground (GND) connection, this is usually a black wire from the power supply.

3. **Fit your GND wire into the appropriate screw-terminal.**

   It's always good practice to fit ferrules to the ends of any wires that will be inserted into a screw-terminal — before tightening.

4. **Connect the 5A+ supply for the motors and other parts of the RAMPS and Arduino board.**

   If your power supply has cables of two different sizes, insert the thinner cable here.

5. **Connect the GND connection for the heated-bed.**

6. **Connect the 11A+ connection for the heated-bed.**

   Make sure this is screwed in nice and tight; this is the final connection, and it carries the most power used on the RAMPS board.

7. **Tidy up any wiring with tie-wraps as required.**

Connecting the motor and position-sensing wiring to the electronics

As an aid to wiring all aspects of the RAMPS control board, you can see a very clear diagram produced by Neil Underwood on the RepRap Wiki here:

http://reprap.org/mediawiki/images/6/6d/Rampswire14.svg

At this stage, we have various components — all with connections — fitted to our 3D printer. In this section, we connect these parts to our RAMPS control board, using the steps that follow:

1. **Connect up the two Z-axis motors that drive the vertical axis.**

   Both motors connect to the same stepper-driver Z connection on the RAMPS board. You'll see two sets of four pins each, near the Z-axis stepper driver. All the motor connections are labeled 2B, 2A, 1A and 1B, depending on the type of stepper motor you have and how it's wired internally. You may need to fit the four-pin connection one way around or the other. Motors are most commonly wired with red, blue, green, and black wires.

   If you reverse the four-way connector, you reverse the motor direction, but you can also do this reverse in software. So, if you have connectors that have locking tabs, don't worry; we can reverse the direction later when we look at the machine firmware.

2. **Connect up the X and Y motors to the four-way motor connectors marked on the RAMPS board.**

3. **Connect the heated-bed to the thermistor (temperature) sensor, and to the heating element (usually fitted with thick wires).**

   a. *Connect the two-pin thermistor wires to the T1 connection on the RAMPS board. The wires can go in either orientation.*

   b. *Connect the power connections of the heated-bed into the D08 connections of the RAMPS board. Be sure to use ferrules here.*

4. **Fit the three end-stops to the RAMPS board.**

   These are clearly labeled on the RAMPS board; they have six connections — marked MIN and MAX — for connecting both home sensors and full-travel sensors.

   Almost all 3D printers do *not* fit the MAX end-stop connections physically. That's because you can state in the firmware where the maximum travel of a machine is. In these steps, we only fit the MIN end-stops. These must be connected in the correct orientation, so check your specific build manual for these connections. It's most likely that you have a red wire and a white wire: red is +5V and white is the signal connection.

5. **Tidy up any wiring with tie-wraps as required.**

6. **Prepare to install the stepper-motor driver modules (see Figure 13-9) to the RAMPS board.**

   Carefully check to ensure that the stepper driver is correctly oriented. The stepper modules fit into rows of pin headers running down the RAMPS printed circuit board.

   Make extra sure to line up Pin 1 on each module with Pin 1 on the RAMPS connector.

Modular Components, Sensors, and Motors

In the preceding section, we installed and wired up most of the electronics required for a 3D printer. The following sections explain these elements of your 3D printer, along with some of the most common types of sensors, options, wiring, and further expansion you may want to add to your 3D printer. For example, you can add an LCD screen and a memory-card interface to RAMPS so your printer can operate without being connected to a computer.

We then discuss the firmware used on RepRap home 3D printers, and look at how to configure our example Prusa i3 build.

Computer-free printing

Popular add-ons for a 3D printer include an LCD screen, a memory card, and a rotary knob. These are usually all found on a separate control "display" board that can connect to the various electronics detailed earlier in the chapter. (See Figure 13-8.) These options allow standalone printing without requiring a computer connection. The use of an LCD screen allows for setup, pre-heating, and printing from a file stored on the memory card — all without having a computer attached to the printer. This arrangement makes a sensible upgrade on 3D printers that will be printing for many hours (even a whole day), or in other situations in which you may not want your computer running all the time. Note that the memory card will store multiple files for printing in the future. These files can also be removed, and G-code files can be stored on your computer and retrieved for 3D printing at any time later.

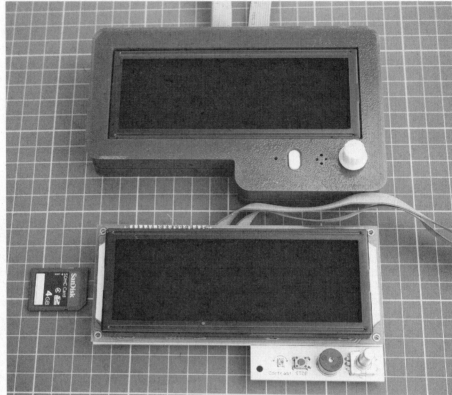

Using motor-driver modules

Every RepRap 3D printer has its movement provided by *stepper motors*. This type of electric motor requires a special driver device to pulse the motor forward or backward; each step rotates (steps) the motor a tiny amount. Our electronics and firmware use many thousands of pulses to make the stepper drivers rotate the motor an exact distance, depending on the gearing and step ratio.

A stepper-motor driver module (see Figure 13-9) can be fully integrated or (more commonly) plugged into the electronics control board. Each module drives one stepper motor, so a minimum of four are required for a 3D printer.

The standard NEMA17 stepper motor used on RepRaps requires 200 pulses to rotate completely around (360 degrees). But our stepper drivers do modes called *microstepping* that step the motor a fraction of that distance. Microstepping reduces motor noise and allows more accurate positioning of the extruder. It's very common to use a stepper driver in 8- or 16-microstep mode.

Figure 13-9:
A stepper-
motor driver
module.

A stepper motor's *microstep mode* is usually set with small jumper switches that are either fitted or removed to turn them on or off. Refer to your set of electronics to set these jumpers; remember what setting you used (it will come in handy when we configure the firmware later in this chapter).

Most RepRap machines run with 16 microsteps (16x): The electronics and firmware are required to pulse 3200 times to make a motor rotate a full 360 degrees. You can see right away that this fine control will give a 3D printer greater positional resolution. Increasingly, electronics and motor-driver modules offer a 32x option, making the motors even quieter and capable of ultra-fine resolution.

There are limits on the maximum step rate your electronics can deliver. Having to drive so many sequences of steps can put an extra processing burden on the firmware to do positional calculations. The extra load can slow down some mechanical processes — for example, rapid acceleration of the extruder — so many 3D printer users prefer to use different motors for different purposes:

✔ 16x for the X, Y, and Z motors (to provide the highest resolution and quiet operation)

✔ 8x for the extruder motor (to allow rapid reversals and acceleration moves).

The resulting boost in reaction speed can increase print quality.

A small aluminum heat-sink is often fixed to the controller device to help reduce its operating temperature. Without a heat-sink, the controller can get hot enough to burn the operator or destroy itself. You can set the amount of power delivered to the motor (known as *current limiting*) by turning a tiny rotary knob (shown in the bottom left of Figure 13-9) with a screwdriver. All stepper motors should be current-limited to operate well within their designed limits so they don't overheat or burn out (which would also destroy the stepper-driver module).

Never remove a stepper-motor connection from the electronics while they are powered up. Doing so can quickly destroy the stepper-motor driver.

Selecting your position-sensing modules

With almost every 3D printer, the electronics need to know where the "home" position is. This is achieved by slowly driving each axis in a known direction until a limit switch or sensor is triggered. This tells the electronics you are at "0" for each axis. When the extruder carriage is at the "home" position, you can start a print job because the printer knows where to begin the many different 3D moves that start and complete the print.

3D printers use the initial *home position* as a universal reference point. From the moment the home position is defined, every move is calculated as a number of steps on each axis, each of which helps position the print head in 3D space. If an axis, carriage, or print head is knocked askew or is out of alignment compared to where the electronics think it is, the 3D printer continues to print but the model will be misaligned and usually ruined as the melted plastic is deposited in the wrong places. Just as the 2D dot-matrix printers of the past kept cluelessly printing, even if the sheet of paper was out of alignment while they were printing, so with 3D printers. Even many professional units are not yet intelligent enough to know when they're going wrong or are out of alignment.

To keep the print job on track (so to speak), we use three main types of positional sensors:

- ✔ The most common sensor is a simple microswitch (shown at the top of Figure 13-10). The carriage mechanically presses into the switch, which sends a signal to tell the electronics that the carriage is "home."

- ✔ An optical sensor (such as that shown in the center of Figure 13-10) breaks a beam of infrared light as the trigger tells the electronics that the carriage is at the "home" position. Because this is a non-contact switch, it's considered more reliable than a mechanical microswitch.

✔ The most sophisticated form of positional sensing (shown at the bottom of Figure 13-10) is a *hall-effect sensor* that detects a magnetic field. Its functioning is very accurate and highly repeatable and (again) it's non-contact. All you need to do is fit a tiny magnet onto the carriage or moving axis and place the sensor at the "home" position. When the magnet comes within a specified distance of that position, it triggers the "home" signal to the electronics. Hall-effect sensors feature a small rotary knob you can turn to adjust the exact trigger distance of the magnet from the sensor. This type of sensor is most often used on the vertical Z carriage to set the position of the nozzle a precise distance away from the print bed, usually with a gap no thicker than a single sheet of paper.

You can use any type of position sensor, or a combination of them. It's highly recommended to use a tunable magnetic type for Z-carriage alignment.

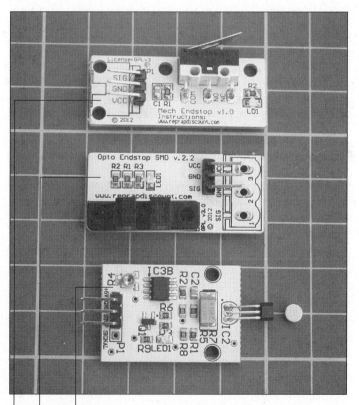

Figure 13-10: Positional sensors set your "home" position for the printer.

Magnetic hall-effect sensor

Optical light

Mechanical switch

Identifying power-supply requirements

Selecting a suitable power supply is a key requirement for any 3D printer. Most RepRap electronics run from a single-voltage supply, usually 12V DC, and generate other voltages as required. Because a 3D printing means melting plastic, home 3D printers can require a significant amount of power to drive the motors and (most significantly) heat the build bed. This brings some challenges — especially sourcing a power supply with enough capacity and making sure that thick enough wiring is used.

Any device that is connected to a household outlet should be treated with extreme caution; 3D printers use lower voltages to run the various parts of the machine, but are still connected to household current via the power supply.

If you decide to run a 200mm x 200mm heated-bed (for example), it will have a resistance of around 1.0 ohms; running with a 12-volt (V) power supply, the device will draw of 12 amperes (A) of current around 150 watts (W) of power. When the bed is first powered up from cold, this draw can spike to 20A. That is a significant load, even for industrial-grade power supplies.

When you also consider that the hot-end may require another 20W to run — and four or five motors need another 20W — it's easy to see that as a minimum you will require 200W at 12V to run most 3D printers.

A low-cost (and readily available) option is the PC ATX power supply, often used and usually rated for high current output on the +12V supply.

Make sure you check how much power can be delivered. You may need to use a 400W (or higher-wattage) supply to ensure that enough power is available on the +12V rail. This is because ATX supplies deliver many different voltages all at once.

The Elefu electronics discussed earlier allow an ATX power supply to be plugged straight in. Most other RepRap electronics require that a number of the output +12V (yellow) wires be joined together to supply enough power to run. It's quite common to have more than one power input on the electronics, usually a dedicated connection for the heated-bed. (See Figure 13-11.) It's more complicated to get an ATX power supply running on other RepRap electronics, but ATX is still commonly used for powering home 3D printers.

Another option is an industrial power supply. (See Figure 13-12.) An industrial power supply offers a less complicated wiring arrangement for most RepRap builds that use ring or blade terminals, but it also requires the direct connection of household mains input by the user rather than the simple IEC three-way plug found on computer ATX supplies. This type of power supply, normally used in large machines, has a number of dedicated screw-terminal outputs that can be directly wired to the RepRap control electronics. It may be slightly more expensive than an ATX supply, but it's designed for this purpose. ATX power supplies are designed to power computer motherboards with many different voltages.

Figure 13-11: An ATX power supply connected to the Elefu electronics.

Figure 13-12: An industrial power supply.

Running at a higher voltage is possible, and this can have some benefits for the motor performance and heating times. It can also help reduce the thickness of wiring from the power supply, but do check carefully if and how to set up your electronics to use greater than +12V power supplies.

Power information will be labeled on a power supply. In Figure 13-13, a 240W industrial power supply clearly lists the maximum 12V and 20A. In contrast, the ATX power supply is rated to 550W and has many power rails (most of which we're not interested in), along with two independent 12V outputs delivering 14A each. So, to stay within the limits specified for the power ratings of our 3D printer, we'd need to connect one of the 12V rails to supply power to the heated-bed, and the other 12V rail to the control electronics.

Figure 13-13:
Power information labeled on a power supply.

SUNPOWER®
MODEL FDPS-240A
AC INPUT 110/220V±15%
DC OUTPUT 12V 20A

ATX12V P4
Switching Power Supply

AC INPUT:230VAC 10A 50-60Hz					Model:A-550BR	
DC OUTPUT MAX	+3.3V	+5V	+12V1	+12V2	-12V	+5VSB
	24A	24A	14A	14A	0.3A	2A
			550W			

CE CB FC ⒸⒸ Ⓑ En60950

8 026155 027121

Without the heated-bed requirement for a 3D printer, the power requirements can drop to a simple 60W brick power supply similar to that used on many laptops.

Adding fans and lighting

Fans are widely used with home 3D printers; they help keep critical parts like the hot-end thermal insulator cool, and can also assist with the printing process. (See Figure 13-14.)

Figure 13-14:
A small fan
mounted
to cool the
part being
printed.

Almost all RepRap electronics have dedicated fan outputs that can be controlled in G-code with both on/off and fan speed. When setting up fans to cool
parts of your extruder or printed part, it's important not to cool the heated-
bed or hot-end of the extruder too much. Doing so wastes power and can
cause lots of problems — for example, parts coming unstuck if the bed temperature drops too quickly, or the hot-end jamming if it's over-cooled.

Other fans can also be constantly powered to keep the electronics — and
sometimes the power supply — cool all the time the printer is running.

Lighting is another favorite for home 3D printing. Having good directed lights,
normally white LED strips or spotlights, can help you align nozzles, check to
see that printing is going as expected, and ensure that plastic is sticking to
the build surface correctly.

LED lighting is normally wired directly to the power supply, but electronics
are starting to provide spare outputs for options like this.

People connect and control many other devices from their 3D printer's electronics. Another fun and simple add-on is a wired or infrared remote signal
for a digital camera or video camera. You can specify that the camera take a

picture at every layer change of your 3D print; these images can be assembled later into a time-lapse video of your entire print.

A common way to signal, which can be controlled in G-code, is to sound a buzzer at the start and end of a 3D print.

If your 3D printers are in another room (or otherwise away from you and out of sight) you can set up a monitored webcam to keep an eye on progress or help you spot problems.

RepRap Wiring and Connections

Even with a full, ready-to-build RepRap kit of parts, you will always have to connect various components and devices to the electronics — and sometimes that means crimping connectors or doing a little soldering.

One of the easiest connection types is a *screw-terminal*. Often used for higher-power connections such as the power supply input, hot-end heater, and heated-bed, the screw-terminal can also be used for motors, fans, and lighting.

It's a very good idea to use *bootlace ferrules* when attaching wires to screw-terminal connections. The ferrule helps constrain the wires so their strands don't spread out when the screw is tightened. Ferrules make for a more secure connection and help reduce chances of frayed cable strands, short circuits, and burnt connections.

Another common connection is the *crimped multi-way terminal;* these are inserted into a plastic shell and form a connector that can be plugged into a mating set of pins on the electronics. (See Figure 13-15.) Multi-way terminals are often keyed so they can only be inserted one way; others use plastic shells that can be rotated or accidentally offset on the mating connection. Be careful when attaching any connection — make sure it's correctly oriented.

Many other types of connectors can be used for RepRap electronics, power supplies, and other board modules. When you buy a full RepRap kit, connectors and wiring often come pre-made; check with the supplier if you have any concerns about the wiring of the electronics. Small mistakes can quickly destroy one of the most expensive parts of your new 3D printer.

Selecting the correct gauge wiring is also important for safe and reliable operation. A NEMA17 stepper motor, for example, will have 7/02-gauge wires fitted: 7 strands of 0.2mm wire are twisted together to form each cable. This size of wire is usually suitable for connecting sensors, fans, and LED lighting. Connections to hot-ends, heated-beds, and power supplies require significantly higher-rated cable; examples can be seen in Figure 13-16.

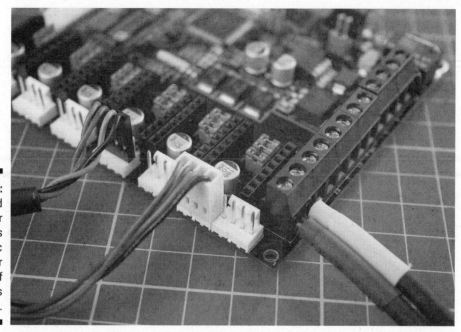

Figure 13-15:
Crimped motor connections and plastic connector shells of various styles.

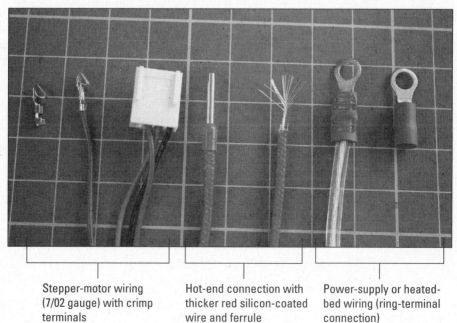

Figure 13-16:
Common wiring types, from left to right: stepper-motor wiring (7/02 gauge) with crimp terminals; hot-end connection with thicker red silicon-coated wire and ferrule; power-supply or heated-bed wiring (ring terminal connection).

Stepper-motor wiring (7/02 gauge) with crimp terminals

Hot-end connection with thicker red silicon-coated wire and ferrule

Power-supply or heated-bed wiring (ring-terminal connection)

Firmware Configuration

If your firmware isn't set up for the mechanical and electrical arrangement of your 3D printer, it's simply not going to print anything, no matter how hard you try.

Further on, we explain how to set up the firmware for our reference build of the Prusa i3 machine. This is an important aspect of any RepRap 3D printer, but you have to do some experimenting to achieve the best results; it's not a one-size-fits-all procedure for all machines.

The firmware of a RepRap 3D printer, although quite complicated, is designed to accommodate many different types of RepRap printer — and even altogether different systems of movement. The important part is correctly setting up the configuration for your chosen printer. You could very easily write an entire book just about the firmware used on a RepRap 3D printer and a lot more resources are available for this aspect of 3D printer setup, so this section just gives you some key pointers on what to change in the firmware as you calibrate your machine. If you bought a kit or decide to build one of the "standard" RepRap machines we have described in this book, it's very likely that a configuration file will be available to download, or settings available online that you can enter.

The Marlin firmware for RepRap, is not only among the most widely used, but is also easy to use. To compile the changes and upload new firmware to your electronics, you'll need to install the Arduino Integrated Development Environment (IDE); version 023 is most often used, although more modern releases of the Arduino IDE (called 1.0x) can now also be used for many versions of Marlin.

Sooner or later, you'll have to change some settings on your RepRap 3D printer, so taking a closer look at the Arduino tools and language is worthwhile. The Arduino software is available from www.arduino.cc. You can find a master version of the Marlin firmware from the lead developer, Erik van der Zalm, on the Github site: https://github.com/ErikZalm/Marlin. (See Figure 13-17.)

Prusa i3 firmware configuration

For our example build, here is a short guide to getting the Marlin firmware running on your RAMPS electronics.

Figure 13-17:
Github is
the master
repository
for the
Marlin firm-
ware used
on RepRap.

We divide the process into four easy stages, as follows:

1. Downloading and installing the Arduino IDE.
2. Downloading and extracting the Marlin firmware.
3. Editing the Marlin firmware for RAMPS and Prusa i3.
4. Uploading the Marlin firmware to the RAMPS electronics.

The next few sections discuss these steps in greater detail.

This section describes many of the settings you can (and most often do) change to get your specific 3D printer set up for using the Marlin firmware. Please refer to the more detailed information available on www.reprap.org. The following steps show how we would set up our reference Prusa i3 machine; use them as a general guide.

In order to compile your firmware and upload it to your electronics, you'll need some applications and the Marlin firmware master from Github. Follow these steps:

1. **Download the Arduino IDE from** www.arduino.cc.

   We will require Version 0023. Run this on your computer; depending on the operating system you're using, it may automatically install drivers the first time you plug in the RAMPS electronics to your computer. If it doesn't, follow the onscreen instructions to install the driver.

2. **Download the Marlin firmware from** https://github.com/ErikZalm/Marlin.

   You can select the Download Zip button on the right side of the screen (as shown in Figure 13-17).

3. **After download, extract the contents of the Zip file.**

   Inside will be the main Marlin firmware directory.

4. **Begin editing the Marlin firmware for RAMPS and Prusa i3.**

   The main file you'll be changing is configuration.h. This file holds most of the key settings for the mechanical arrangement and electronics type.

Editing the Marlin configuration.h file

Editing this file is the heart of the configuration process. This section provides an overview and specific recommendations. Keep in mind that the configuration.h is a text file in computer programming language. Do not fundamentally change its structure or add extra items; it you do, it won't compile and operate.

You'll see a lot of helpful comments in the code that start with //. Anything after the double slash is a comment that the firmware ignores; it's just there to help you configure your machine and remember why you made specific changes. You can add more comment lines in the code to make it clear what parts you are changing and why.

Note that some of the code has been *commented out* — having // in front of it. Such code is inactive; you may have to re-enable lines and disable others, as indicated in the comments. You'd normally do so only for nonstandard settings, but this capability may be important, depending on the electronics type you're using with your RepRap printer.

Another key setting in firmware is a #define value, which is an important way to let the firmware know what parts of your machine are enabled.

For example, the firmware needs to know if your printer has more than one extruder and a heated-bed.

At the top of the file, you can find the choice of electronics used on the RepRap 3D printer. Here you see a long list of comments that give each different set of electronics a unique number. (For example, Figure 13-18 shows RAMBo as 301 and different versions of RAMPS as 3, 33, or 34.) The section below this list shows a #defineMOTHERBOARD 80 (see Figure 13-18), indicating that this firmware is currently configured to use RUMBA electronics. If we want to change the firmware to use RAMBo electronics, all we do is use the comments to change the setting to #define MOTHERBOARD 301.

Figure 13-18: Changing the electronics number tells the firmware what other settings to use for pin configuration, wiring, and more.

You can use the same approach to the other settings by reading down the rest of the configuration.h file and taking one of three actions:

- ✔ Changing the #define numbers.
- ✔ Un-commenting the parts you want to make active.
- ✔ Commenting out the parts you want to make inactive.

The key settings to check are as follows:

✔ TEMP_SENSOR: This setting usually has more than one value, indicated by _0 _1 _2 and will have a list of types with a number for you to enter from the information. The most commonly used is type 1 (EPCOS 100k). It is essential you match the type being used in your hot-end with one on this list and enter the number for all active hot-ends.

✔ TEMP_SENSOR_BED: Exactly the same as the setting just listed, normally this one uses the same electronics type as your hot-end.

✔ PID settings: These settings determine the proportional control loop that takes care of heating your hot-end correctly to a target temperature that you set in Slic3r. The settings below indicate to the firmware how your hot-end responds to temperature heating and detection of change. It's very important to have this correctly set. We discuss how to get this information later on in this chapter because we need to let the hot-end run up to temperature and perform a test sequence to get it calculated.

The settings you will need to change are

• DEFAULT_Kp (the proportional element)

• DEFAULT_Ki (the integral element)

• DEFAULT_Kd (the differential element)

All these settings may sound complicated but don't be too worried; we look at how the electronics can actually give us this information automatically. All we need to do is enter in the numbers that the RepRap printer's firmware calculates from doing a number of test heating and cooling cycles with the machine's hot-end.

Setting the switches

The 3D printer has switches to let the electronics know when the X, Y, and Z carriages are at the home position. These can very often require an inverted signal for the electronics to understand they're being activated. If your new RepRap machine refuses to move when you first set it up, it's quite likely you need to change the following settings either to true or to false:

✔ X_ENDSTOP_INVERTING = true (or change to false)

✔ Y_ENDSTOP_INVERTING = true (or change to false)

✔ Z_ENDSTOP_INVERTING = true (or change to false)

You have to do likewise with the motor directions if the carriage moves away from your end-stop when you home the machine. You'll have to change the motor direction, using the settings that follow. Then you'll have to do the same with the extruder if it pushes the filament in the wrong direction when you drive it forward. Change it here:

✔ INVERT_X_DIR = true (or change to false)

✔ INVERT_Y_DIR = true (or change to false)

✔ INVERT_Z_DIR = true (or change to false)

✔ INVERT_E0_DIR = true (or change to false)

✔ INVERT_E1_DIR = true (or change to false)

✔ INVERT_E2_DIR = true (or change to false)

With X_MAX_POS and the all other axes, you can set a maximum travel distance. This is handy if something goes wrong or if you accidentally try to print an object bigger than your platform; the firmware will stop the axis rather than crash it into the end of the machine. Movement settings are as follows:

✔ The HOMING_FEEDRATE setting tells how fast the X,Y, and Z axes move when doing the home command. If it's set too fast, motors will skip and cause machine misalignments.

✔ DEFAULT_AXIS_STEPS_PER_UNIT has a sequence of numbers — for example, {55.5, 55.5, 500, 200}. This number sequence relates to the X, Y, and Z axes, and to all the extruders fitted to the printer.

It's crucial to enter this set of numbers correctly; doing so tells the firmware exactly how many steps each stepper-motor must move the axis or filament to move exactly 1mm. If this setting is not correct, your machine won't produce accurate parts, and will under- or over-extrude material. To start with, we use 200 for the number of extruder steps. Read on to see why this figure is a good starting point — but expect to change this number after we've completed extruder calibration. The axis movement is determined by what belts and pulleys you've fitted; the kit or machine type will give you that information.

✔ DEFAULT_MAX_FEEDRATE is the maximum speed at which your 3D printer can safely move while printing without causing skips or motor stalls. Again, an example of the setting for X, Y, Z, and Extruder is {300,300,300,25}.

✔ DEFAULT_MAX_ACCELERATION defines the fastest rate of change in acceleration, printing, and travel moves. An example for X, Y, Z, and Extruder is {500,500,500,380}.

✔ DEFAULT_ACCELERATION is connected to the maximum setting mentioned earlier; this is the starting speed for acceleration. If it's set too fast, it won't allow the stepper motors enough time to ramp up to speed and they'll stall or skip. An example is 300 for all motors apart from the that of the extruder.

✔ DEFAULT_RETRACT_ACCELERATION is the same as the previous setting, but it's specific for all extruder retractions; they have to be fast to be effective in combating strings and blobs on your emerging 3D prints. An example of such a setting is 380.

The last movement settings you can alter are the JERK values; these define the safe levels of instantaneous movement of the axis and extruder. It's common for a Z axis — which usually consists of threaded rods moving in a nut — to move slowly. The fastest acceleration of a Z axis is still usually much slower than that of all the other motors. Extruders also require a lot of torque and for that to develop correctly, they need a low starting point for their acceleration. Finally, the X and Y axes can't start moving fast instantly; they need a setting value that tells the machine so. Typical JERK values for a Prusa i3 machine could be XYJERK 20.0, ZJERK 0.4, and EJERK 12.0. Values are in mm/second.

With a Delta printer such as the RostockMAX, you don't have a slow Z axis, so the ZJERK value would be the same as that of the XYJERK setting.

Uploading the Marlin firmware to the RAMPS electronics

When you've made your printer-specific setting changes to the configuration.h file, you can save the file. Then check to ensure that the following settings are appropriate:

✔ Make sure that you have the correct Arduino board selected for your electronics under the Tools/Board tabs. For Our RAMPS electronics on the Prusa i3, we would select Arduino Mega 1280 or 2560 (depending on the model of the Arduino board that came with our kit).

✔ Select the serial port to which you've connected your electronics via the USB cable; from the Sketch tab, select Verify/Compile.

If you have no errors in the electronics connections, you can upload the revised firmware to the electronics via a USB lead. (See Figure 13-19.)

We calculate and go into further details about the critical settings required for your 3D printer in Chapter 15. Those settings include calibrations for motion, heating, and extruder flow rate. You'll have to come back to the firmware, make other changes depending on the calibration stages — and then re-compile and upload the changes, using the information given in this section. It's worth spending some time becoming familiar with the Arduino software; further information can be found on the www.arduino.cc website.

TIP

We also highly recommend *Arduino For Dummies* by John Nussey (Wiley). It's a fantastic book if you want a deeper understanding of the Arduino programming language (and of the processes described in this section) — especially if you want to develop parts of the Marlin firmware.

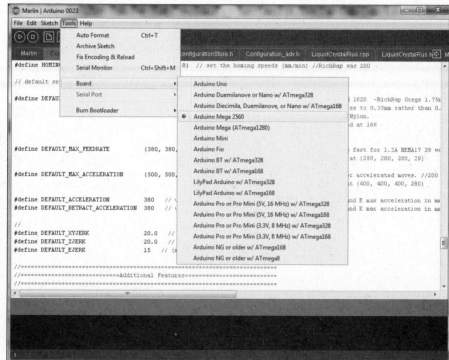

Figure 13-19:
Most RepRap electronics like RAMBo, RAMPS, RUMBA, and RepRapEasy require that you select the Arduino MEGA 1280 or MEGA 2560.

Chapter 14

Assembling the RepRap Extruder and Upgrading RepRap

*I*n this chapter, we show you how to assemble a RepRap extruder and describe how it operates. Here you find our advice for keeping everything working well as you print. We look at alternative materials and explain how you can print with them on your RepRap. We then show you how multi-color printing is possible and even give you some tricks to make it easier to achieve colorful prints of your own.

Thermoplastic Extrusion

As mentioned previously, the extruder is one of the most important parts of the 3D printer: This is where the quality and reliability of parts is critical.

You can make all the parts required for an extruder with basic tools and a lot of time, but for this part of any 3D printer, it's well worth paying for well-machined parts that fit smoothly together and won't leak or melt on you.

All extruders are required to do the same job: Grip the round plastic filament and drive it, in a controlled manner, to the hot-end where it's melted and ejected from the nozzle. It sounds easy, but when you take a look at the many parts of an extruder (and for that matter, of a hot-end), it's the one area that causes the most problems for people using home 3D printers.

Start with the *filament drive* mechanism. This part almost always takes the form of a round bolt or rod with concave-cut teeth that grip around the plastic. (See Figure 14-1.)

Filament-drive mechanisms can be machined in a wide variety of different ways. It's important to look for even and well-cut drive teeth that will grip but not strip or grind through your filament. Too-sharp teeth can be as bad as too-blunt teeth.

Filament drives used in thermoplastic extruders can all perform the same job, but are manufactured in various ways. At the top of Figure 14-1 is a traditional *hobbed-bolt* filament drive; this is the most common type of filament drive, and performs adequately. In the middle is a professionally machined drive wheel, which usually provides the most grip around the filament as it is pushed into the extruder. This wheel is usually mounted directly onto the shaft of the extruder motor, or on a gearbox attached to the motor. At the bottom of Figure 14-1 is another machined bar, but this time with shallow, blunt grooves; this design won't grip as firmly, and if over-tightened, may deform your filament.

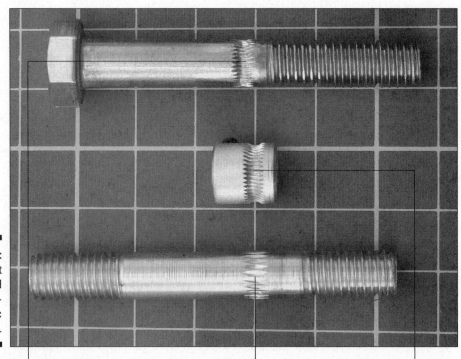

Figure 14-1:
Filament drives used in thermoplastic extruders.

Hobbed-bolt filament drive   Shallow and blunt grooves   Professionally machined drive wheel

There are a number of different ways to assemble an extruder. In its simplest form, the filament drive wheel fits directly onto the shaft of the extruder's stepper motor, and drives the filament directly by rotation of the motor shaft. This method provides the lowest torque but requires fewest other components.

The most basic filament extruder can perform adequately, but only if you have a powerful drive motor and well-machined hot-end to reduce the forces required to push the filament. On the left of Figure 14-2 is the same professionally machined drive wheel shown in Figure 14-1. On the right is a very basic drive cog that has been machined with a groove for the filament; this cog costs little to manufacture, but it also has the lowest performance. It has no gearing to improve torque, and should be avoided if at all possible. These direct-drive extruders do have one advantage: Two can be placed close together to provide dual extrusion.

Figure 14-2:
The most basic filament extruder can perform adequately.

Professionally machined
drive wheel

Machined drive cog

A compact gearbox can be attached to the output of a stepper motor and greatly improve the torque and rotational resolution from the direct drive types we discuss earlier. (See Figure 14-3.) These can also be very compact, allowing dual extrusion.

Figure 14-3:
A
profession-
ally made
gearbox
attaches to
the stepper
motor,
improving
performance
(even with
a smaller
motor).

With RepRap 3D printers, it's more common to see the motor connected to a series of 3D-printed gears. (See Figure 14-4.) When the gearing drives the motor faster, this increases the torque, allowing the filament to be driven very quickly into the hot-end. This arrangement allows fast printing and fast retraction.

Another common type of extruder is the Bowden, which works on the same principle as the brake-lever cable of a bicycle: A slippery Teflon (PTFE) tube separates the extruder drive motor from the hot-end. This tube allows the driven filament to be constrained and pushed into the hot-end section.

The Bowden extruder is often used on smaller or lightweight machines. Doing so has several advantages:

- ✔ The design removes the bulk, mass, and weight of the motor from the moving carriage, leaving only the hot-end.
- ✔ You can mount more hot-ends on one 3D printer.
- ✔ The design can be ideal for machines that need a lightweight head that can move around fast.

Figure 14-4:
The 3D-printed geared extruder has more parts to assemble, but can produce greater power and speed for faster printing.

A Bowden extruder does have a few downsides:

- The printer design has more parts and complexity.
- The printer must perform a longer filament retraction after every print move, to minimize any oozing due to the pressure and "spring" of the filament being pushed down the tube.
- The design is often harder to control and tune.

The Bowden model shown in Figure 14-5 uses a 1-meter PFTE tube; this would be used on a large 3D printer that produces models with widths greater than 500mm.

Any extruder also needs an *idler wheel* to push the filament into the teeth of the drive wheel. An idler wheel is usually a round bearing being pushed with a spring or with rubber bushing. Figure 14-6 shows an idler bearing/wheel fitted to a printed lever; the spring on the left causes the bearing to be pushed into the drive wheel, keeping the filament tightly gripped.

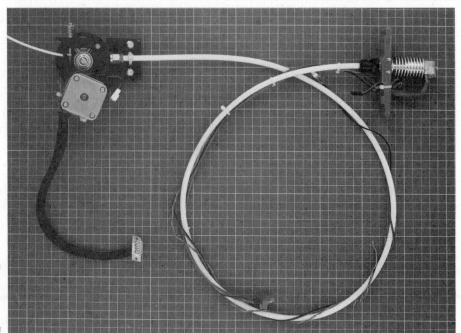

Figure 14-5:
A Bowden
extruder.

Figure 14-6:
The idler
wheel is
essential
and must be
tightened
just enough
for the drive
wheel to
grip the
filament.

Do not overtighten the idler bearing. If the grip on the filament starts to squash it out of round, it will be much harder to force down the thermal insulator of the hot-end and may jam. Check how much the drive wheel is biting into the filament: You should see small, regular marks where each tooth bites in, and the filament should not be crushed.

The hot-end is normally attached into the extruder body with bolts to allow removal if the extruder jams or gets blocked. A finished extruder also requires a heating element on the hot-end and a temperature sensor. (See Figure 14-7.) This wiring, along with the four motor connections, must go back to the RepRap electronics wiring, as discussed in Chapter 13.

Never try to drive the motor or rotate the gears driving the filament if the hot-end is not at the correct temperature. This can cause the filament to strip and get chewed up. If this happens, you'll have to clean out the teeth on your drive wheel before you can print again.

A thermoplastic extruder needs to be carefully calibrated to operate well; we discuss all the steps of achieving a good calibration in Chapter 15.

As shown in Figure 14-8, the extruder is a highly active area for new development in RepRap. Many different designs exist and some are more specialized than others, offering higher temperature, faster extrusion, or fine detail. Most will usually cover the requirements of home 3D printing with thermoplastics.

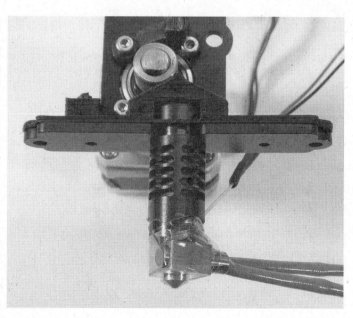

Figure 14-7:
Our wired-up hot-end, fitted onto the motor and drive assembly. This is a complete thermoplastic extruder with a machined gearbox.

Figure 14-8:
A represen-
tative range
of RepRap
extruder
designs.

Prusa i3 Extruder and Hot-End Assembly

The final procedure in our example build is to assemble the extruder and hot-end — in this case, a modern, compact, geared extruder (refer to Figure 14-7) with a J-head hot-end (refer to Figure 11-17).

We've divided the process into five general steps, as follows:

1. Fitting the filament drive to the motor shaft.
2. Assembling the extruder idler pressure bearing.
3. Fitting the J-head hot-end.
4. Fitting the assembled extruder to the X carriage.
5. Wiring up the Hot-end heater and thermistor to RAMPS.

The next few sections discuss these steps in greater detail.

Fitting the filament drive to the motor shaft

Fitting the filament drive to the motor shaft is pretty straightforward. Our stepper motor already has a gearbox fitted to it; this is a very compact and lightweight way to make a small, powerful extruder. Other types of extruder assembly use printed gears to do a similar job, but a more popular option is to use an off-the-shelf gearbox-and-motor assembly to improve operational life of the printer and to increase print quality. So all we need to do is fit the drive wheel onto the motor gearbox shaft and tighten with an Allen wrench.

An example of this type of drive wheel is shown in Figure 14-1. Another type is fitted to the geared motor shown in Figure 14-3. They all perform the same job.

You may have to mount a bracket or printed adapter as well, depending on the type of motor you're using and where it was sourced. (See Figure 14-3 for an example of a suitable mounting bracket.)

Assembling the extruder idler pressure bearing

The *idler pressure bearing* performs a very important job of firmly pushing the filament toward the drive wheel so the rotating motor can force the filament down into the hot-end. See Figure 14-6 for reference; these general steps provide an overview:

1. A 3D-printed lever is usually supplied for the idler; to this we fit a small 623-size bearing, as shown in Figure 14-6.

2. The idler assembly is attached to the motor body, forming a lever.

3. A spring is pushed in between the idler assembly and the mounting bracket to lever the idler bearing into the filament drive wheel.

4. A small, 3D-printed guide is attached to the motor body with an M3 x 10mm bolt; this helps guide the filament into the gap between the drive wheel and the idler bearing.

Fitting the J-head hot-end

The J-head hot-end will most likely come as a ready-assembled unit. Fortunately, other compatible hot-ends such as the Pico from B3 Innovations, the Prusa V2 nozzle, or the V5 from E3D can also be used in exactly the same fitting. See Figure 11-17 in Chapter 11 for examples of such compatible hot-ends, and Figure 11-17 for an exploded view of an MK5 J-head for reference. Here's what to look for while fitting the J-head hot-end:

✔ The J-head (or compatible) hot-end will have a groove mount at the top of the unit. Use this to clamp into a matching recession of the metal plate or 3D-printed adapter found on most extruder assemblies.

   Make sure you don't trap any wires — and be careful with the fine thermistor wiring attached to the J-head body.

✔ Some mounts will just slot in, others will require either M4 x 16mm bolts or M3 x 20mm bolts to lock them in place.

Fitting the assembled extruder to the X carriage

This is usually a simple task, requiring two M3 or M4 bolts to fit the extruder body onto the X carriage of your machine. For the Prusa i3 design, various mounts can be downloaded from the main repository site at

```
https://github.com/josefprusa/Prusa3-vanilla
```

or from Thingiverse at

```
http://www.thingiverse.com/search?q=prusa+i3+extruder&sa=
```

Wiring the extruder to RAMPS

The last part of our build is to wire up the extruder motor, hot-end heater, and thermistor sensor to our set of RAMPS electronics. Remember to check the RAMPS wiring guide (as we did in Chapter 13) at

```
http://reprap.org/mediawiki/images/6/6d/Rampswire14.svg
```

Then follow these general steps:

1. Wiring the Extruder motor is exactly the same procedure used for wiring up the X, Y, and Z motors as described in Chapter 13.

2. When the Extruder motor is wired up, fit it to Extruder E0 on the RAMPS board.

3. Connect the thermistor. Its two-way header can go in either orientation, and connects to T0.

REMEMBER

4. Connect the hot-end heater can to the D10 screw-terminal connectors, in either orientation.

   Use ferrules on the wire ends if possible.

You can now calibrate your machine as described in Chapter 15. When that's done, you can perform your first 3D print.

Syringe and Paste-Based Extrusion

The use of paste and clay materials is not widespread in RepRap, but is one of the most straightforward forms of 3D printing. You can print out a syringe-based extruder to use on your RepRap 3D printer and start experimenting today.

In the early days of home 3D printing, the Fab@Home project (`http://www.fabathome.org/`) chose to develop open-source printers using various pastes instead of thermoplastic materials. RepRap has been a little slow to adopt paste materials for printing, but they can be ideal for some uses. (See Figure 14-9.)

Figure 14-9:
The open-source Fab@Home 3D printers pioneered the use of paste extrusion rather than thermo-plastic materials.

Photo courtesy of Floris Van Breugel

Richard had a particular interest in syringe-based 3D printing. When trying this out on his own RepRap, Richard discovered why it isn't as popular as you might imagine: Controlling the material was difficult. Many early attempts as paste extrusion used compressed air to force the material out of the syringe, often without controlling the stop and start of the flow. When the object began printing, it had to keep going until the end. That was fine for printing (say) a flat cookie, but it didn't allow much truly *three-dimensional* printing.

Richard set out to equip his 3D printer with an extruder design that could be used and controlled in much the same way as a traditional thermoplastic extruder. After a few models and a flash of inspiration, he ended up with a design for a *universal paste extruder.* (See Figure 14-10.) Instead of using compressed air, his design used a normal stepper motor to drive a timing belt that mechanically pulled down a syringe plunger, extruding paste materials onto the build platform layer by layer. This design was released as an open-source project; before long, people all over the world were using it, developing variations on the design, adapting it for different uses, and fitting it onto all manner of machines. That's how open-source technology is supposed to work.

Figure 14-10:
The
universal
paste
extruder.

The universal paste extruder is easy to use on any RepRap. That's because as far as the control electronics know, the stepper motor is performing the same job as a thermoplastic extruder. To work this bit of magic, you need only re-calibrate the number of steps that the motor requires to extrude a set amount of material. With a paste extruder in place, you have all sorts of material options available to experiment with. (See Figure 14-11.) Richard's favorite materials are clays and ceramics — after all, if you make a mess, you can just scrape them off your build platform, add a little more water (if required), and try again.

When using paste materials, it's a good idea to fix a sheet of greaseproof paper or aluminum foil onto your platform. This keeps materials like clay from drying out too fast and allows easy removal.

Precious-metal clays and other ceramic materials can also be extruded into 3D models or jewelry in this way. Then, when dry, some of the parts can also be successfully fired or finished by hand as needed.

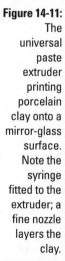

Figure 14-11:
The universal paste extruder printing porcelain clay onto a mirror-glass surface. Note the syringe fitted to the extruder; a fine nozzle layers the clay.

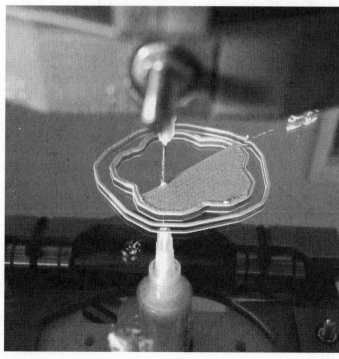

In addition to clay-based materials, you can print with gels, various types of silicon sealants and (of course) with many different foods (including sugar paste, heated chocolate, marzipan, and frostings) if you can get a smooth enough paste to form. People have even experimented with various batter mixes that 3D-print out directly over a hot frying pan, for custom waffles and pancakes! (See Figure 14-12.)

Figure 14-12: Using chocolate muffin mix requires just the basic syringe without a needle, and provides a 3mm bead of extrusion.

Pastas and fondants make for great food-based 3D-printing experimentation. Also, masa flour (used to make corn chips) is a perfect food for 3D printing: It sticks to itself, and after it's extruded onto a baking tray or silicon sheet, you can bake it for the ultimate custom-designed crunchy treat. (See Figure 14-13.)

If you want to print your own universal paste extruder, here's where you can see the full build instructions and download the 3D model parts to print out: http://richrap.com/?p=60.

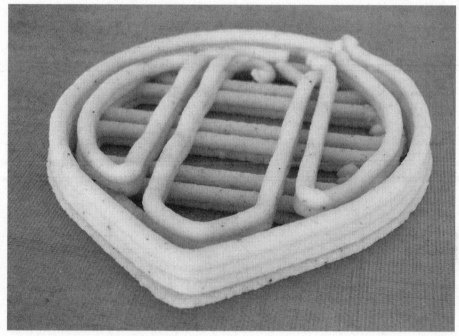

Multi-Color Printing

Another RepRap development goal for home 3D printing is to print objects in many colors — even mix, on demand, the exact color of your choice from a set five or six master materials. Full-color home 3D printing is still a little way into the future, but a number of methods now exist to help brighten up your 3D-printed objects. This section explores multi-extruder printing, color mixing, and simple ways to achieve impressive results, even with only a single extruder.

In one of the many RepRap experiments at Bath University in the U.K., Myles Corbett and Dr. Adrian Bowyer investigated the mixing of two different colors into a single nozzle. They discovered that the plastic materials don't blend naturally. Instead, they come out fused together in a similar manner to striped toothpaste. (See Figure 14-14.) Myles and Adrian continued to develop the extruder. Eventually, after trying all sorts of baffles, chambers, and passive methods of achieving a mix, they concluded that only an active method of stirring the melted plastic together *inside* the hot-end would provide a true mixed-color output. This they did — and it worked.

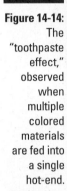

Figure 14-14:
The "toothpaste effect," observed when multiple colored materials are fed into a single hot-end.

If you'd like to read more about this work, the excellent report on color mixing at Bath (all 50+ MB of it) can be found on the RepRap wiki here:

```
www.reprap.org/mediawiki/images/0/05/
RepRapColourColorMixingReport-jmc.pdf
```

Richard's development efforts with color and material mixing led to the creation of a three-way extruder that feeds three materials into one single nozzle. He found that each extruder could be controlled, and that the toothpaste effect would be interesting, so he decided not to implement an active mixing system. This approach produced a number of unique prints, with two or three sides of an object showing different color tints. (See Figure 14-15.)

Further details of this approach to three-way color mixing can be found here: `http://richrap.com/?p=121`.

A much more common way to produce a dual-color print is by using two separate extruders and two hot-ends. (See Figure 14-16.) You can load one color into the first extruder and a different color into the second; for that matter, you could load different types of materials if you find they'll print out together. It's then a slightly more complex process whose general stages (using thermoplastic) look like this:

Figure 14-15:
A three-way blending nozzle combines cyan, magenta, and yellow feeds to produce a psychedelic printed frog that changes color from different angles.

1. Design two separate 3D objects that fit together and load them both into your slicing software.

2. Specify a different extruder for each printed object, and slice both objects together into a G-code file that the printer can understand.

3. The 3D printer heats up both extruders; while it prints the first object with Extruder 1, it drops the second extruder's temperature enough to keep the plastic from oozing out.

4. Extruder 1's temperature is then lowered and Extruder 2 is used to print the first layer of the second model.

5. The whole process repeats until both models are printed, fused together as one object in two different colors.

In Figure 14-16, the dragon and heart are separate 3D objects, placed together in the slicing software. One extruder is specified for each object; each extruder is fitted with a different color filament. We go over using multiple extruders in more detail in Chapter 15.

What if you only have a single extruder, but want to try out some multi-color prints? Here are a number of ways to achieve some really impressive and colorful results on almost any RepRap 3D printer.

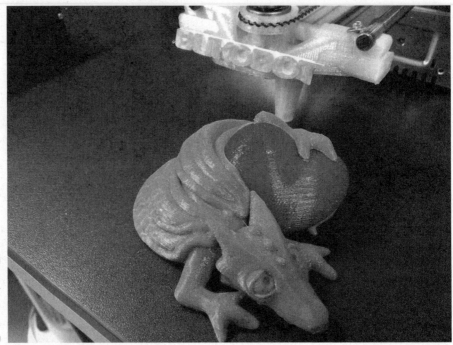

Figure 14-16:
A dual-extruder print.

When Richard first made multicolored objects, he designed a simple filament joiner. This approach allowed sections of different filaments to be melted together; when the fused filament line was used in a 3D printer, it made objects with stripes of different colors.

It became obvious that you could produce all sorts of objects in many different colors by (a) designing the object's features to have different layer heights and then (b) printing different colored layers on top of each part. The flag in Figure 14-17 (for example) was designed to have the red, white, and blue features at slightly different heights; when one color finishes printing, another color can be printed on top of it. Selecting which parts of which layers to expose produces a multicolored object. Similarly, Matthew Bennett's iPhone cases (shown in Figure 14-18) use the same method, but with many more color changes, using clear filaments give the final product even more variation. This was all done with a single extruder.

Figure 14-17: Multi-color printing with a single extruder, (layer selective color printing) using different layer heights.

Figure 14-18: These iPhone cases are another fine example of some extreme layer-selective color printing that uses a single extruder.

Photo courtesy of Matthew Bennett

A simpler method is deciding not to join the filaments together, but to use a two-stage cut-and-follow-on method instead:

1. Carefully cut the filament close to the extruder while an object is being printed.

2. Feed another color manually as the extruder draws down the cut end.

With a little patience and practice, all sorts of interesting color effects become possible.

The only downside with this method is that you get oozing with the filament during printing. With a normal, solid length of filament, the extruder can retract a little after each print move; if it retracts while a section of cut filament is not joined to the last section, the filament is not retracted — so it oozes a little out of the hot-end. A very fast travel move can compensate for the ooze, but such fast moves weren't possible in the early days of home printing. In general, filament joining was a better solution.

If you print an entire plate of many different parts, and if you can time to cut and load a new color every 15 minutes or so (or however often you desire), you could end up with an entire set of printed parts in fabulous colors. Figure 14-19 shows the same set of 3D-printer parts we used in the frame construction of the Prusa i3 printer described in Chapter 12. These parts, however, were printed in rainbow colors using just a single extruder and following the cut-and-follow-on method for continuous printing.

If you're not feeling confident enough to use the cut-and-follow-on method, most 3D-printing software interfaces (such as Pronterface) allow you to pause a print, so you can make changes. Just follow these general steps:

1. Manually release the extruder idler.

2. Pull out the color filament just used.

3. Replace the filament with a filament of another color.

4. Tighten the extruder idler again and continue the print.

This approach works the same as the cut-and-follow-on method; it just takes a little longer.

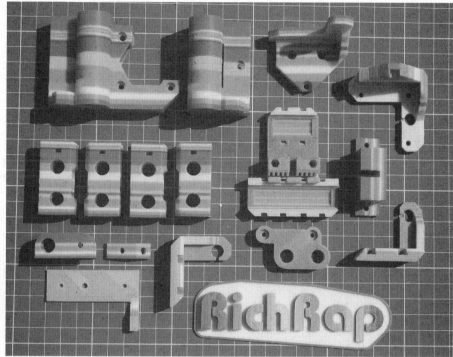

Figure 14-19:
Continuous
multi-color
printing
using the
cut-and-
follow-on
method.

Extruder Operation and Upgrades

This section is full of tips to keep your extruder and 3D printer happy. Following the advice here will help make your 3D printing go smoothly, help you avoid failed prints, and keep your new 3D printer in action. Keeping your extruder in tip-top condition is really important: It's the device that takes the most wear and tear from operating your 3D printer. In the following list, we give you some advice and tips for good printing methods and for looking after your extruder:

✔ **Check the accuracy of your software/firmware:** Always make sure that the temperatures reported by your firmware and software are accurate. This can help resolve a lot of common problems, and also extend the life of your 3D printer. You can check the temperature in a number of ways. One of the very best is to insert a thermocouple probe down into the hot-end nozzle. If this is not possible, you could try investing in a non-contact digital laser temperature sensor, which can be purchased for around $30 (See Figure 14-20.) To use it, just point the laser at the place you want to measure. This device is good for checking the temperature of your heated print-bed, or to see whether your motors or your drive electronics are getting too hot.

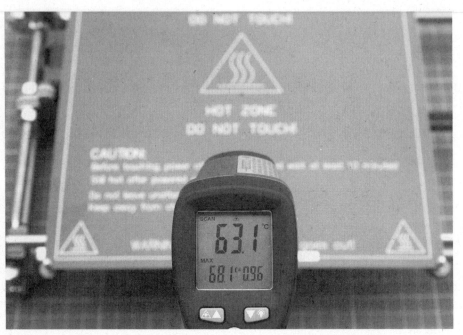

Figure 14-20:
A no-contact laser temperature sensor makes sure your 3D printer is running at the correct temperatures.

✔ **Verify the temperature of your cold-end:** Once you have a way to measure temperatures, it's a great idea to check how hot the cold-end (thermal barrier) is getting on your hot-end. As you may recall from Chapter 11, the cold-end needs to be kept below the glass-transition temperature of the material you're printing. This is most critical for PLA, so check your extruder after it has been on and printing for 20 minutes or so. If it's heating up over 50 degrees Centigrade, consider adding a cooling fan; just make sure this fan points across the cold-end part of the extruder and is not pointing toward the hot-end or the object being printed.

Some 3D-printer kits come with a fan to cool the cold-end of your extruder — usually a very good idea. It's not always needed, but having your incoming filament go quickly from cool to melting is much better than trying to push a plug of heated, semi-soft, rubberlike material into your extruder nozzle.

✔ **Clean your filament:** Add a fluff-capturing device to your 3D printer. This may sound a little odd, but dust and fluff on the filament going into your hot-end can clog it up and eventually jam the nozzle. Such gunk is also very hard to clear out. A simple cut section of sponge, secured around the filament with a zip-tie, will catch the fluff and stop it from entering your extruder. (See Figure 14-21.)

Figure 14-21:
A simple dry sponge catches fluff, grease, and dust to keep it from entering (and jamming) the tiny nozzle of your hot-end.

Fixing a blocked hot-end or extruder

When you get a hot-end blockage or your extruder's filament drive fails, the signs are usually obvious: The stream of plastic starts to lessen, and then stops; the printer keeps trying to print, but extrudes layer after layer of nothing.

The first thing to do is stop the print and check to ensure that the heater block on your hot-end is still at the expected temperature. (Ideally, for maximum safety, you should use a non-contact temperature sensor.) If the heater temperature is significantly below 160 degrees Centigrade, it may have failed or it may have developed a problem in the wiring or the electronics controlling the heaters.

Unfortunately, it's common for wires on home 3D printers to break due to the constant movement of the machine. Wiring should always have plenty of room to move around gently, with enough slack that it's not tightly bent or yanked back and forth as the machine moves. Using silicon-coated wire can help, especially with extra resistance to heat. Increasingly, newer machines use gently curved *ribbon cable,* (a ribbon of many separate, parallel wires instead of a thick wire). This tends to alleviate issues with cable strain and damage.

If your heater block is jammed but is at the expected temperature, here's the general procedure:

1. **Keep the heater block turned on.**

2. **Check to ensure that the filament drive hasn't become blocked or that the filament is not buckled in or wrapped around your extruder drive wheel.**

3. **Release the idler bearing and gently pull out the filament.**

   It's not common for a filament to become so jammed that it cannot be pulled out while the hot-end is at temperature. More commonly, the removed filament shows signs of being overly compressed — a little fatter where it melted inside the hot-end. Usually the action of pulling out the melted filament removes contaminants from the hot-end nozzle.

4. **Cut off the melted filament end and manually push it back down into the hot-end.**

   If you can push down and material is extruded from the nozzle, you have cleared the blockage.

5. **If you can't get the material to extrude, then allow the end of the material to melt and pull it back out again.**

   Doing this several times should clear most blockages. If you still have a blockage, you have two more options to be done extremely carefully:

   • Push a pin or small drill bit into the nozzle end while pulling out the melted filament.

   • Allow your hot-end to cool down and *when it's cool,* use a chemical solvent (such as acetone) to help dissolve any build-up.

   Before using any chemical cleaners, check with your supplier and mention the type of material that was last used in the hot-end when the jam occurred.

You may be starting to think that having a few different extruders is a good idea. Well, it usually is; in the event of a blockage, a backup extruder can get you printing again while you repair. Another reason for having a choice of extruders is that your machine becomes much more capable at printing different types of objects, which can widen your selection of available printing materials.

Acquiring an assortment of extruders

For thermoplastic printing, it's a good idea to have two or more extruders of the same type, but with different nozzle sizes and maybe a choice of 3mm and 1.75mm filament. Some materials — especially the more experimental — tend to come in 3mm size (less often in 1.75mm); 3mm filament can also cost less, depending on the manufacturer. A choice of nozzle size is great if you intend to print a variety of different-quality parts. Although you can always just print with a smaller nozzle, the print job may take a lot longer with certain parts. Having the option of a bigger nozzle can be handy when you want to create rough drafts of your models, or if you intend to finish the resulting object with paints or fillers.

A good all-around nozzle size is 0.4mm, which allows fine detail while also a reasonable print time for most parts. You can also select layer heights of around 0.3mm or lower.

This is not to say that a bigger nozzle can't provide high quality. You can still select very low layer heights if you're using a bigger nozzle which makes the vertical quality of a print almost identical to what you'd get with a smaller nozzle, though some fine horizontal details may be lost if the model has a lot of sharp corners and features. Think about a 3D-printing nozzle as similar to a paintbrush: You can use smaller for finer details and sharper edges; a bigger brush or nozzle "paints" faster but can't resolve intricate details as clearly.

A typical large nozzle for a home 3D printer is 0.6mm or 0.8mm. Some (much larger) RepRap printers use 1.2mm nozzles to produce models a meter or more long.

Don't set a layer height of more than the size of the nozzle. It's always a good idea to keep the layer size at least a little smaller or, for that matter, much smaller than the nozzle. Doing so ensures a good bonding of plastic, layer on layer.

- ✔ A good all-around nozzle size is 0.4mm, which allows fine detail, a reasonable print time for most parts, and layer heights of around 0.3mm or lower.

- ✔ A nozzle size of 0.6mm will allow you to print layers of 0.5mm or lower and usually give you a much faster print time.

You can try using as small a nozzle as your machine mechanics will allow. Keep in mind, however, that normal minimum layer heights are around 0.1mm (100 microns) about the thickness of a sheet of office paper. Most RepRap machines will also allow 0.05mm (50 microns), and even smaller, but the time taken to print will be dramatically increased and the extra quality is hard to distinguish.

It's common to print with 0.2mm or 0.25mm layer heights. The result is a highly presentable surface. As you become more accustomed to 3D printing and tune your printer to run faster, you'll find a more pleasing resolution at layer heights around 0.15mm or 0.1mm.

If you do decide to keep more than one extruder available for your 3D printer, you don't need to fit them all on your machine at the same time. In many situations, it makes a lot of sense to have a quick-fit mechanism that allows you to change extruders easily.

Richard struggled with the issue of multiple extruders when some of the first RepRap machines were being developed. At the time, all extruders were mounted permanently on the moving X-axis carriage with nuts and bolts. Changing extruders was time-consuming and tricky and never mind even thinking about using more than just one type.

Richard developed a quick-fit carriage and various extruder bases for the most common hot-ends and paste extruders. The idea was to allow easy experimentation and to make entire extruders easy to change and lock in place on RepRap printers. (See Figure 14-22.)

Figure 14-22:
A replacement X-carriage compatible with many RepRap 3D printers. The yellow lever at left allows the quick fitting and removal of extruders.

Cooling extruders with fans

A final point about 3D printing extruders: Use fans. We have already discussed using a small fan to keep the cold-end insulator of your hot-end below the glass-transition point of your plastic. This is a good idea, but when you start experimenting with printing ultra-tiny objects with fine details or printing objects at great speed, you quickly discover an interesting problem with the 3D printing of thermoplastic materials: controlling layer temperature.

If you print very tiny parts that have little layer surface area or turn out an object at very high printing speeds so each layer is completed in a matter of seconds, often the layer of plastic just laid down doesn't have time to cool. It's still a little molten when the next layer is laid down. With the radiated heat from the nozzle and more hot plastic being extruded, the model can end up a messy blob instead of the object you had intended. You can slow down the speed, but this may not resolve the problem; you shouldn't have to wait even longer to print an object anyway. This is where a controlled cooling fan can make a massive difference.

The cooling fan used to cool a printed object is usually around 80mm wide. It's controlled by the electronics: In your Slic3r-generated G-code, you can specify how fast a cooling fan runs, and when to turn the fan on or off. With a cooling fan fitted, Slic3r can still run the print at full speed — even when printing fine details of a model. Without a fan, Slic3r would have to instruct the G-code to slow down to allow for natural cooling of the plastic before adding more. As you can imagine, fine structures can be tricky to print without a cooling fan.

We discuss setting up the fan settings with Slic3r in Chapter 15, but here we want to point out a fan's ability to allow *bridging* of extruded material. This is an essential part of many 3D-printed objects. *Bridging* is when a model has to span a gap, essentially making a bridge in thin air. If you extrude plastic with nothing underneath it, the extruded material will naturally sag down and sometimes break. Although you can bridge filament without using a fan, you will usually have some strings of snapped extruded filament hanging down, and a little sagging. With a fan to help cool the plastic as it's extruded, you can make a tight bridge and get smart-looking results. (See Figure 14-23.)

 A very important point about fan cooling is to mount the fan so it's cooling the top layer of the part being printed. If you cool the heated-bed, your part will pop off in the middle of the print. If you accidentally cool the hot-end, your extruder may jam. It's quite common for a cooling fan to have a 3D-printed duct to direct a stream of air across the printed object while it prints; this minimizes unwanted cooling of the heated-bed and hot-end. (See Figure 14-24.)

Figure 14-23:
Bridging a filament. With good cooling and a few alternating layers, this becomes a solid surface that can be printed on.

Figure 14-24:
A printed duct cools the part being printed and does not accidentally cool the hot-end heater.

In almost all cases, it's not advisable to use a cooling fan for printing in ABS material. The fan makes a part's edges cool too fast and curl up; the next layer may be worse. Eventually the part can be so deformed and warped that the print head can knock it off the build platform. With PLA, however, the exact opposite is true: PLA likes a fan; ABS does not.

Chapter 15

Identifying Software and Calibrating Your 3D Printer

*W*e are now on the final phase of RepRap machine setup: processing and calibrating 3D models. In this chapter, we think about the best ways to print models (including the use of "support material"), and look at various sources for 3D models and some of the common 3D-modeling packages you can use to generate designs. We go into more detail about the preparation of the model files and producing output G-code with Slic3r that you can use with your RepRap 3D printer. Then, before getting into the nuances of printing parts, we make sure the machine is calibrated and ready to print your first object. Finally we look at some common types of 3D objects and how you can use specific settings to achieve the best 3D-printed results.

3D Design Software and Model Resources

The entire 3D-printing process starts with a model — but how are these models created, and where can you get digital models of objects ready to be printed? And what can't be 3D-printed easily?

Objects designed for home 3D printing are exactly that: ready-made models. Usually the designers of these objects have home 3D printing in mind, expecting that their models will be 3D-printed before any modeling process starts. After all, if you get a taste of the results, you have a clearer goal when you start making your own models.

The promise of home 3D printing doesn't mean you can print anything and everything. This practical limitation can frustrate users who expect to jump right in and start printing high-quality parts for product development, model-making, or as a substitute for products crafted by hand or manufactured traditionally.

Well, consider that 3D printers are good at producing objects that *can't* be made by other manufacturing techniques. Figure 15-1 shows two such examples; most users, however, aren't faced with creating such complex models, at least not as first projects. Most home users of 3D printing face the more standard limitations of simply getting what they need out of a 3D printer.

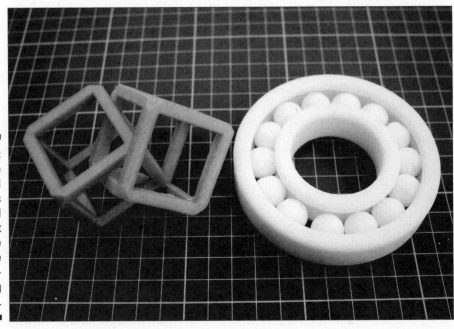

Figure 15-1:
Two 3D-printed objects that would be almost impossible to produce by injection-molding machines.

As an example, if you wanted to print out a model of a person for a scale-model railroad, you might want that person in a seated position with arms stretched out. (See Figure 15-2.) Software packages like Poser or Google Sketchup make this sort of modeling easy to do. If you were sending this model off to a 3D-printing bureau that uses a professional Selective Laser Sintering (SLS) 3D printer, such a professional operation would have no problem printing this model. However, trying to do this yourself on a home 3D printer — especially as an ambitious early project — can be a real challenge.

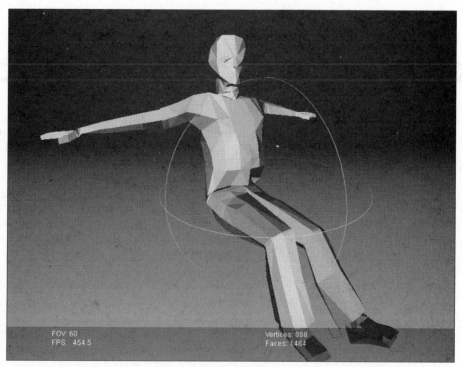

Figure 15-2: A posed person is a challenge to print on a home 3D printer; the model has overhangs where the printed material would lack support.

FOV 60
FPS: 454.5

Vertices: 888
Faces: 1484

The main difficulty for Fused Filament Fabrication (FFF) printers such as RepRap is that they can't extrude into free air; the object must always be supported while the printing is going on. Each new layer needs a supporting layer to build on. In printing a model of a seated person, then, the feet and lower legs would print just fine, but the 90-degree overhang of the upper legs and the outstretched arms will present a problem: The extruded filament has nothing to attach to. With nowhere to go, the filament just collapses into a mess of extruded spaghetti.

A professional SLS 3D printer works differently: It builds up objects by using fine nylon powder. A laser melts the nylon layer and fuses the shape of the object; then another complete layer of fine powder is spread over the build surface and the process repeats. The main difference here is that all that spare unfused powder provides support for the fused parts as they build so the parts that eventually will extend from the model into free air can be built with support, and will stay in place while being printed. When the model cools and the excess powder is brushed off, the model is complete, and can be of almost any shape and complexity. That process isn't possible with home 3D printers, at least not yet.

To help with this problem, we can use a support structure that builds up a fine column of material from the base of the bed (or from the printed part itself) to support any overhanging features. Our Slic3r software (discussed in the next section) can detect where to add support. You can even use a second extruder to put a different support material into the build.

Normally, home 3D printers use the same material for the model as for the support material. All the extra material will have to be snapped off, and the model cleaned up a little, after the print is complete. (See Figure 15-3.) Slic3r model processing software can add support material automatically wherever it's required. This approach works well, but remember that the support material is temporary; it must be cut away after the print is finished. This cutting can leave marks and scarring. If the printed parts are intricate, removing the support by hand can be difficult. (See Figure 15-4 and Figure 15-5.) Using a second extruder to provide a more workable support material say, a thermoplastic such as PVA allows the object to be trimmed just by submerging it in warm water: The PVA dissolves away, revealing the finished model. Dissolvable support material will probably be a commonplace addition to future home 3D printers.

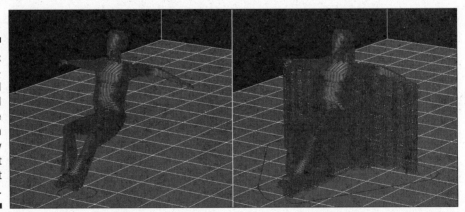

Figure 15-3: The unprintable model (at left) and the same model with breakaway support material (at right).

Basic model

Basic model with support material added

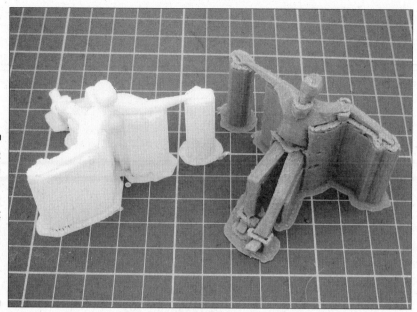

Figure 15-4:
Take care when removing the support material; small, fragile parts can be damaged or snapped off.

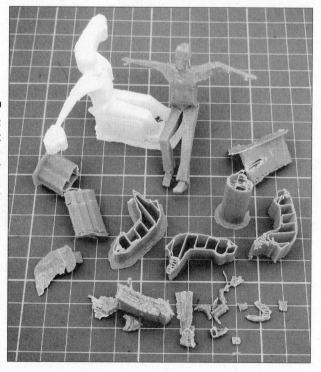

Figure 15-5:
This support structure is mostly hollow, easily removable with needle-nose pliers; further cleanup may require using a sharp blade or small files.

We can often get around (or minimize) the use of support material by rotating the model in Netfabb before printing (see Chapter 11 for a Netfabb overview). For example, if we rotate the model of the seated person so the back and arms are on the base of the print surface, we may not have to use support material at all. (See Figure 15-6.)

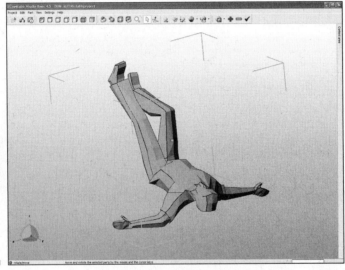

Figure 15-6:
Rotating a model in Netfabb so it can be printed more easily.

No wonder 3D-printing sites often provide models designed for home 3D printing. The model of a person would most likely be posed standing straight up with hands down by the sides of the body, or posed in contact with the upper legs. In either case, no extra support material is needed, so it can be printed easily on home 3D printers. If more complicated posed positions were posted, most people would have a struggle to print them, due to the way 3D printers build up a model layer by layer. For this reason, if you require a model of a seated person, you may have to settle for the use of support material (as shown earlier in Figures 15-4 and 15-5).

Another way to avoid adding supports is to divide a complex model into two or more parts that each require less support material (or none at all). After printing these parts, you can join them with glue.

Complicated objects are often better off being divided into separate parts; all parts are printed flat on the build-plate and assembled later into complex, functioning objects. The planetary gearbox shown in Figure 15-7, for example, is still a real challenge even for a professional-grade 3D printer to build as one complete, functioning object with no manual assembly required. But stay tuned; we're getting closer to this goal all the time.

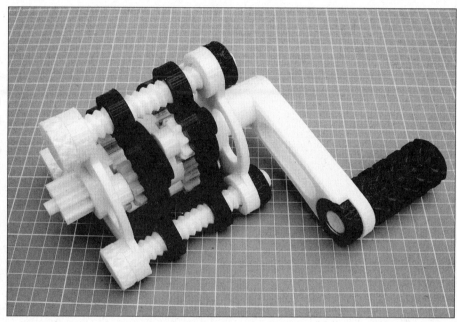

Figure 15-7:
A multi-stage planetary gearbox. Home 3D printers can make all the parts, but some assembly is still required.

Using design software

Many software packages for the design of 3D models are available. Many are open-source or can be downloaded for free and include export options that support the .STL model format used by RepRap 3D printers.

A very popular option for RepRap developers is OpenSCAD (`www.openscad.org`). This open-source 3D modeling program has an amazing array of examples, libraries, and resources. It allows *parametric modeling,* in which a design can have almost any of its dimensions, shapes, or features changed by altering the appropriate parameters. For example, with parametric modeling you could specify a new motor and the model would be retooled automatically to be more suitable for the motor you want to produce. The downside with this software is that it's complex. Unless you're familiar with programming and have a good mathematical grasp of geometric 3D space, this software may present you with quite a struggle. (See Figure 15-8.)

Figure 15-8:
The para-
metric
nature of
OpenSCAD
can accom-
modate
many
physically
different
options with
just a small
change of
code.

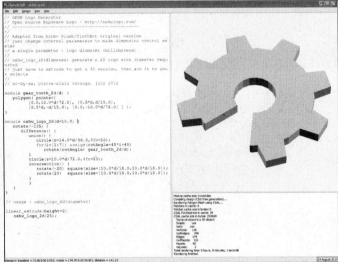

Another commonly used package is Google Sketchup. This visual modeling tool is a good way to experiment with your own designs or alter existing 3D models. Find it at `http://google-sketchup.en.softonic.com/`.

You can use almost any type of 3D-modeling program; many now exist as cloud-based applications that produce customized 3D models (or allow them to be made easily).

Many more consumer-level software products are specifically usable with 3D printing; these include Tinkercad, 3DTin, Meshmixer, and the suite of Autodesk123 programs. All provide easy-to-use applications for the 3D modeling of objects designed for home, hobby, or business 3D printing.

Professional tools such as Solidworks are intended for the complete design and functional analysis of products. Packages such as Rhinoceros (used by jewelry designers and 3D artists) provide options for almost any use of a 3D printer.

The output format you require for a 3D printer is .STL. This common file format is usually available as a standard export option, although some packages may require a plug-in.

If you've already obtained an STL model file from an object repository, or as an export from your 3D modeling program, use the upcoming section to check the model and make sure it works with your software.

Model verification with Netfabb

If you have an STL model file, you have to *verify* the model before you can print it. Software programs and slicing tools for 3D printing see all 3D models, including solids, as a series of triangles joined together to create a hollow *mesh* surface. The triangles in your model must not intersect through the faces of other triangles — that's an *invalid mesh* that would cause problems if you try to 3D-print it.

It's always a good idea to verify that your model export or download is a *valid mesh,* that it's in the correct orientation for 3D printing, and that its size is what you expect and require. Netfabb Basic is ideal for doing this sort of object pre-checking; it highlights problems with exclamation marks and shows you the orientation onscreen. Then you can repair, scale, and reorient a model as needed for export and 3D printing. (See Figure 15-9.)

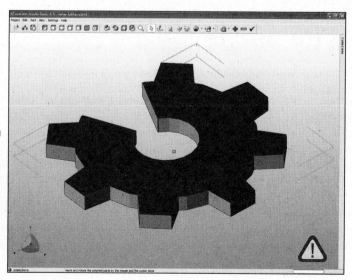

Figure 15-9:
Netfabb highlights problems in your model with exclamation marks.

When mesh errors are present, you can use Netfabb to make repairs. After rotating and scaling the model as needed, you click the + button to attempt a repair. Then you select Standard Repair and click Apply Repair to obtain a new model that you can export for 3D printing. (See Figure 15-10.)

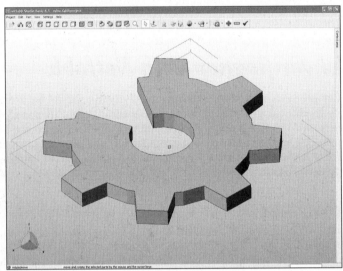

Figure 15-10:
Here Netfabb detected that the model was not solid. After repair, the solid model can be 3D-printed.

Working with Slic3r

Slic3r is a print-slicing program we introduced back in Chapter 11. It helps process 3D models for printing. The Slic3r software can be downloaded for PC, Mac, and Linux at www.slic3r.org. Before working with the material in this chapter, we recommend that you download and install Slic3r on your computer.

Configuring Slic3r

When Slic3r has been installed successfully, you can go about configuring it. Before an object can be sliced up into layers for printing, Slic3r has to know a number of key settings for your particular 3D printer. You enter these settings in a configuration wizard that appears when you first start Slic3r.

Don't worry — all these settings can be changed later if you need to change them after you use Slic3r. For now, just enter all the specified details you can. You can save different configurations later. This arrangement is useful when you're running several different machines, testing upgrades, or trying different material types.

To configure Slic3r, follow these steps:

1. **In the wizard, select the particular style of G-code to use with the firmware you'll be running on your RepRap 3D printer.**

   This is usually RepRap (Marlin/Sprinter). (See Figure 15-11.)

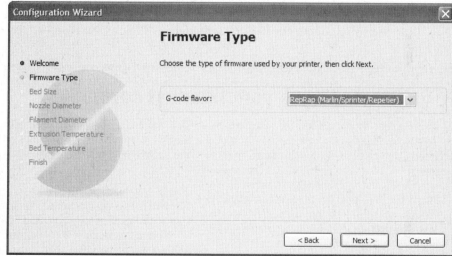

Figure 15-11:
Choosing
the G-code
for your
firmware.

2. **Enter the size of your printer's build bed.**

   • For a RepRap using a Prusa-style heated-bed of PCB material (as described in the previous section), enter a size of 200mm x 200mm.

   • A Delta printer has a rounder build area, which has to be considered when you're printing objects, but you can still enter size as X and Y coordinates.

3. **Enter the size of the output nozzle on your 3D printer's hot-end.**

   Enter the size of your extruder nozzle; common sizes are 0.5mm, 0.4mm, and 0.35mm. Slic3r uses this information to help calculate the space necessary to extrude each layer so that each layer is bonded securely to the one beneath it. This setting serves as a guide for Slic3r; tuning the width and height of the extrusion path is a separate, independent part of the calibration process.

The actual extruded width of the output also depends on many tiny aspects of the hot-end design. It's common to have some *die-swell* from a small hole under pressure: The output filament expands from the nozzle as it exits. Print calibration, then, is important to prevent extruding plastic layers from extruding too close together or too far apart for your 3D models to look right and function correctly. We show you how to handle die-swell later in this chapter.

4. **Enter the filament diameter.**

   Be sure to measure the diameter of your filament, get the best average, and enter that result as the filament diameter for Slic3r, preferably after you ponder the cautionary sidebar, "Check your filament carefully."

Check your filament carefully

A consistent filament diameter that extrudes with a round, not oval, cross-section is critical to 3D-printing success. Slic3r needs to know the size of your input filament so it can calculate the volume of plastic that it commands the 3D printer to push out of the hot-end while the head is moving around the object. If this setting is not correct — or if your material changes in diameter during a print — you've got trouble:

- You run the risk of over-extruding. Then your print head may jam or skew off-position and ruin your print.

- Equally bad, the print head may under-extrude your material, resulting in a weak print, layer delamination, or just an ugly object.

Good filament should have a round cross-section that does not deviate more than 0.1mm. Oval filament is a potential 3D-printing disaster; it changes in volume in your hot-end, depending on how the extruder pinch-wheel is gripping it.

The result is a mess. If you find that your filament has an oval cross-section, complain to the supplier and reject the filament if it causes problems.

The best way to get an average size for your filament is to measure ten points along a good few meters of material using a micrometer; check that the filament is round by rotating the micrometer at the same point. Take these measurements and add together, then divide by ten. You should have an average value that shows a tolerance of around 0.1mm deviation if you're using suitable-quality filament.

You can trust the information for diameter provided by your supplier, but it's well worth taking the time to measure your material size, especially if you have different suppliers or different types of material. And note that the actual size of 3mm filament is often around 2.85mm. This is normal; it allows the filament to be driven down tubes used in 3mm-diameter hot-ends and extruders.

Newcomers to 3D printing who discover a lack of material or an over-extrusion on their printed objects often change the filament diameter setting to adjust the volume of material. It can work, but as a rule, don't do it. Inaccurate extrusion often masks a bigger problem with extruder calibration or machine setup. These problems will manifest themselves as poor print quality, overextrusion of material giving poor results, and bad size tolerance for holes and apertures. And any fudge of settings will lead to inaccurate calculation of print time and material being used. Use an accurate measurement for filament diameter, and never adjust this number to tweak the volume of plastic being extruded.

5. **Continue with the Slic3r configuration wizard, setting up your extrusion temperatures, and selecting heated-bed temperature settings.**

   The extrusion temperature of a thermoplastic, when used in 3D printing, has to be high enough to allow your extruder to push material consistently into the hot-end without stalling but not so high that the plastic gets runny and overheated, and starts to break down and smoke. Earlier we set up the extrusion temperatures for common types of plastic you are likely to extrude in your 3D printer. For PLA, the temperature is around 200 degrees C; for ABS, around 240 degrees C.

   Printing temperatures usually need to be increased if you print significantly faster than "normal" or if you're trying to print a tiny detailed object slowly. (More about extrusion temperature later in this chapter.)

6. **If your RepRap 3D printer has a heated-bed, enter a temperature value for the material you intend to print.**

   Again, don't worry if you plan to print different materials; you can set up multiple configurations in Slic3r later. As a guide, use 60 degrees Centigrade for PLA and 110 Degrees Centigrade for ABS. If you want to print without using a heated-bed, then leave this value set to 0.

   Almost every RepRap 3D printer needs to be tuned for specific printing temperatures. It's fine to use other people's suggestions as a guide, but exact locations of the temperature sensor and small variations in the electronics and firmware setup may give you a very different reading.

Model processing with Slic3r

When Slic3r is installed and configured, you can use it to process your valid model. Slic3r will process your model to create an output G-code file, ready for printing.

Note: We're running Slic3r in Simple mode during this example. After you become more familiar with your 3D printer and its capabilities, you can change to Expert mode for many more settings and options. We explain some of the expert features later on in this chapter.

Open-source software tools such as Slic3r are constantly modified and upgraded, so use the following steps as a guide to the general process of preparing an object for 3D printing and outputting the G-code file. Expect changes in the near future to include the user interface, options, and degree to which the program becomes more self-intelligent about detecting the best settings for objects.

Follow these general steps to process your valid model:

1. **Position the model for printing by loading it into Slic3r.**

   When you have a valid model correctly oriented and scaled, load it into Slic3r by dropping the file onto the Plater window, which provides a scale view looking down on the outline of your model. More objects can also be loaded and moved around, if necessary, on the virtual build-plate. (See Figure 15-12.)

Figure 15-12: The Plater window provides a virtual build-plate on which to place your 3D objects before processing.

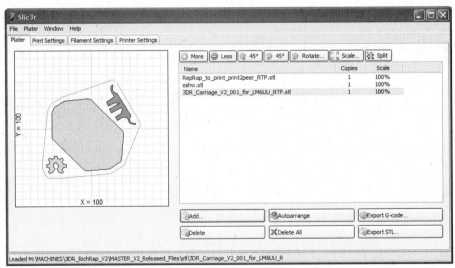

2. **Select suitable print settings for your model.**

   On the Print Settings tab (see Figure 15-13) are options that tell Slic3r how you want the model to be printed, and at what speed and quality:

- *Layer Height:* This determines how finely your model is vertically sliced. The finer the layers, the better your finished print will look but the longer it will take to print. A typical layer height would be 0.25mm for a 0.4 or 0.5mm nozzle.

- *Perimeters (minimum):* This is the number of times the extruder draws the outer surface of a layer before doing the infill. It's normal to use at least two perimeters to ensure a solid, good-looking object.

- *Solid Layers (Top and Bottom):* These settings are used to ensure that the top and bottom of an object are solid. For most models, it's good to start with three top and bottom layers.

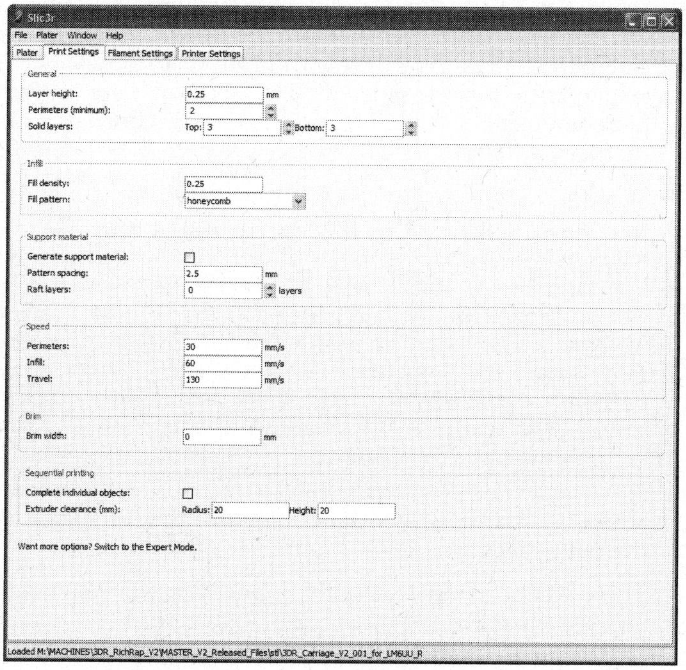

Figure 15-13:
The Print Settings tab in Slic3r allows you to describe how solid your part will print, and at what speed.

If you select zero top layers and select no infill, your model will be printed as an outer shell with as many perimeters as you selected. This is ideal for printing pots, vases, or other types of hollow objects. We discuss other options for printing pots later on in the chapter.

- *Fill Density:* This is represented in percentage, so a setting of 0.25 will give a 25% level of plastic infill for an object. A level of 0.3 (30%) is a good setting for most functional parts.

The objects you print will almost never require an infill of 100 percent. There's no need to use more plastic for only a slight gain in strength. It's quite normal for display models to be printed with less than 15 percent infill. Functional parts such as those needed to build a 3D printer usually require an infill of 25 to 50 percent.

- *Fill Pattern:* This allows you to select how the interior of an object is filled. The most common fill patterns are rectilinear and honeycomb; concentric is often used for round parts or for vases, pots, and so on. For mechanical parts, honeycomb is the strongest, but it's slightly slower to print than rectilinear.

- *Generate Support Material:* You can select to generate automatic support material if your object has significant overhanging features. The Raft option is not commonly used; it builds a plastic raft on the build platform before the object is printed. Doing so can help minimize warping with some types of plastic, and can also help correct for unlevel build platforms, but it will have to be removed from the print and uses more material (which is then discarded).

- *Speed — Perimeters, Infill, and Travel:* The Speed settings govern how fast the machine attempts to build the object. Your electronics firmware will limit the maximum speed and acceleration. Experiment with this setting, but start out slowly to get a good working sense of how fast your particular RepRap can go and what issues you face when speeding up or slowing down. With most modern RepRap 3D printers, it's quite normal to print Perimeters at 50mm/sec and Infill at 70mm/sec or faster. *Travel speed* is the speed that the machine can move from one point to another between extrusions of material. You want the print head to move as fast as possible to each a new position between stops and starts of a layer; the goal is to minimize the print time and improve overall quality.

  There will be a maximum limit to how fast you can move the motors and mechanical parts of your 3D printer. Start out at 150mm/sec and move up in small steps. Top travel speeds for a RepRap printer with an extruder mounted on the moving carriage will be around 280mm/sec. A lightweight Bowden extruder or a Delta printer should be able to exceed 400mm/sec, which is fast to watch, but only a few years ago home 3D printers were 10 times slower.

- *Brim Width:* We discuss this setting at the end of this chapter.

- *Sequential Printing:* Set this if you want to print each object on your build-plate one at a time. Normally an entire plate of parts will be printed layer after layer, which is usually the fastest way to print. However, printing the entire plate at once means that if you have a fault in the print or if one of the objects becomes detached, the entire build will be ruined. With sequential printing, you print each part one at a time, and this can limit the failures, but it takes longer. Also, because your extruder must be able to print around an already-printed object, you'll have to enter the clearance distance of your hot-end so it doesn't crash into an already-finished part. This arrangement also limits how many parts you can place on the build platform.

3. **Select print material size and temperature.**

   Go to the Filament Settings tab (see Figure 15-14) to tell Slic3r the diameter of your filament and the temperature at which to extrude it based on the material being used. You can also tell Slic3r to use a heated-bed, if one is fitted. Make sure the measured diameter of your filament is correct. Note that if you're printing with PLA, you should set an extruder temperature of around 200 degrees, and a heated-bed temperature of 60 degrees. Here you also have the option to increase the temperatures a little for the first layer. This is useful if the plastic isn't sticking too well to the build platform, but don't go too high; excess heat may actually keep the material from sticking.

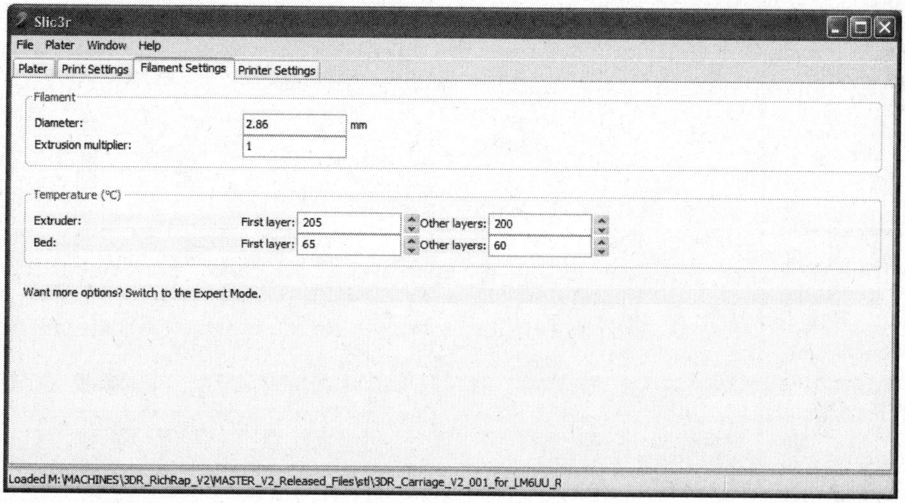

Figure 15-14: The Filament Settings tab tells Slic3r what material you're using and how hot it should be set.

4. Set your 3D printer size and firmware type.

Click the Printer Settings tab. (See Figure 15-15.) Here you should see the value for the mechanical size of your 3D printer, as you set it when you first ran the startup wizard. Make sure the bed size and print center are what you expect for your machine. The other options on this tab include the following:

- *Z Offset:* This setting is useful if you're running different extruders that may have different hot-end lengths, or if the nozzle is fractionally too far away from or close to your build surface. Enter a positive value here to raise the hot-end away from the build surface before printing starts. Depending on how your 3D printer is configured, it may not be possible to enter a negative number here to lower the hot-end before printing. If that's the case, you can usually adjust the hot-end mechanically; we discuss this in more detail later when we set up and calibrate the printer.

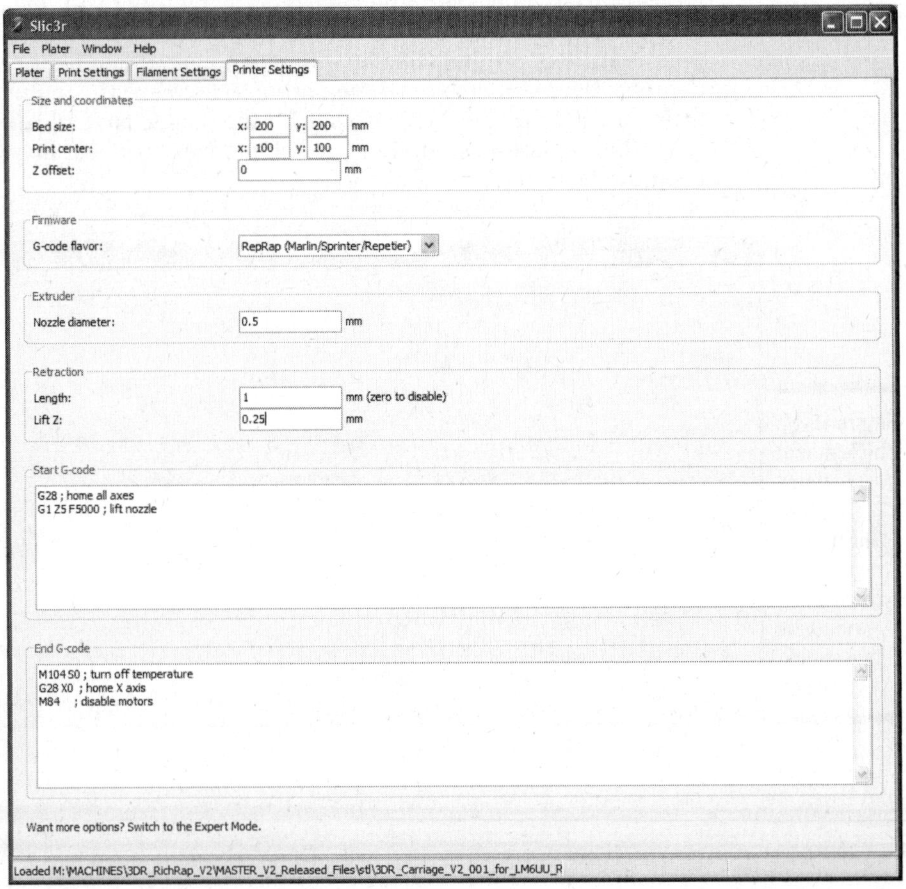

Figure 15-15:
On the Printer Settings tab, enter the dimensions of your RepRap 3D printer and the type of firmware in your electronics.

- *G-Code Flavor:* This specifies the type of open-source RepRap firmware you have on your electronics. Check with your supplier if your 3D printer is not a RepRap. The option here is usually (Marlin/Sprinter/Repetier).

- *Nozzle Diameter:* Check to ensure that your nozzle diameter is correct.

- *Retraction — Length:* A very important part is adding a retraction element to the extruder movement. This retraction length is a move to suck back the melted filament into the hot-end after a section of printing. Usually it happens before the hot-end travels to a new point on the build-plate where another section of material will be deposited. You only need to specify a retraction; the firmware knows to move the filament back the same distance when it reaches the next printing point before it starts extruding. We use this setting to prevent blobs and fine strings of melted plastic from making a mess of our print. Without retraction enabled with at least 0.5mm, you're likely to have messy-looking printed objects.

Every extruder setup is different. Experiment to find the best degree of extruder retraction; keep in mind that this figure must also be adjusted to suit the type of material being used. With a geared or direct-driven extruder, it's normal to start with 0.5mm of retraction and expect that up to around 1.5mm may be required to stop strings and blobs. Don't set the retraction value too high; doing so can force air to be sucked into the nozzle, and will cause many other problems. A Bowden requires a significantly longer retraction, due to the sprung nature of the filament being pushed inside the PTFE tube: Approximate values can range from 1.5mm up to 5mm of retraction.

- *Retraction — Lift Z:* This setting allows the extruder to lift a little above the object being printed right after the extruder retraction is done and just before the machine-travel move starts. This gives the fast-moving print head a little more clearance when it's moving across a printed layer to get to a new point to print. Again, you only need to specify a positive number here, usually one extra layer height (which you specified in the Print Settings tab for example, 0.25mm). As with the extruder retraction, the firmware knows to go back down by the same amount when the travel move is completed and before the next extrusion starts. This setting can help if your objects are being knocked off the print-bed during printing (or if layers are skewed out of alignment) because the motors are hitting corners or already-printed components of the object.

If Lift Z doesn't keep objects from being knocked off or printed layers from shifting, it may be because the travel moves are too fast. In such a case, try slowing down the travel in the Print Settings tab. If that doesn't resolve the issue, then it's most likely that the extruder is over-extruding plastic material that's getting caught on the hot-end during printing. There's more about ensuring correct extruder calibration later in this chapter.

- *Start and End G-Code:* These are commands that start up and finish off every print. This G-code is added to the output of every part printed and can specify to the firmware how best to set up the specific RepRap 3D printer for printing and how to shut it down.

The standard "start" G-code in Slic3r tells your printer to go to the home position and to lift the nozzle a little. Your print will start after the extruder head and heated-bed have reached the temperature you specified in the Filament Settings tab of Slic3r. The "end" G-code shuts off the extruder and bed heaters, and then homes the printer, but only on the X axis; you don't want to crash the carriage into the now-printed object. Finally, all the stepper motors are disabled, so the machine is in a running-but-shut-down state.

Eventually you may want to add more custom G-code commands. For example, many RepRap electronics now have a *sounder* onboard that can play beeps and alerts. You can control it by specifying (at the start G-code) three short beeps at the start of a print; you may want to specify a long and loud beep to signal the end of the print at the end G-code. Many other operations can also be controlled with G-code, such as turning fans on at the end of the print to cool down the printed object and build bed. Another option, in the Expert mode of Slic3r, allows you to trigger a digital camera to take an image after every layer is printed, which can provide a stop-motion high-speed video of your object growing as it prints.

5. **On the Plater tab, click the Export G-code button.**

Depending on the complexity of the objects being printed, the performance of your computer, and how fine the layers you selected are, exporting the G-code file can take a few seconds, many minutes, or (in extreme cases) hours. Things take time; complex things take more time.

When you've finished your tweaks, provided no warnings were displayed, your G-code should be ready for your printer. Before you print, however, make sure the 3D printer is calibrated. That's what we look at next, starting with the all-important firmware setup.

Calibrating Your 3D Printer

With our firmware set up and the RepRap printer's mechanical movement mostly calibrated, final preparation for 3D printing encompasses these procedures:

✔ Final calibration of the extruder and hot-end

✔ Entering these details into the firmware

✔ Compiling and downloading the firmware once more

Don't be tempted to skip this next section. Correct calibration of the extruder and hot-end makes all the difference between an awful-looking print and a stunningly good one.

For this next section, we run Pronterface. You can also run other host programs we've discussed, but we chose Pronterface for this initial setup because it's easy to use. (See Figure 15-16.) Pronterface was designed and programmed by Kliment Yanev as an open-source control interface for RepRap 3D printers; you can obtain the full package (called Printrun) from Github here:

`https://github.com/kliment/Printrun`

As with Marlin from Github, you can download by clicking Download Zip on the right side of the Github page.

Figure 15-16: Pronterface running and connected to our RepRap printer with G-code loaded ready to print.

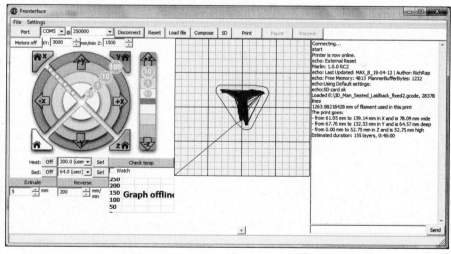

Unlike 2D paper printers that simply appear in all applications as a "printer," most 3D printers require a host program to prepare, control, and send the specific G-code file. Thus, at this point, we can't just turn on the machine and hit Print. You need to do a little more with a 3D printer. Here are the steps you take in Pronterface:

1. **Power the 3D printer on and connect it via USB.**

2. **Select the communication port from the list.**

3. **Make sure you have the correct speed selected.**

   This speed is normally 250,000 for Marlin firmware.

4. **Click Connect.**

   If the communication port and speed are set, you see a sign-on message in the right-side window. This signals that you have control of the printer and it's ready to accept commands.

Leveling your print-bed

The first order of business here is to make sure your hot-end nozzle is a set distance away from the print surface and that your printing surface is flat and level.

This overall procedure is described in many RepRap resources, and varies from one 3D printer to the next. Usually it involves tightening up or slackening three or four specific points on your build-bed, usually one made of PCB material and either fixed or held by spring bolts that allow the user to level the bed.

Before you start to level the bed, make sure that the other major assemblies of your 3D printer, especially the moving X carriage and vertical Z movement, are also level and at equal distance on each side.

The main sensor used to position the hot-end correctly away from the build-bed is the *Z-axis end-stop*. This is usually a mechanical switch that can be moved up and down or a magnetic sensor that can be tuned to a set distance by turning a small rotary knob known as a *potentiometer*. It's common for a small LED to light up as an indicator when the end-stop position has been reached. If your axis doesn't stop, or if the LED doesn't light when the axis is sent to the home position, you may have an incorrect orientation set in your firmware (as discussed in Chapter 13). In such a case, change the X_ENDSTOP_INVERTING = true setting to false in your configuration.h file of the Marlin firmware.

If you use a heated-bed, be sure it's powered on and at full temperature for a few minutes (to allow everything to expand to where it will be when printing) before you set the mechanical distance of the hot-end nozzle from the bed.

Check the operation of the end-stop switches by commanding each axis in turn to the home position. (See Figure 15-17 for the controls in Pronterface.) Then you can set the Z-axis distance so the hot-end nozzle is spaced appropriately far from the bed. The best way to do so is to move the print head to the center of the bed. On a standard RepRap, you set this space by moving X by 100mm and Y by 100mm.

Figure 15-17: You can use Pronterface controls to position the print head for leveling the bed, setting the correct distance for the hot-end nozzle and pre-heating before printing.

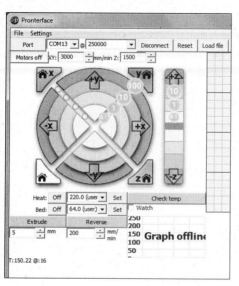

The distance you need to achieve will depend somewhat on the nozzle size and on how well you've managed to level the build-bed surface. Partly for this reason, a sheet of glass (which tends to be reasonably flat) is a good choice for the build surface. As a starting point, make sure you can just slide a single sheet of office paper under the nozzle when it's at the Z home position. Check this gap for uniformity at all four corners and in the center. Use the Z-movement buttons in Pronterface to lift and lower the nozzle. You can then move the position of your Z end-stop on the Z axis to activate at the correct distance away from the print-bed (use the office paper as a spacer). When you home the Z axis in Pronterface by clicking the Z Home button (see Figure 15-17), the nozzle should raise and then lower until the Z end-stop is triggered. If the spacing is still not correct, move the Z end-stop slightly and press the Home button again.

Tuning your hot-end temperature control

The next stage of setup is to calibrate the temperature-control requirements of your specific hot-end. For this procedure, you have to enter the command M303 into the bottom-right corner of the Pronterface screen and then click Send. (See Figure 15-18.) This command has the printer perform a number of heating and cooling cycles; at the end of these cycles, it gives you the settings you need to enter into the firmware (as discussed in Chapter 13) for DEFAULT_Kp, DEFAULT_Ki, and DEFAULT_Kd in configuration.h.

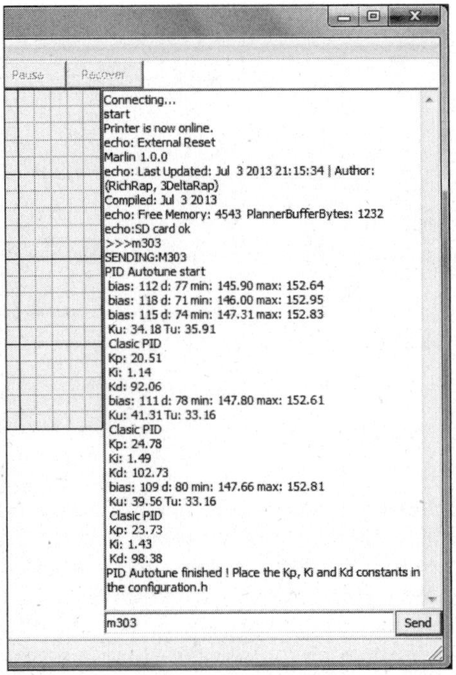

Figure 15-18:
The G-code command M303 runs an auto-tune routine that calculates the ideal control loop settings for your firmware.

```
Pause      Recover

Connecting...
start
Printer is now online.
echo: External Reset
Marlin 1.0.0
echo: Last Updated: Jul  3 2013 21:15:34 | Author:
(RichRap, 3DeltaRap)
Compiled: Jul  3 2013
echo: Free Memory: 4543 PlannerBufferBytes: 1232
echo:SD card ok
>>>m303
SENDING:M303
PID Autotune start
bias: 112 d: 77 min: 145.90 max: 152.64
bias: 118 d: 71 min: 146.00 max: 152.95
bias: 115 d: 74 min: 147.31 max: 152.83
Ku: 34.18 Tu: 35.91
Clasic PID
Kp: 20.51
Ki: 1.14
Kd: 92.06
bias: 111 d: 78 min: 147.80 max: 152.61
Ku: 41.31 Tu: 33.16
Clasic PID
Kp: 24.78
Ki: 1.49
Kd: 102.73
bias: 109 d: 80 min: 147.66 max: 152.81
Ku: 39.56 Tu: 33.16
Clasic PID
Kp: 23.73
Ki: 1.43
Kd: 98.38
PID Autotune finished ! Place the Kp, Ki and Kd constants in
the configuration.h

m303                                    Send
```

Write down the values displayed for Kp, Ki, and Kd. You'll enter these into the firmware after you complete the final stage of calibration.

Extruder distance calibration

Before you can calculate the last value, you need to ensure that the correct amount of plastic is extruded for a set extruder distance, perform a simple test extrusion, measure the results, and calculate the change. Don't worry — it's not difficult. We take you through it step by step.

This extruder calibration is really important. It ensures that the firmware knows exactly how much material is being deposited, and that Slic3r can rely on your machine for accurate calculations when producing the G-code to print objects.

We discuss the key firmware settings in Chapter 13. Pay particular attention to the fourth number in the DEFAULT_AXIS_STEPS_PER_UNIT list; it specifies how many steps the extruder motor uses to feed 1mm of filament into the hot-end.

You can extrude and reverse the extruder, but only when it's up to temperature. This manual control is essential for loading and removing filament, and for purging any old material. In Pronterface, you can command the extruder to extrude or reverse the stepper motor a set distance (specified in millimeters, as shown in the bottom-left corner. (See Figure 15-19.)

Figure 15-19:
Controlling the extruder in Pronterface.

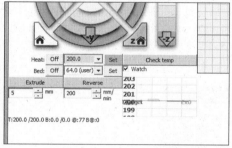

Calibrating your extruder ensures that the extruder axis moves exactly the number of steps per unit (unit being 1mm) and exactly the distance you specify in Pronterface. This way, when the G-code produced by Slic3r commands a 2mm extrusion you can be sure the correct amount of material will be deposited. Calculate the correct value by following these steps:

1. **Heat up your extruder to the temperature of the material you're going to use. (200 degrees C for PLA and 240 degrees C for ABS.)**

   No need to heat your heated-bed for this calibration.

2. **When the hot-end is at temperature, insert the filament.**

   Pushing down and using the Extrude button in Pronterface about 5mm at a time should grip and drive the filament into your extruder.

   At this point, if you notice the extruder stalling or spinning around and attempting to drive what looks like a lot more than 5mm you may need to simply lower the number in the firmware just so you can calibrate more accurately.

Depending on the type of extruder, the type of gearing it has, the electronics that were selected for it, and the way the micro-step value was set, the steps-per-unit value should be somewhere between 50 and 1100. If you're using 200-step-per-revolution motors with 16x micro-stepping, one rotation would be set at 3200 steps. One full rotation usually drives a significant amount of filament into your extruder, so if you don't have any other advice about your extruder, try using a number around 200 for the first test.

3. **Mark the filament: Wrap a strip of tape or a sticker to the incoming filament at a distance of about 50mm from the extruder's filament-entry hole.**

4. **Measure the exact distance between the mark you've just made and the extruder body before and after extruding 20mm of filament. Write this number down.**

   As a working example, say it was 48mm between the mark and the extruder body. The best way to measure this is with a digital micrometer, another very good tool for 3D printing. (See Figure 15-20.) A digital micrometer can help you in many ways, including (a) checking whether your printed parts come out as they were designed and (b) in measuring the filament diameter of different coils for setting in Slic3r.

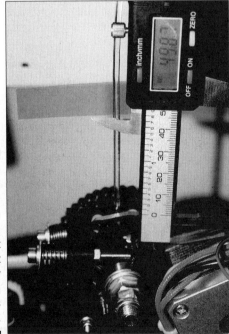

Figure 15-20:
Use a digital micrometer to measure the distance the input filament actually moves when 20mm is extruded.

5. **Extrude 20mm of plastic filament in 5mm steps, with a delay of a few seconds between steps.**

   The delay is to ensure that you don't extrude too fast; it reduces the risk of the motor skipping.

   You should have had a smooth motion of filament driven down into your hot-end and extruded out.

6. **Measure the new distance of the gap between the mark and the extruder as you did before.**

   If your extruder was ideally calibrated, the new remaining distance (in this instance) would be 28mm; we drove the extruder in Pronterface for 20mm. Chances are, however, that this new gap size is either bigger or smaller than the 28mm we wanted. For our working example, then, say that we actually measured 32mm, meaning that the extruder actually drove the filament only a distance of 16mm instead of the 20mm we expected.

7. **Calculate the steps-per-unit value.**

   We now use the existing number of extruder steps per unit in our firmware (which we set to 200 in Step 2), and the distance extruded, which in this case was 20mm, to calculate the number of motor steps your firmware just moved. Because 200 x 20 = 4,000, this is the number of motor steps your firmware moved for the 20mm of extruder motion we set. Since we achieved only 16mm of movement, however, we can calculate our actual steps-per-unit value by dividing that 4,000 by 16 to get 250.

   The same calculation can be made if you found the number was higher than 20. The result will just be lower than the 200 steps we first tested.

8. **Enter the new steps-per-unit value in the firmware.**

   If we enter the change in the extruder's steps-per-unit value in our firmware from 200 to 250, we achieve the 20mm of movement we requested the next time we perform this operation.

After updating your firmware with these changes, you're ready to print your first 3D object.

Be sure you routinely check to ensure that your 3D printer hasn't been knocked out of alignment and that your hot-end is still a suitable distance away from the build-bed before you print. Fortunately, you don't need to calibrate the temperature of your hot-end and do extruder calibration every time you print; you've entered these values into your firmware, and such settings don't require constant adjustment.

3D-Printing Objects

Now you're ready for your first 3D print. This is an exciting moment, but don't get overly ambitious for this first object. Instead of jumping in with a complex object at this stage, try printing something easier — like a simple cube. You can print cubes to test all sorts of things, including materials and settings; they're a great way to check things out. They don't take too long to print and can show you how settings such as Infill and Solid Layers change the way an object looks.

You can download a simple 20mm cube (20mm x 20mm and 10mm high) from www.thingiverse.com/download:17279.

To print it, just follow these steps:

1. **Load your cube object into Slic3r. Select an Infill of 20% and 3 solid top and bottom layers.**

2. **Export the G-code and then load that G-code into Pronterface.**

   Pronterface shows the object loaded in the middle of the virtual print-bed. You can click the object and scroll through the various layers. Above you can see the base layer with a ring around it. This ring is not part of the object being printed; it's added by Slic3r as the first part to be printed, which primes the plastic flow of the extruder before the object starts to print. The middle sections show the hexagonal infill and (finally) the solid top surfaces. (See Figure 15-21.) You're now ready to print your first object.

3. **Set your print-bed and hot-end to the required temperatures for the material you're printing and allow the printer to reach temperature.**

   This is always a good idea, but if you forget to do this, the G-code will do it for you.

4. **Manually extrude some material.**

   This is done to check that everything is working correctly and to home the printer axis.

5. **When you're at print temperature, press Print.**

   After a slight delay while the G-code checks and stabilizes the temperatures the print head moves to the middle and starts printing your cube, usually with a border outline to start the flow of plastic. While the first border is being extruded, look to see whether the plastic is sticking; make sure that the print head is not scraping across the surface and is not too far away.

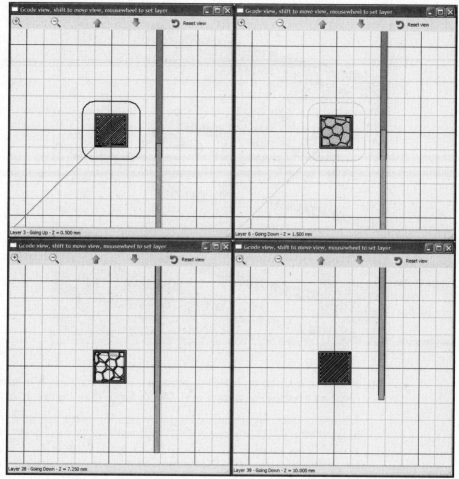

Figure 15-21: Pronterface shows your cube loaded in the middle of the virtual print-bed.

One of the trickiest settings is the correct distance of hot-end nozzle over the print-bed. Figure 15-22 shows an example of a well-bonded first layer. Here the printer has completed two perimeters. Note the slight ridge; the infill will look solid and have similar ridges. For the first layer, you shouldn't see any gaps between the individual extruded lines.

If you're not seeing a good bond of the plastic, stop the print and adjust your nozzle head a fraction closer. If material doesn't escape and you see the flow stop and start or if you're seeing a lot of material squashed out (leaving very high ridges) and the nozzle being dragged through the plastic, the extruder is a little too close. Move the nozzle head away from the build bed.

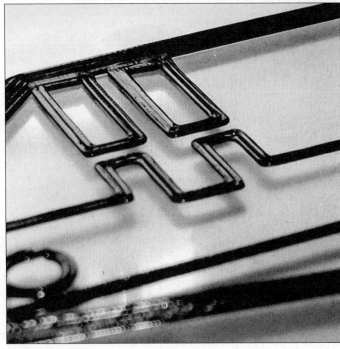

Figure 15-22:
A well-bonded first layer.

6. **When your cube is finished, measure it and confirm it measures as close as possible to 20mm and 10mm high. (See Figure 15-23.)**

If it has printed significantly larger or smaller — for example, if it measures 40mm — the number of DEFAULT_AXIS_STEPS_PER_UNIT is probably set incorrectly for the Z and Y axes. Work out the new value by performing the same calculation we did for the extruder. For this to be useful, be sure you mark and remember the orientation of the cube when it's printed:

- The distance from front to back of the cube on the build-plate is the Y measurement.

- The distance from left to right is the X axis.

New users most often find that the Z axis is more likely to be set incorrectly. That's because many RepRap 3D printers use similar belt-and-pulley drives for X and Y, but different machines may use quite a range of threaded rods, belts, or lead-screws for the Z-axis motion.

7. **Check that your cube corners are nice 90-degree right angles.**

If they aren't, then check to make sure your X-axis carriage is aligned straight across the moving Y axis.

Figure 15-23:
Make
sure your
printed cube
measures
correctly.

You should now be able to print more objects and start exploring the capabilities of your 3D printer. It takes time to learn the different speeds, temperatures, and settings required for printing different objects. The best way is by experimentation; many factors influence different 3D printers in various ways.

The next few sections describe a few tricks and tips, along with Slic3r settings, to think about for various common types of 3D-model printing.

Printing vases, pots, and cups

Many models are designed to be printed as hollow. (See Figure 15-24.) Such models are sealed at both ends, and usually have surface detail, patterns, or other designs on the outside surface. They look solid but are intended to be printed as a single-wall-outline pot or vase. Such designs often give the best surface quality, but can only be used for single-walled objects.

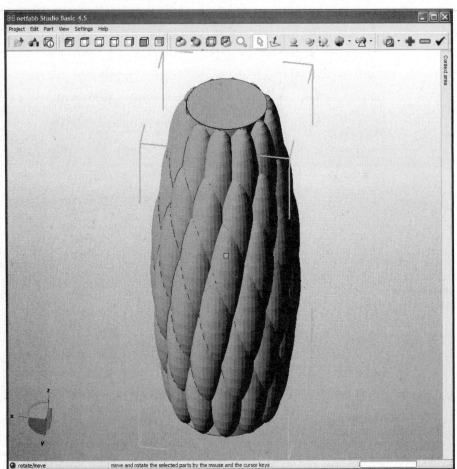

Figure 15-24:
A hollow-pot
design.

Slic3r has a specific setting for cylindrical versions of such objects; it also allows for almost continuous printing without any extruder retractions or machine moves. This setting is called *Spiral Vase*. (See Figure 15-25.) You need to access the Expert mode on Slic3r and select the Spiral Vase mode. You can then still select the layer height, and number of solid bottom layers. Slic3r will automatically remove the top layers for you, so you end up with a single-wall outline of the object and a solid base.

What's even more impressive with this sort of printing is that after the solid base layers are printed, the single wall outline is one single extrusion, usually just spiraling around while the Z axis moves ever so slightly up as the print head rotates around and around. All this movement can make printing

Figure 15-25:
The hollow-pot 3D model printed as a Spiral Vase, where the vertical Z axis never stops being slowly raised, resulting in a seamless print.

much quicker, with no visible seam on the printed object because the extruder flow is not stopped for a change of layer height, as would happen normally.

Using a bigger nozzle size is ideal for single-walled objects being printed with the Spiral Vase setting. You can still select fine layers, and the wider nozzle provides a thicker single wall, giving your printed object more strength.

Printing large single-piece objects

Printing certain objects — especially large single parts — can be tricky; the edges of a big part often curl up while it prints. Some parts are more likely to suffer from this problem than others. If you're printing parts larger than 100mm, even when using PLA on a heated-bed (which doesn't allow much warping), you may still get some issues. But using ABS for big parts will certainly challenge most home 3D printers. Fortunately, Slic3r has a trick that addresses this problem and you may find it useful for all sorts of parts.

The Brim option provides a horizontal ring of extending perimeters on the first layer of an object. This option can be highly useful if the object you're printing is sticking to the base of your build-platform, or if an object's corners start to warp up during a print.

The Brim option was invented mainly to help big objects stick to the build-plate during an extended print. It can also be helpful, however, even essential, if you're printing tiny objects that don't have a lot of surface area in the first layer: The printed brim will peel away from a finished object with minimal cleanup required.

Printing tiny or highly detailed objects

If you can choose to print tiny objects, consider printing many of them together. This approach allows a layer to print while each part layer is printed; by the time it gets around to the first part again, the plastic will have cooled enough for the next layer. This technique has one downside: You may not want more than one of the same part, and you may also start seeing tiny defects on the outside surface of an object where the head is moving between the parts. These visual flaws may not be a problem for functional parts but if they're models or intended for display, you'll probably require the best possible appearance.

To address this speed problem, you could just slow down the entire print speed, but there's a better option: Define a minimum print time per layer in Slic3r. In Expert mode, choose Filament Settings and Cooling ⇨ Enable Auto Cooling. You'll probably find that this is a good setting to keep enabled all the time. Read on to find out why.

When we define a minimum layer time, Slic3r knows that it has to automatically calculate and slow down any layer to this set speed. The result is that tiny objects automatically print slowly, and bigger parts automatically take longer than the minimum layer time and so will not be slowed down. Thus the Auto Cooling setting gives you the best overall print speed and quality.

That's really important with some objects; a pyramid is a good example: It starts off with big layers at the base, and you can print quickly as the layers get smaller (and so quicker to print) toward the top. If you don't set a minimum layer time, the pyramid still looks great *until* the print reaches the top, where it's ruined by the very fast printing of tiny layers — which usually results in a blob of plastic instead of a defined, sharp peak. When you set a layer time of around 15 seconds, the print automatically slows down as it gets closer to the top, and the model prints well.

It's possible to print objects very quickly without using the slowing-down method just described, but it takes some time to discern just when this technique is appropriate. The general way to achieve this result is to use a directional fan to force-cool the layers immediately after they print — but this trick is usually only recommended for materials such PLA and non-heated printbeds (using a mechanical bond to tape rather than a heat bond).

Printing many objects at once

As you get more confident with 3D printing, you'll want to set up a plate of parts and print them all at once. Normally this approach doesn't cause any particular problems but it's worth using the nozzle-lift function we discussed earlier. Raising the print nozzle just a fraction before a travel move is a good idea when you have a lot of parts on a build surface; it can reduce the chance of accidently knocking off a part or making the print carriage shift out of alignment.

With some objects and 3D printers, you may find that rotating a part by 45 degrees on the platform makes it easier to print, may reduce warping, and can minimize the possibility of travel moves hitting corners or the edges of parts. If a print fails or has problems, consider this simple rotation or reposition the object on the bed before changing other settings.

Improving print quality

As a general rule, slowing down the print speed usually helps improve overall print quality. A fast travel speed can affect print quality; the print head gets to a new point quickly, and the high acceleration and deceleration sometimes cause unwanted shadows and artifacts on the print. Experiment with machine travel speed before changing other settings.

Temperature plays an important role in print quality; it's especially linked to print speed and layer height. As a general rule, if you start to slow down your printing speed below 20mm/sec, it's also a good idea to reduce your printing temperature.

You may decide to print more slowly for a variety of reasons, for example when printing a single small object or a part that's proved tricky to print in the past. Most thermoplastic materials can print perfectly well at many tens of degrees lower than you'd normally print. Reducing the temperature also helps stop the self-oozing of hot plastic from the extruder nozzle. Such a reduction in self-oozing can make a really big difference in the print quality of fine parts being printed slowly; you have more control over the plastic being extruded. Such an approach usually also lowers pressure in the extruder nozzle, which further improves final print quality.

If you find you're getting more print failures when printing plates of multiple parts, it's often a sign that you probably have a small mechanical-alignment problem. Check your belts to see whether they're tight enough. Also check carriage speed; if you're moving the carriage around too fast for the frame design of your 3D printer, try slowing it down. If that doesn't help, consider tweaking another Expert setting in Slic3r: Avoid Crossing Perimeters. Once set, this option tries always to move the print head around the outside of a printed layer instead of moving across the part to reach the other side of the build-bed or other object. The setting does extend the time taken to print out an object, but it can also improve the quality and reliability of the print.

PLA will print at temperatures as low as about 160 degrees Centigrade when you're printing parts slowly. Doing so can produce less oozing and finer detail for smaller parts. You can still use a fan to force-cool the plastic layers, even at such lower temperatures.

This concludes our journey into home 3D printing. We hope you decide to try it out for yourself and even build up a RepRap 3D printer of your own.

Part VI
The Part of Tens

Check out another list of ten online at www.dummies.com/
extras/3dprinting.

In this part...

- ✓ Check out ten examples of additive manufacturing and personalization.
- ✓ See ten ways additive manufacturing may disrupt the traditional manufacturing economy.
- ✓ Take a look at ten 3D-printed designs that would be impossible to fabricate using traditional manufacturing techniques.
- ✓ Take ideas from these concepts to use in your own 3D printing projects!

Chapter 16

Ten Ways That Rapid Prototyping Will Disrupt Traditional Manufacturing

. . . .

Major transitions rarely happen without stress. Additive manufacturing offers exciting new capabilities, but it also abbreviates the production process that underlies modern mass manufacturing — creating new opportunities as it threatens others. Early adopters of these technologies are already making key discoveries — using them for rapid prototyping, direct-digital manufacturing, and highly personalized short production runs. Some such runs are so short that they produce only a single item — such as a medical implant custom-fit to the consumer — without the need for the fundamental tooling that would make traditional manufacturing equivalents cost-prohibitive. Retooling to produce (say) a single custom component would be very expensive, or perhaps even beyond the capability of existing custom manufacturers and craftspersons.

Such advantages allow 3D printing to offer many new potential opportunities in additive manufacturing — but the more this technology catches on, the greater its potential to disrupt aspects of the traditional manufacturing cycle. This chapter discusses ten ways additive manufacturing may upset this cycle.

Reducing Time to Market

Additive manufacturing equipment can be used on-site, allowing design upgrades to be conducted in a far shorter time frame between initial measurements and final implementation of product designs. Today, a new design can be described in a planning session, prototyped for testing the same day, and then transmitted electronically for production fabrication. Updates in the middle of production runs can be made as simply as uploading a new corrected 3D model to the fabrication systems — without the need for changes to custom tooling, even when complex internal geometries and voids are present in the final product. This greatly reduces the time it takes to bring a product to market, reducing the demand for machine operators, tooling fabricators, or skilled tradespersons specializing in the creation and production of material goods.

Eliminating Mass Manufacturing

New product rollouts can be performed globally, using a standard model electronically transmitted to production facilities in close proximity to the intended consumers. No need to design products in one country, have individual components assembled in other countries, and then ship the final assembly to the end consumer somewhere else. Additive manufacturing allows the direct production of increasingly complex end products; eventually it may eliminate the need to produce components in low-wage economies that have fewer safety mandates for factory environments. This will allow even complex production to be performed locally, which threatens economies that depend upon mass-manufacturing practices currently used in the global market.

Displacing Transportation Industries

Current production of goods relies on long production cycles, with items distributed globally using large cargo vessels that burn fossil fuels and inevitably risk ecological damage from exhaust byproducts or toxic spills in the course of their operation. The products shipped around the world by these massive cargo ships are transferred to ground distribution through huge ports. Long supply chains have always been vulnerable to attack and abuse; these days hackers and other opportunists regularly compromise shipping automation to pass illegal materials amidst legitimate goods. Bulk items are shipped by trucks to warehouses in each region, according to regional or seasonal demand, and there the products are stored until needed in stores. Ultimately, the items are shipped again via truck to the final store where customers can purchase and pick up their goods. Consider the inefficiency of such a system.

As more complex products can be fabricated using additive manufacturing, consumers will be able to go online to a local fabricator's website, order their products with customizations applied, and then pick up their items on the way home from work. There will be no need for mass goods shipment, transportation, storage, and multi-level distribution — with the attendant pollution, fossil-fuel consumption, and cost associated with traditional manufacturing. By reducing the volume of material passing through ports and international gateways to the basics — for example, raw materials only for the fabrication centers — transactions of contraband materials will be easier to identify and thwart in this new economy.

Consuming Alternate Materials

Additive manufacturing allows the use of materials other than those currently used in traditional mass manufacturing. Thermoplastics and hybrid materials can be combined in granular form for laser sintering. Polymer bindings can enable the fabrication of materials with complex new structures that vary in material qualities throughout its volume, depending on what's needed (whether rigidity, flexibility, or variations in color). If this process proves economically viable, many industries that currently supply raw material to the traditional fabrication process may have to change to supplying new materials if their former product lines are no longer in demand. A 3D-printed house, for example, might not need wood products, gypsum wallboard, fiberglass insulation, or asphalt roofing tiles, using instead custom mixtures of concrete, Styrofoam granules, and other materials in their place.

Reducing Material Requirements

While some raw materials will remain the same, because (for example) a metal hammer is simply more durable than a plastic hammer, additive manufacturing allows the fabrication of objects that include structural voids and other material reductions — while retaining the same strength in use as their cast or milled solid equivalents. Like birds' bones, materials produced by new additive manufacturing techniques allow for a solid outer shell filled with a porous inner structural material that can allow coolant (or simply air) to fill the remaining voids, reducing the total amount of metal needed to fabricate the same engine block or tool head.

Going Green

The porous internal structure will not only require less material to manufacture, but also reduce weight in the final product. Vehicles made using these structures will need less fuel to perform the same task, reducing their operational environmental impact more than simple reductions in fuel requirements. The key to this improvement is the abbreviation of the transportation cycle. Changes in material requirements also allow the use of environmentally friendly materials such as plant-based PLA plastic in place of traditional fossil-fuel-based polymers, provided the trade-off between environmental cost and structural qualities is favorable. Materials such as concrete used in building construction can be recovered and recombined to allow recycling of structural members in construction — to a degree not possible when a house consists of complex assemblies of wood, glass, and other materials. Even materials such as sand and other local resources — why not lunar regolith? — may soon be formed into structures using little more than solar energy to convert the raw local resources into useful final products. As this practice gains momentum, it will disrupt trades such as carpentry and roofing, as well as the industries that supply the raw materials for traditional construction — mining for gypsum, sawmills for structural wood and fiberboard, asphalt and tar producers for shingles and roofing materials, even brickmakers and bricklaying tradespersons.

Curtailing Planned Obsolescence

The ability to print new parts even for old equipment and outdated designs allows the continued re-use of existing items without need for full fabrication of a replacement object. The ability to fully fabricate copies of existing intellectual property once they have fallen out of patent protection also means that if you truly love your old 1960s Shelby Mustang, there is no reason you cannot keep it running — or even replace it completely when the original one wears out. Current production depends on the cycle of planned obsolescence that forces people to replace old items when they wear out, because repairs become increasingly difficult and more costly as spare parts for old designs become scarce. From musical instruments to old cars, replacement parts are already being fabricated using 3D printers to produce plastic, wood amalgams, and even metal parts — in some cases, more durable than the original parts used in original designs. This will impact existing industries that depend on the resale of outdated capital goods and parts for them, as well as industries that depend on the replacement of existing equipment once the items wear out as planned.

Eliminating One-Size-Fits-Most

Mass manufacturing, as presently done, is clearly evident in any crowd of people waiting in line or sitting in a class. The omnipresent white ear-buds of the latest i-Whatever products dangle from half the ears present, and discussions of the relative qualities of the latest gold-versus-white cases, relative qualities of Android-versus-IOSx, or the newest tablet form factor can occur spontaneously between total strangers. This buzz grows out of the cycle of planned obsolescence, coupled with the drive to have the newest model in the never-ending race to "keep up with the Joneses." As a result, traditional mass-manufacturing is content to produce and sell millions of identical units when the latest product update becomes available.

Personalization of individual items is already being provided through 3D-printed cases and stands to hold these standard designs of (say) this year's model phone or tablet. As the technology improves, soon the phone itself may be fashioned entirely with 3D printing, or as a wrapper for the basic electronic "guts" of the phone, tweaked to express the unique preferences of each individual owner. Obviously, this type of personalization is necessary in critical applications such as medical implants (see Figure 16-1) and prosthetics, but it's also becoming possible for nearly any type of product through additive manufacturing. Want your car to look like your school's mascot or your guesthouse to model the latest A-list actor's face? Just use 3D-modelling software to capture the design and print it out in a personalized fabrication perfectly fit to your body proportions and preferences (assuming you properly license that design, of course). Additive manufacturing could have created Bilbo Baggins' hobbit-hole with a room just suited to Gandalf's taller frame, if 3D construction printers had existed in the world of *The Lord of the Rings*. The potential disruption in planning for mass upgrades and marketing for the new year's model will probably take on a new focus: providing a continuous stream of personalization. You'll be encouraged to upgrade or replace your existing items to suit the holiday, season of the year, region you live in, or even just to fit your hand while you wear a bandage and finger splint from the unfortunate bowling accident over the weekend.

Figure 16-1:
A tiny implant-able stent designed to perfectly fit the recipient's blood vessel size and curvature.

Image courtesy of NanoScribe

Crafting What You Wish

In addition to simple personalization, many are taking the potential of 3D printing and applying it to new creations and designs entirely of their own creation. Where the personal color printer replaced the scribe, typesetter, press operator, and illuminator of past book creations, today the home 3D printer allows a single individual to create original holiday decorations, party favors, or even robots without needing a detailed understanding of casting, injection molding, or the other workshop skills traditionally necessary for these tasks. Many tools exist online that can take a crude drawing or sketch and convert it into a design that can be fabricated in plastic at home — or in metals and ceramics online — with little more than a few clicks of the mouse. Creativity is the sole limiting factor today. Even now, many components can be handled through automation — say, to allow a couple to create custom gold wedding bands with the names of the affianced inscribed on each band, without having to speak to a custom goldsmith (or even to a salesperson at the local jewelry store). These tools place the capability to create dreams into the hands of the populace, displacing the traditional trades and businesses that provided services in the traditional world, replacing those relationships with services that transform electronic designs into solid objects. The object can be a custom wedding ring or a cake-topper that presents likenesses of the couple's faces in full color — garbed as bride and groom, Imperial Stormtroopers, or mythical creatures, with equal ease.

Providing Basic Necessities

Beyond 3D-printed cake-toppers at a wedding, new designs are being tested that eventually will print out the cake as well. Research into food preservation is moving past canning and pickling and into the realm of science fiction. Powders and pastes can be combined and prepared in a few minutes to provide nutritional and attractive meals created from materials that can be stored years ahead of time. Research in bioprinters is exploring not only how to create new body parts as we age or get injured, but also how to directly fabricate animal muscle tissue in a form suitable for the grill. From 3D-printed steaks that do not require the factory farming of animals to 3D-printed pizzas that come out of the printer ready to share with your kids, all that's needed is sufficient development of edible materials and suitable printers. We are entering a time when we may see the displacement of many traditional businesses involved with food production, storage, and preparation.

Speaking of muscle and other tissues, the capability to print out new body components — and even augment what nature has provided — may also create wholly-new businesses. We might check into a clinic on our way home and have those fashionable new cheekbones installed, or have a personalized pharmacopeia fabricate entire courses of treatment for our bodies' needs. We'll still need the raw materials, of course, but industries that currently exist to provide for basic bodily needs — or market products meant to improve our bodies or health — will surely see a change in the years ahead.

Chapter 17

Ten Examples of Direct-Digital Manufacturing and Personalization

● ●

*A*dditive manufacturing is not a futuristic technology; it's already in place and in use across many industries from medical implants to aerospace technologies. Originally created for rapid prototyping, additive manufacturing has steadily migrated into direct digital fabrication of consumer products and goods. As material options expand and complexity of 3D-printed objects increases to include integrated electronics and enhanced structural designs, a broader spectrum of products can be manufactured directly from electronic files and raw source materials. This chapter discusses ten examples of this sort of direct-digital manufacturing.

Producing 3D-Printed Food

Cornell University and other research sites are exploring 3D-printed foods such as vegetable wafers and meat pastes. Under a NASA grant, a small company in Austin, Texas is currently working on a 3D printer using materials from long-storage powders, suspended oils, and water to create 3D-printed pizzas that will cook to completion on the heated build plate of the food printer. Future astronauts will depend on such systems to prepare their food during long-term travel to the moon, Mars, and beyond. Other researchers are testing the use of lab-grown meat cells to create 3D-printable hamburgers and steaks that don't require the raising and feeding of entire animals. If successful, this development would provide travelers and explorers with some practical, portable supplies and allow sufficient protein consumption even in the absence of farm facilities or open land. Cornell's students already print out custom cakes and finger-foods using a growing array of food options.

Printing Tissues and Organs

Beyond the simple biological materials needed to 3D-print muscle tissues and foodstuffs, additive manufacturing bioprinters are being developed with the capacity to create complex multi-cellular matrices that can grow into functional organs and replacement tissues for human recipients. One benefit of these designs is that they can make use of a recipient's own cells, producing implantable replacements that don't require a lifetime regimen of immuno-suppressive medications to prevent transplant rejection. The current state of the art allows the creation of simple organs — for example, frameworks into which bladder cells can grow — but the first examples of complex critical organs such as multi-cellular livers are currently under test. Small 3D-printed organs of different types are currently being used to test new pharmaceuticals and medical treatment protocols outside living bodies.

Fashioning Biological Replicas

Until such time as bioprinters can create replacement living tissues, 3D printing still has a promising medical role: It allows the fabrication of prosthetics and implants perfectly matched to the original body part (or mirrored from functional body parts) to provide individualized replacements. Gone are the days of the crude wooden "peg leg" or articulated "hook" for missing limbs. The prosthetic can be transformed through 3D printing into not only a functional replacement, but also a work of art, one that accurately reflects the wearer's personality. The current state of the art cannot yet replace missing limbs with fully functional bioprinted replacements, but the non-biological alternatives now possible can result in implants capable of growing into existing biological structures — already an improvement on the past.

Crafting Clothing and Footwear

Looking beyond the bounds of our bodies, 3D printing allows the creation of textiles and other body adornment. One such product would be custom-fit athletic wear capable of giving the athlete better traction and reduced weight; another would be stylish full-body coverings uniquely tailored to each wearer's body measurements (see Figure 17-1). Then, even if two people were to "wear the same dress to the ball," the "same dress" would appear as two different creations suited to each wearer individually. The potential for custom-manufactured (rather than simply custom-tailored) garments has cropped up in fictional works, but today it is en route to becoming a reality — using materials, colors, and designs entirely selected by the wearer and designed to suit mood, desire, or occasion. Branding can go well beyond stitched alligators on the lapel of a shirt to include trademarks (or marketing messages) in every aspect of the design — or embedded solely within the garment's solid components to mark an original design in a way that would not be easily duplicated without a copy of the original design file, in copies matching only the outward makeup of the original. With photogrammetry making duplication across town possible almost before the fashion model steps off the runway, internal patterns of voids can help to protect a designer's intellectual property.

Figure 17-1:
A precise fit was possible for Dita's gown by mapping the design to her body's unique measurements.

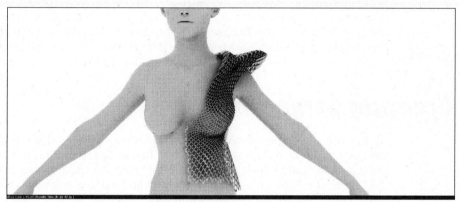

Image courtesy of the Francis Bitonti Studio (Designer: Michael Schmidt, Architect: Francis Bitonti)

Customizing Artwork

One of the earliest uses of small 3D-printed items was in the creation of customized plastic earrings and pendants. Today this has grown to include magnificent creations that capture the beauty of math in solid form, using precious metals that can be worn to suit the preferences of a wearer or the requirements of the designer. Even plastic components are being used to fashion dioramas of entire rooms in full scale, and to build massive works of art representing the participation and preferences of individual artists in crowd-crafted consolidated fabrications. From small fashion assets worn as jewelry to designs applied to furniture and displayed for public viewing, 3D-printed artwork is already creating entirely new cottage industries for designers who would not previously have been able to transform their dreams into solid form.

Making Hollywood Spectacular

Model makers have long created sets and props for movie productions, but the potential of 3D printing has made it possible to personally fit a costume to an individual actor. An example is Tony Stark's magnificent Iron Man costume, created to fit actor Robert Downey, Jr.'s exact dimensions— through the magic of 3D printing. Similarly, when Hollywood wanted to blow up James Bond's classic 1964 Aston Martin DB5 from Sean Connery's time in the role (complete with the original BMT 216A license plate), the original car ($4.6 million USD) was spared; a 3D-printed replica stood in as the "stunt double." Even the outer costuming for actors and actresses can be fashioned of transparent materials — for example, armor wrought of bright, metal-seeming compounds without the weight of a true metal, or integrated illumination added to enhance the wonder. Use of these 3D-printed fanciful devices is only beginning.

Creating Structures

3D-printed artwork does not have to stop at simple artworks, but can now produce entire structures big enough to live in. Using natural raw materials such as sand and lunar regolith, this capability will enhance our ability to explore new worlds or to fashion habitats and satellites in space — using materials derived from asteroids and other sources already to be found abundantly in the solar system, rather than carrying materials from Earth at great cost. Eventually entire houses may be crafted in place, but right now concrete 3D-printed modules are already being used to repair denuded reefs and other damaged elements of our ecosystem. Researchers at the University of Washington and in Europe are already testing systems aimed at scaling up printers so they're capable of crafting entire buildings. Other artisans are reinventing how our furnishings, flatware, and even ceramic or glass designs can elevate the simplest elements of our homes into personalized works of art. Fans of the *Portal* video game series, for example, can easily craft a cup in the form of a Companion Cube design from the game. Headboard finials in wood composites — or larger objects such as end tables — could be similarly themed to create a custom living environment, using technologies that already exist today.

Reaching Beyond the Sky

Aerospace designs for high-performance turbines and jet-engine compressors can be crafted as single-print objects rather than traditional assemblies of smaller components. One advantage is that having to join components can create weaknesses and require finishing and tooling during assembly into their final form — but a 3D-printed object is already one piece. GE is already taking advantage of this capability, updating designs mid-process simply by changing the design file used to fabricate jet engine components. Looking even higher, NASA is currently testing 3D-printed rocket nozzles and other high-compression components needed to let our eager aircraft and spacecraft "slip the surly bonds of earth" as John Magee wrote in his poem "High Flight". As private industry begins to join with governments in the exploration of space, they will take along with them the capability to create what they need from the materials they discover during their travels.

Constructing Robots

Automation and robotics are transforming the world into a highly interactive and self-controlling environment. Factories once filled with hundreds of workers exposed to hazardous environments are now automated and managed (from positions of relative safety) by remote operators. The tools they use for these purposes are often custom-built designs, but 3D printers are making the same potential available to individual makers and designers who are learning about robotics or who are developing small-production runs of custom robotics suited to a particular purpose too narrow to draw commercial production of custom designs by large industries. Complex linkages and connections between components can be easily created using 3D printers to form one-off brackets and other elements fit to exactly the need of the moment, with new innovations being added and tested easily to enhance the capability of robots as new uses are identified.

Printing 3D Printers

Beyond basic robotics, 3D printers are now making it possible to fashion more 3D printers using basic robotic controls and linkages together with custom brackets and common off-the-shelf hardware. When fundamental patents on FDM/FFF thermoplastic extrusion expired in 2006, Dr. Adrian Bowyer's self-REPlicating RAPid prototyping (RepRap) system was released to the world as an open-source design — and a capability once only available in labs and high-end manufacturing facilities became a household appliance costing less than the first LaserJet printers. Today, RepRaps of dozens of different designs and their offspring are available in makerspaces, schools, and even office supply stores. Each of these can be used to print many of the components for another printer in turn, using open-source designs freely available online.

More possibilities wait for expression as additional fundamental patent controls expire over the coming decades. The original stereolithographic (SLA) technology has fallen out of patent protection and is being used in systems like the Form 1 — already in production for high-resolution printouts using photopolymers. Selective laser sintering (SLS) patents expire in 2014, potentially opening up new commercial and hobbyist-level innovations and making personal fabrication possible for plastics, metals, ceramics, and other granular-powder materials.

Sintering has additional requirements that are still slowing its wider adoption — for example, environmental controls, specialized gasses, and high-powered lasers that require special enclosures to protect their users. Granted, a sintering setup is presently more complex, elaborate, and costly than a FDM/FFF thermoplastic printer, but the community behind this exploration builds atop the growing Maker movement and the tremendous creativity of open-source designs present there.

Chapter 18

Ten Impossible Designs Created Using Additive Manufacturing

• •

*M*any of the designs made possible through additive manufacturing are "impossible" using traditional manufacturing technologies — or, if they're not outright impossible, they're at least so expensive or difficult to produce that they may as well be. This chapter discusses ten designs you can achieve only by using additive manufacturing.

Personalized Objects

When Kirk created small whistles to give away at his daughter's last birthday party, each whistle included the initials of the recipient. For two girls who showed up without RSVPs, he was able to print the last two whistles while party games were played outside. Details such as serial numbers or small spiders (see Figure 18-1) can simply be included in the design file so that each printed object is created with its own identity apart from all others like it.

Medical Implants

Unlike traditional implants — which use standard rods and other adjustable components — 3D-printed implants can be designed to perfectly complement the recipient's existing body dimensions. Another advantage is that such objects can be printed with complex inner patterns, such as Within Labs' trabecular lattice that allows bone tissue to grow directly into the implant itself (a process called *osseointegration*). The resulting cranial cap or joint replacement, incorporating the patient's natural tissues, can become a part of the recipient's body without having to be attached with screws and other mechanical fasteners (which can wear away at tissues and cause further damage to bones over long-term use).

Figure 18-1: This guitar has been customized with a unique spider-and-web motif to meet the customer's whim and prefer-ences.

Self-Deploying Robots

New designs for robotic insects can be created using 3D printers to fashion integrated components capable of popping into their useful configuration directly out of the printer. Traditional equivalents would require sub-assembly steps before they could be deployed while their 3D-printed cousins could be deployed using only an automated fabrication facility.

Printed Aircraft

3D-printed drone aircraft allow for the on-site fabrication of remote sensing tools for gathering intelligence in disasters or military settings. These drones are lighter in weight than their traditionally manufactured equivalents because their structural strength does not depend on the solid measure of their material form. This reduction in mass allows more drones to be fabricated using the same pool of raw materials, and each can operate for a greater length of time using the same amount of fuel. Airbus and other manufacturers hope to apply these same efficiencies to their full-sized aircraft once 3D printers capable of printing entire airliners are available.

On-Demand, On-Site Manufacturing

The U.S. military has developed 3D fabrication facilities that fit within a standard cargo transport container, allowing the deployment of a rapid fabrication and testing lab along with troops in the field. Such compact but full-featured facilities allow immediate solutions to be identified, tested, and produced on site in limited quantities. Full fabrication is managed back home, using tested electronic designs transmitted directly back from the testing module. In fact, end users can come up with new designs or needed modifications without leaving the operational theater.

Custom Objects Created in Space

Because additive manufacturing techniques like FDM/FFF do not rely on gravity for layer construction, they can operate upside-down or in microgravity environments such as Earth orbit on the ISS (International Space Station). NASA is currently developing a variation of electron-beam welding that will allow metal in wire form to be built up into solid objects in vacuum. This development will let future astronauts travel without having to carry spares of every possible tool they might need in their explorations — just another 3D Printer that can print spare parts for its twin.

Printed Finger Foods

Another example of space technology being tested using 3D printing involves printed foodstuffs, intended to break up the monotony of extended-duration travel in space. These "finger foods" can be produced in artistic designs that also fulfill nutritional requirements for astronauts. Current designs are being tested using materials with multi-year shelf life in storage — vital to the preparation of landing sites ahead of our future explorers.

Locally Fabricated Items

Markus Kayser's design for the Solar Sinter and current work at the NASA JPL — or at EU sites for space technologies — are demonstrating the fabrication of complete objects using nothing more than local solid materials and sunlight. Whether these printed objects are bowls formed of glass fused from sand or structures formed of the local version of rocks, these technologies represent one of the "purest" forms of green engineering: Final products could be ground back up and returned to their natural state after use, with no further chemicals or fuels required.

Body Parts

Perhaps one of the most amazing range of "impossible" designs possible through 3D printing — but not through traditional manufacturing — is that of body parts; organs with complex inner configurations at the cellular level are the best example. Apart from the capability to create replacements without rejection risk, these structures could even extend our natural capabilities to add extended breath capacity, resistance to toxins, or many other capabilities beyond our body's natural limits. At the present time, organic 3D-printed objects are only available for use outside the body to test new medications and treatments before they're certified for use on a living body. Complete, implantable organs — at full scale — will soon be available.

Custom Drugs

Custom-fabricated 3D-printing formulary systems can print individual pills, each containing a combination of basic drugs unique to a patient's needs, across the entire course of treatment. Custom formulary systems that use traditional manufacturing do exist, but their products tend to be sustained combinations of existing medications, scaling traditional standard doses by body weight alone. The cost of producing individual treatment programs has been high — and never mind custom-creating pills tailored to the patient. 3D-printed pharma systems can manage such feats, completing each pill's mixture as easily as they'd create a pill with only a single source chemical. The mixture can be adjusted to match the patient's body mass, absorption rates, daily food and water intake, and general health, and might even include a mix of new medical nanomaterials as well as the simpler compounds of today.

Index

• C •

• *U* •

• *V* •

About the Authors

Kalani Kirk Hausman has been involved with the Maker Movement for several decades, and has followed the evolution of additive manufacturing since the first SLA system was demonstrated in a 1980s future-tech television show. If you follow 3D printing, Ardunio microcontrollers, or many other technologies found in local makerspaces, odds are that you have visited one of Kalani's topic-curation sites to learn more. He visits makerspaces any time he travels near a new one. His STEMulate Learning workshops have incorporated 3D printing into STEM (Science, Technology, Engineering and Mathematics) educational lessons, building the SOLID Learning model being explored at public schools in Australia, the United Kingdom, Hawai'i, and various parts of the mainland United States of America. Kalani has many prior books from his professional career in information technology, but this is the first book drawn from his personal passions alone.

Richard Horne (RichRap) has two decades of experience in the electronics industry, first as an electronics engineer and more recently in sales and marketing. His work spans a wide range of technologies and industries, in both the consumer and industrial sectors. From arcade games to washing machines, Richard has designed and developed products used by millions of people around the world.

Richard is also a highly passionate advocate of DIY-based 3D printing, for the open-source Maker Movement. Joining the RepRap project in 2009, and then blogging, developing, and sharing ideas to encourage greater consumer interest and collaboration in 3D printing, Richard continues his efforts to make this high-tech movement easier to join — while also pushing the technical boundaries of design and personal manufacturing.

Dedication

From Kirk: To my wife, Susan, and our two magnificent, brilliant children who make every day worth waking up.

From Richard: To Samantha, my true love and my best friend, for providing support and understanding, listening to me talking about 3D printing (even in my sleep); to Amelia and Sophia for lighting up my life and being so inspiring.

Authors' Acknowledgments

From Kirk: This book would not have been possible without the tremendous assistance of a multitude behind the scenes — foremost, my co-author, Richard Horne, whose expertise with the RepRap platform places him in the top tier of practitioners working in this exciting field! The book could not have gotten off the ground without the engagement of Wiley Publishing's acquisitions editor, Kyle Looper, who brought this project through a year's worth of review before getting the green light! Kyle was surrounded by others in the editorial team, from Christopher Morris, who gathered the pieces I provided and trimmed to make them look like an actual book, to copy editor Barry Childs-Helton, and technical editor, Nathan Chapman. In addition to the team that polishes my crude efforts into a product worthy of a title, this book also received support from many who provided material to visualize the amazing potential of additive manufacturing. My thanks to MaxBots at Maker's Tool Works for the excellent MendelMax Cartesian printer kit, to Os1r1s who helped me get it calibrated properly, and also to John at SeeMeCNC for the towering RostockMax Delta printer kit (always a hit when I show it off and talk about this book). Creaform provided one of their excellent Go!Scan3D scanners, which captured our model with amazing precision, even during fits of giggling. Others whose figures appear in this book include Ondrej Doule, Cody Wilson, Karl Willis, Sean Charlesworth, Olaf Diegel, Markus Kayser, Lee Perry-Smith, Stephanie Riker, Anke Werner, Berok Koshnevis, Siavash Mahdavi, Liz von Hasseln, the Francis Bitonti Studio, Vince Rossi, the Smithsonian's "Laser Cowboys" and any others I missed in this truly globe-spanning group! And I cannot miss out on thanking the one who makes all my books possible — my agent, guide, and very good friend, Carole Jelen!

From Richard: I would like to thank my co-author Kirk for a really enjoyable and fun experience writing this book together. Also thank you to my agent Carole Jelen and all the folks at Wiley for their support, guidance, and excellent feedback.

And finally, a really big thanks to all my friends, family, and the entire RepRap community for their encouragement and enthusiasm. I hope this book inspires you discover the same joy and creativity with 3D printing that I have.

Publisher's Acknowledgments

Acquisitions Editor: Kyle Looper

Sr. Project Editor: Christopher Morris

Sr. Copy Editor: Barry Childs-Helton

Technical Editors: Nathan Chapman

Editorial Assistant: Annie Sullivan

Sr. Editorial Assistant: Cherie Case

Cover Image: Prototype of an automotive shock absorber, 3D printed on a Stratasys Dimension 3D Printer using ABS thermoplastic, courtesy of © Stratasys

Apple & Mac

iPad For Dummies,
5th Edition
978-1-118-49823-1

iPhone 5 For Dummies,
6th Edition
978-1-118-35201-4

MacBook For Dummies,
4th Edition
978-1-118-20920-2

OS X Mountain Lion
For Dummies
978-1-118-39418-2

Blogging & Social Media

Facebook For Dummies,
4th Edition
978-1-118-09562-1

Mom Blogging
For Dummies
978-1-118-03843-7

Pinterest For Dummies
978-1-118-32800-2

WordPress For Dummies,
5th Edition
978-1-118-38318-6

Business

Commodities For Dummies,
2nd Edition
978-1-118-01687-9

Investing For Dummies,
6th Edition
978-0-470-90545-6

Personal Finance
For Dummies,
7th Edition
978-1-118-11785-9

QuickBooks 2013
For Dummies
978-1-118-35641-8

Small Business Marketing Kit
For Dummies,
3rd Edition
978-1-118-31183-7

Careers

Job Interviews
For Dummies,
4th Edition
978-1-118-11290-8

Job Searching with
Social Media
For Dummies
978-0-470-93072-4

Personal Branding
For Dummies
978-1-118-11792-7

Resumes For Dummies,
6th Edition
978-0-470-87361-8

Success as a Mediator
For Dummies
978-1-118-07862-4

Diet & Nutrition

Belly Fat Diet For Dummies
978-1-118-34585-6

Eating Clean For Dummies
978-1-118-00013-7

Nutrition For Dummies,
5th Edition
978-0-470-93231-5

Digital Photography

Digital Photography
For Dummies,
7th Edition
978-1-118-09203-3

Digital SLR Cameras &
Photography For Dummies,
4th Edition
978-1-118-14489-3

Photoshop Elements 11
For Dummies
978-1-118-40821-6

Gardening

Herb Gardening
For Dummies,
2nd Edition
978-0-470-61778-6

Vegetable Gardening
For Dummies,
2nd Edition
978-0-470-49870-5

Health

Anti-Inflammation Diet
For Dummies
978-1-118-02381-5

Diabetes For Dummies,
3rd Edition
978-0-470-27086-8

Living Paleo For Dummies
978-1-118-29405-5

Hobbies

Beekeeping
For Dummies
978-0-470-43065-1

eBay For Dummies,
7th Edition
978-1-118-09806-6

Raising Chickens
For Dummies
978-0-470-46544-8

Wine For Dummies,
5th Edition
978-1-118-28872-6

Writing Young Adult Fiction
For Dummies
978-0-470-94954-2

Language &
Foreign Language

500 Spanish Verbs
For Dummies
978-1-118-02382-2

English Grammar
For Dummies,
2nd Edition
978-0-470-54664-2

French All-in One
For Dummies
978-1-118-22815-9

German Essentials
For Dummies
978-1-118-18422-6

Italian For Dummies
2nd Edition
978-1-118-00465-4

 Available in print and e-book formats.

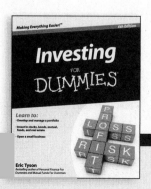

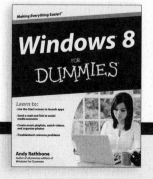

Math & Science

Algebra I For Dummies,
2nd Edition
978-0-470-55964-2

Anatomy and Physiology
For Dummies,
2nd Edition
978-0-470-92326-9

Astronomy For Dummies,
3rd Edition
978-1-118-37697-3

Biology For Dummies,
2nd Edition
978-0-470-59875-7

Chemistry For Dummies,
2nd Edition
978-1-1180-0730-3

Pre-Algebra Essentials
For Dummies
978-0-470-61838-7

Microsoft Office

Excel 2013 For Dummies
978-1-118-51012-4

Office 2013 All-in-One
For Dummies
978-1-118-51636-2

PowerPoint 2013
For Dummies
978-1-118-50253-2

Word 2013 For Dummies
978-1-118-49123-2

Music

Blues Harmonica
For Dummies
978-1-118-25269-7

Guitar For Dummies,
3rd Edition
978-1-118-11554-1

iPod & iTunes
For Dummies,
10th Edition
978-1-118-50864-0

Programming

Android Application
Development For
Dummies, 2nd Edition
978-1-118-38710-8

iOS 6 Application
Development For Dummies
978-1-118-50880-0

Java For Dummies,
5th Edition
978-0-470-37173-2

Religion & Inspiration

The Bible For Dummies
978-0-7645-5296-0

Buddhism For Dummies,
2nd Edition
978-1-118-02379-2

Catholicism For Dummies,
2nd Edition
978-1-118-07778-8

Self-Help & Relationships

Bipolar Disorder
For Dummies,
2nd Edition
978-1-118-33882-7

Meditation For Dummies,
3rd Edition
978-1-118-29144-3

Seniors

Computers For Seniors
For Dummies,
3rd Edition
978-1-118-11553-4

iPad For Seniors
For Dummies,
5th Edition
978-1-118-49708-1

Social Security
For Dummies
978-1-118-20573-0

Smartphones & Tablets

Android Phones
For Dummies
978-1-118-16952-0

Kindle Fire HD
For Dummies
978-1-118-42223-6

NOOK HD For Dummies,
Portable Edition
978-1-118-39498-4

Surface For Dummies
978-1-118-49634-3

Test Prep

ACT For Dummies,
5th Edition
978-1-118-01259-8

ASVAB For Dummies,
3rd Edition
978-0-470-63760-9

GRE For Dummies,
7th Edition
978-0-470-88921-3

Officer Candidate Tests,
For Dummies
978-0-470-59876-4

Physician's Assistant Exam
For Dummies
978-1-118-11556-5

Series 7 Exam
For Dummies
978-0-470-09932-2

Windows 8

Windows 8 For Dummies
978-1-118-13461-0

Windows 8 For Dummies,
Book + DVD Bundle
978-1-118-27167-4

Windows 8 All-in-One
For Dummies
978-1-118-11920-4

ℯ Available in print and e-book formats.

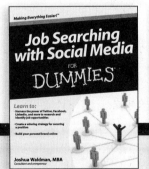

Take Dummies with you everywhere you go!

Whether you're excited about e-books, want more from the web, must have your mobile apps, or swept up in social media, Dummies makes everything easier .

Dummies products make life easier!

- DIY
- Consumer Electronics
- Crafts
- Software
- Cookware
- Hobbies
- Videos
- Music
- Games
- and More!

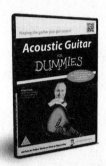

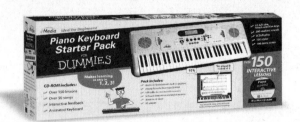

For more information, go to **Dummies.com®** and search the store by category.

FOR
DUMMIES
A Wiley Brand

Illustration by Alex Ross

THE REBELLION

FROM THE BATTLE OF YAVIN TO FIVE YEARS AFTER

Open resistance begins to spread across the galaxy in protest of the Empire's tyranny. Rebel groups unite, and the Galactic Civil War begins. This era starts with the Rebel victory that secured the Death Star plans, and ends a year after the death of the Emperor high over the forest moon of Endor. This is the era in which the events in *A New Hope*, *The Empire Strikes Back*, and *Return of the Jedi* take place.

The events in this story take place shortly after the events in *Star Wars: Episode IV—A New Hope*.

VOLUME ONE | IN THE SHADOW OF YAVIN

Script	Art	Colors	Lettering
BRIAN WOOD	**CARLOS D'ANDA**	**GABE ELTAEB**	**MICHAEL HEISLER**

THE ASSASSINATION OF DARTH VADER

Script	Art	Colors	Lettering
BRIAN WOOD	**RYAN ODAGAWA**	**GABE ELTAEB**	**MICHAEL HEISLER**

Front Cover Art
ALEX ROSS

DARK HORSE BOOKS

LUCAS BOOKS

President and Publisher
MIKE RICHARDSON

Collection Designer
JIMMY PRESLER

Editor
RANDY STRADLEY

Assistant Editor
FREDDYE LINS

NEIL HANKERSON .... Executive Vice President
TOM WEDDLE .... Chief Financial Officer
RANDY STRADLEY .... Vice President of Publishing
MICHAEL MARTENS .... Vice President of Book Trade Sales
ANITA NELSON .... Vice President of Business Affairs
SCOTT ALLIE .... Editor in Chief
MATT PARKINSON .... Vice President of Marketing
DAVID SCROGGY .... Vice President of Product Development
DALE LAFOUNTAIN .... Vice President of Information Technology
DARLENE VOGEL .... Senior Director of Print, Design, and Production
KEN LIZZI .... General Counsel
DAVEY ESTRADA .... Editorial Director
CHRIS WARNER .... Senior Books Editor
DIANA SCHUTZ .... Executive Editor
CARY GRAZZINI .... Director of Print and Development
LIA RIBACCHI .... Art Director
CARA NIECE .... Director of Scheduling
TIM WIESCH .... Director of International Licensing
MARK BERNARDI .... Director of Digital Publishing

Special thanks to Jennifer Heddle, Leland Chee, Troy Alders, Carol Roeder, Jann
Moorhead, and David Anderman at Lucas Licensing.

This volume collects issues #1–#6 of the Dark Horse comic-book series Star Wars, as well as "Star
Wars: The Assassination of Darth Vader," first published in Free Comic Book Day 2013.

Published by Dark Horse Books, a division of Dark Horse Comics, Inc.
10956 SE Main Street, Milwaukie, OR 97222

DarkHorse.com StarWars.com

International Licensing: (503) 905-2377
To find a comics shop in your area, call the Comic Shop Locator Service toll-free at 1-888-266-4226

Library of Congress Cataloging-in-Publication Data

Wood, Brian, 1972-
Star Wars. Volume one, In the shadow of Yavin / script, Brian Wood ; art, Carlos D'Anda ; colors, Gabe
Eltaeb ; lettering, Michael Heisler.
      pages cm
Summary: "Princess Leia forms a stealth squadron of her best pilots--including Luke Skywalker--to
expose a spy and find the Rebel Alliance a safe home"-- Provided by publisher.
ISBN 978-1-61655-170-4
[1. Graphic novels.] I. D'Anda, Carlos, illustrator. II. Title. III. Title: In the shadow of Yavin.
PZ7.7.W65St 2013
741.5'973--dc23
                                        2013015114

First edition: September 2013
ISBN 978-1-61655-170-4

10 9 8 7 6 5 4 3 2 1
Printed in China

Illustration by Alex Ross

IN THE SHADOW OF YAVIN

The Rebel Alliance destroyed the Galactic Empire's fearsome space station, the Death Star, but the losses they suffered in the midst of that victory were substantial.

Rebel leader Princess Leia Organa witnessed the destruction of her homeworld; farm-boy-turned-hero Luke Skywalker lost the only family he knew, as well as a boyhood friend; and smuggler Han Solo made a decision to fight the Empire that will have consequences he can't even begin to anticipate.

Now, in the quest for a new base from which to continue the war against the Empire, Leia, Luke, and ace pilot Wedge Antilles have journeyed to the edge of the Outer Rim.

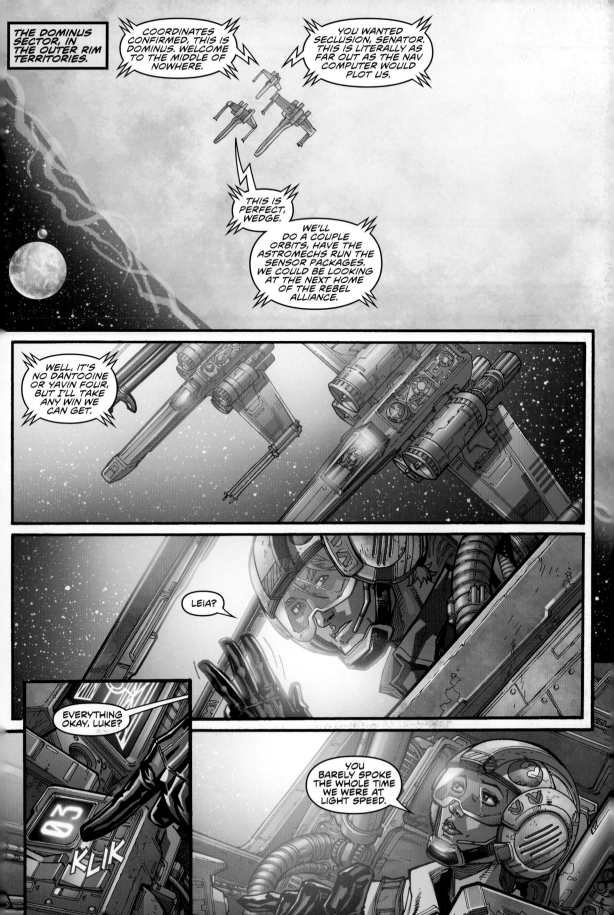

8

NOT ENOUGH.

I LOOK FORWARD TO THESE LONG TRIPS. IT GIVES ME TIME TO *THINK*, SOMETHING I HAVE PRECIOUS LITTLE OF AS AN OFFICER OF THE ALLIANCE.

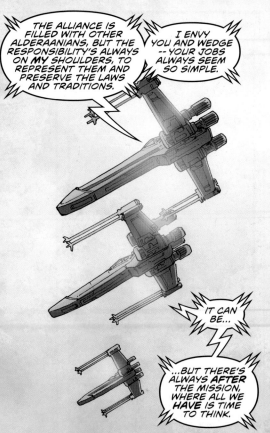

THE ALLIANCE IS FILLED WITH OTHER ALDERAANIANS, BUT THE RESPONSIBILITY'S ALWAYS ON *MY* SHOULDERS, TO REPRESENT THEM AND PRESERVE THE LAWS AND TRADITIONS.

I ENVY YOU AND WEDGE -- YOUR JOBS ALWAYS SEEM SO SIMPLE.

IT CAN BE...

...BUT THERE'S ALWAYS *AFTER* THE MISSION, WHERE ALL WE *HAVE* IS TIME TO THINK.

IS THIS WHY YOU'VE BEEN FLYING THESE MISSIONS WITH US?

THAT'S HOW I SOLD IT TO MON MOTHMA. LUKE, LISTEN...

WE'VE *ALL* LOST MORE THAN A LIFETIME'S WORTH OF LOVED ONES, ALL IN A FEW SHORT MONTHS.

IF GENERAL KENOBI WAS TEACHING YOU HOW TO FIND A BALANCE, A WAY TO USE THE FORCE TO TURN THAT PAIN INTO SOMETHING POSITIVE...

...YOU SHOULD STICK WITH IT. WE NEED YOU.

THANKS, I THINK I WILL. FOR BEN, *AND* FOR MY FATHER.

KRRSSSHHKK... SORRY TO BREAK IN, KIDS, BUT WE GOT TROUBLE. SWITCH TO THE TACTICAL CHANNEL, AND CALL SIGNS FROM HERE ON OUT.